Y0-DNC-377

+DS481 .G3 G278+

AUDREY COHEN COLLEGE
50664000146870
/Gandhi's significance for today / edite
DS481 .G3 G278 1989 C.1 STACKS 1989

Gandhi's signifi-
cance for today

DS
481
G3
G278
1989

DATE DUE

GANDHI'S SIGNIFICANCE FOR TODAY

Also by John Hick

AN INTERPRETATION OF RELIGION
ARGUMENTS FOR THE EXISTENCE OF GOD
CHRISTIANITY AT THE CENTRE
DEATH AND ETERNAL LIFE
EVIL AND THE GOD OF LOVE
FAITH AND KNOWLEDGE
FAITH AND THE PHILOSOPHERS   (*editor*)
GOD AND THE UNIVERSE OF FAITHS
GOD HAS MANY NAMES
PROBLEMS OF RELIGIOUS PLURALISM
THE MANY-FACED ARGUMENT
(*editor with A. C. MacGill*)
CHRISTIANITY AND OTHER RELIGIONS
(*editor with Brian Hebblethwaite*)
CLASSICAL AND CONTEMPORARY READINGS IN THE
PHILOSOPHY OF RELIGION (*editor*)
PHILOSOPHY OF RELIGION
THE EXISTENCE OF GOD   (*editor*)
THE MYTH OF GOD INCARNATE   (*editor*)
THE SECOND CHRISTIANITY
THREE FAITHS – ONE GOD
(*editor with Edmund S. Meltzer*)
TRUTH AND DIALOGUE   (*editor*)
WHY BELIEVE IN GOD?   (*with Michael Goulder*)

Gandhi's Significance for Today

Edited by

John Hick
Danforth Professor of the Philosophy of Religion
The Claremont Graduate School, Claremont, California

and

Lamont C. Hempel
Associate Director, Center for Politics and Policy
The Claremont Graduate School, Claremont, California

Foreword by John David Maguire

St. Martin's Press
New York

© The Claremont Graduate School 1989

All rights reserved. For information, write:
Scholarly and Reference Division,
St. Martin's Press, Inc., 175 Fifth Avenue, New York, NY 10010

First published in the United States of America in 1989

Printed in the People's Republic of China

ISBN 0-312-02798-2

Library of Congress Cataloging-in-Publication Data
Gandhi's significance for today/edited by John Hick
and Lamont C. Hempel; foreword by John David Maguire.
p. cm.
Includes bibliographies and index.
ISBN 0-312-02798-2
1. Gandhi, Mahatma, 1869–1948 — Philosophy.   I. Hick, John.
II. Hempel, Lamont C.
DS481.G3G278 1989
954.03'5'0924 — dc19   88–7791
                                          CIP

Contents

Foreword *John David Maguire* — vii
Acknowledgements — ix
Notes on the Contributors — x

INTRODUCTION

    Overview: The Elusive Legacy *Lamont C. Hempel* — 3

1 Gandhi's Relevance Today *James W. Gould* — 7

PART I GANDHI THE MAN

    Introduction *John Hick* — 21

2 The Heart of Satyagraha: A Quest for Inner Dignity, Not Political Power *Paul Mundschenk* — 24

3 Shoring Up the Saint: Some Suggestions for Improving Satyagraha *Mark Juergensmeyer* — 36

4 Gandhi and Celibacy *Arvind Sharma* — 51

5 Gandhi in South Africa *James D. Hunt* — 61

PART II GANDHI ON RELIGION AND ETHICS

    Introduction *John Hick* — 85

6 Gandhi's Concept of Truth *Rex Ambler* — 90

7 Gandhi's Moral Philosophy *Steven A. Smith* — 109 ✓

8 Gandhi on Civilization and Religion *Raghavan Iyer* — 122

9	Gandhi's Interpretation of the Bhagavad Gita *Kees W. Bolle*	137
10	Gandhi and Christianity *Margaret Chatterjee*	152
11	Gandhi's Religious Universalism *Elton Hall*	166

PART III   GANDHI ON POLITICS AND ECONOMICS

	Introduction *Lamont C. Hempel*	185
12	The Core of Gandhi's Social and Economic Thought *Sugata Dasgupta*	189
13	The Gandhian Movement in India Since the Death of Gandhi *Geoffrey Ostergaard*	203
14	Gandhian Feminism *Sushila Gidwani*	226
15	The Influence of Gandhi on Martin Luther King, Jr. *Thomas Kilgore, Jr.*	236
16	An Anti-Secularist Manifesto *Ashis Nandy*	244

Glossary — 265
Index — 266

Foreword

While it is commonly agreed that Mahatma Gandhi is a figure of world significance, debate continues about the precise nature of his contribution. What is the essence of his greatness, then and now? Was it his ability to fashion a coherent world view of nonviolence, one that would withstand the unavoidable tests by people of violence? Was it his willingness to make painful sacrifices for the sake of ideals that he found precious? Or was it, perhaps, his enormous capacity for empathy with the poor and afflicted of his society? No simple answer will suffice. Gandhi's life was a complex blend of revolutionary thought and symbolic action; one that exhibited a remarkable integration of moral and political fervor. Surely it was a life that merits scrutiny for what it can teach us about perseverance and selfless leadership.

In 1984, The Claremont Graduate School held an interdisciplinary colloquium on 'Mahatma Gandhi and his Significance for Today'. Organized under the auspices of the Graduate School's James A. Blaisdell Programs in World Religions and Cultures, the conference included presentations by more than thirty scholars from India, Canada, Britain, Central America, and the United States. Many of the papers presented have been included in this volume.

In his keynote address to the conference, Rodrigo Carazo, former President of Costa Rica and Acting Rector of the United Nation's University for Peace, declared that Gandhi was 'a clear symbol of what he practiced and preached: the local and the universal, joined in the task of emancipation through the means of nonviolence.' For Gandhi, nonviolence entailed more than a renunciation of bombs and bullets; it was above all concerned with what President Carazo called 'the lethal weapons represented by human exploitation, abuse, and ignorance'. The emancipation from colonial domination that Gandhi inspired was merely the first step in his quest for universal emancipation from poverty and injustice.

Many of the contributors to this book agree that part of Gandhi's legacy lies in his powerful use of symbols. Symbols, however, are by their character subject to a variety of interpretations. Many of these essays describe an imposing little man, sitting behind his spinning wheel, who boldly changed the course of history. But the meaning of that change, and its significance for today, is less clear than the ideas that fostered it. Hence the elusive nature of the legacy.

In this book, the authors have tried to make the legacy more understandable by relating the character of the man, his style of leadership, his ethical, religious, and social concerns, to the political actions through which he expressed them. This is a book about Gandhi, the man, formed from the dust of India and from the misery of its people; but it is also a volume about the Mahatma, a visionary leader, whose ideas speak to us today with just as much relevance and force as they displayed in South Africa and India in the years before an assassin's bullets cut him down.

JOHN DAVID MAGUIRE

Acknowledgements

The editors gratefully acknowledge the help and support of the students, staff and faculty colleagues who assisted us in this endeavor. In particular, we would like to thank Dr Edward Hughes for his help in coordinating The Claremont Graduate School's colloquium on Gandhi – the conference from which most of the essays in this book originated. We are also indebted to Rena Brar, Marilyn Scaff and Karen Kidd for their assistance with proofreading and editing, and to Fay Rulau and Elisabeth Duran for their excellent secretarial skills in preparing the manuscript. Special appreciation is due to Pauline Snelson, Sophie Lillington and Jill Lake of Macmillan for their patience and skill in guiding us through the preparations for publication. Lastly, we are indebted to the James A. Blaisdell Programs in World Religions and Cultures for its sponsorship of our work and for its commitment to the ideals for which Gandhi stood.

Notes on the Contributors

Rex Ambler is Lecturer in Theology at the University of Birmingham.
Kees W. Bolle is Professor of History at the University of California, Los Angeles.
Margaret Chatterjee is Professor of Philosophy at Delhi University.
Sugata Dasgupta (deceased, 1985) was the Director of the Jayaprakash Institute of Social Change, Calcutta.
Sushila Gidwani is Associate Professor in the Department of Economics and Finance at Manhattan College, Riverdale.
James W. Gould is Professor of History and International Relations at Scripps College, Claremont.
Elton Hall is Professor of Philosophy and Sociology at Oxnard College, Oxnard, California.
James D. Hunt is Professor of Religion at Shaw University in Raleigh, North Carolina.
Raghavan Iyer is Professor of Political Science at the University of California, Santa Barbara.
Mark Juergensmeyer is Associate Professor of Ethics at the Graduate Theological Union and the University of California, Berkeley. He is also co-director of the Berkeley-Harvard Program in the Comparative Study of Social Values.
Thomas Kilgore, Jr. is Senior Pastor of the Second Baptist Church, Los Angeles.
Paul Mundschenk is Professor of Religious Studies at Western Illinois University.
Ashis Nandy is Senior Fellow at the Centre for the Study of Developing Societies, Delhi.
Geoffrey Ostergaard is Senior Lecturer in Political Science at the University of Birmingham.
Arvind Sharma is Lecturer in the Department of Religious Studies, University of Sydney.
Steven A. Smith is Associate Professor of Philosophy, Claremont McKenna College, Claremont.

Introduction

Overview: The Elusive Legacy

Lamont C. Hempel

The 1980s mark another decade of senseless killing in Ahmedabad – the city where Mohandas K. Gandhi launched some of his most celebrated campaigns of nonviolent resistance. The feelings of terror and grief that grip this city are not fundamentally different from those that prevailed nearly forty years ago in the months leading up to Gandhi's assassination. Today, as then, Hindus and Muslims wage war across the narrow lanes and rooftops that divide their communities. Lingering caste hatred is reignited by battles over job quotas and educational reforms designed to help the Untouchables – the people Gandhi lovingly called *Harijans*. Nightfall brings deadly confrontations between feuding families and gangs armed with rocks, clubs and knives. Meanwhile, children taunt riot police with bonfires and makeshift barricades on Gandhi Road.

How easy it would be to conclude that Gandhi failed; that his impassioned pleas for *satyagraha* (holding fast to the Truth) and *ahimsa* (nonviolence) had no lasting effect. In retrospect, Gandhi's influence seems to have been crushed under the enormity of injustices he set out to correct. Apartheid continues in South Africa; untouchability remains in India; Pakistan and India are still sharply divided; and the world as a whole seems to drift perilously closer to thermonuclear annihilation.

But are we to measure Gandhi's success by what he accomplished or by what he overcame? Comparing his lofty goals with his brittle accomplishments will give us a Gandhi who, by his own standards, ultimately failed. Gauging his vision of peace and social justice, on the other hand, and the courage and skill with which he moved nations over seemingly impossible obstacles, presents us with a Gandhi of astonishing achievements. His violent death cannot serve as a denial of all that he lived for, anymore than his failure to unify Muslims and Hindus can be counted a bitter legacy of Indian *swaraj* (self-government). The Mahatma – the 'great soul' – is perhaps best remembered precisely because he was ready to die for what he believed in and was willing to set his objectives sufficiently high to make failure probable, perhaps almost inevitable. As Gandhi himself said, 'Our task is to make the impossible possible.'

What is the real legacy of Mahatma Gandhi? What is his relevance for today? The contributors to this volume have all sought, in one way or another, to answer these questions. Some have focused on the spread of Gandhian movements during recent years, finding significance in their rapid growth and in their fidelity to Gandhi's doctrine of nonviolence. Others have concentrated on the character of the man himself, noting his importance as a symbolic figure and the sustained contribution his life represents as an example to millions of what the selfless and totally dedicated individual can achieve. A few have called attention to the idiosyncrasies and flaws that kept Gandhi human, thereby countering the tendency to deify him and to remove his example and accomplishments from the realm of human potential. Several contributors have emphasized the relevance of Gandhi's spiritual and intellectual thought, and the unifying force it represents for connecting religion, politics, ethics and economics. Still others have sought to present Gandhi's legacy in terms of his influence on subsequent leaders, such as Martin Luther King; and on social issues, such as world peace, civil rights, poverty, women's liberation, appropriate technology, and ecology.

In all of these approaches, the picture of Gandhi that emerges is one of a moral activist who joins the personal with the political; the spiritual with the struggle for justice. To be sure, many of the important aspects of Gandhi's life and thought, and their relevance to modern society, are not addressed here. That task, even after the publication of 85 volumes of Gandhi's collected works, is far from complete. This book, then, is intended to be only one step in the completion of that task. Its purpose is to explore those aspects of Gandhian thought which have endured to this day and which continue to inspire us and to enrich our collective sense of what is possible and desirable in a world plagued by hunger, violence and discrimination.

Gandhi stated many times that he was willing to sacrifice those

Overview: The Elusive Legacy

things that were most precious in his life, including life itself, in his quest for God and Truth (which were essentially one and the same in his eyes). This quality of self-sacrifice in pursuit of *moksha* (liberation from the cycle of death and rebirth) or in defense of deeply held principles is what made Gandhi so formidable as a *satyagrahi*. It is also, ironically, what allowed his assassin to ignore personal risk and brazenly approach within three feet before firing the fatal shots. Surely ideas and causes worth dying for can reveal much about the human condition. They are the ultimate tests of what it means to be human, for they remind us of the differences between mere biological survival and a purposeful life.

Thus, Gandhi's crowning achievement may have been his ability to inspire *homo humanus* out of *homo sapiens*. Although many will claim that little, if any, inspiration remains, Gandhi's life still affects millions of people in powerful ways, as the response to Richard Attenborough's (1982) film about Gandhi demonstrates. What is more important, however, is that Gandhi's *ideas* remain powerful. Their legacy may grow and develop in the decades ahead in ways that we can only dimly perceive now. It may be that the world has not yet had sufficient time to discover the lessons behind the man. As Ralph Buultjens, a prominent scholar of Asian philosophy and international relations, notes:[1]

> Thirty-five years after the crucifixion of Jesus Christ there was no indication that Christianity would emerge as one of the great spiritual forces of history. Around 450 B.C., three decades after the death of Confucius, nobody could have predicted how influential his ideas eventually became. And around 1915, thirty years after Karl Marx, the Communist movement seemed doomed to be an inconsequential political aberration. Perhaps, then, we are too near Gandhi to evaluate his impact on history.

While acknowledging that this may be correct, the editors and contributors to this volume have focused on Gandhi's relevance for our time without attempting to prejudge his importance for future generations or across recorded history. As James Gould notes in the introductory essay which follows, Gandhi's influence has expanded both geographically and theoretically through the non-violent struggles of diverse political, religious, labor and ethnic groups. Its significance today does not invite dramatic news coverage, as it did during the Quit India movement, but that may be because Gandhian actions today are culturally dispersed, more decentralized politically, and less reliant upon charismatic leadership and dramatic symbols of the type that foster major news events (e.g. Gandhi's Salt March). Regardless of the degree of public visibility, the legacy of Gandhi's Truth remains intact and powerful. As the following essays reveal, it is indeed an 'elusive' legacy – one that is difficult to pinpoint – but one whose presence can be deeply felt.

To assist the reader in forming his or her own assessment of Gandhi's significance for today, this book is divided into three parts: (I) Gandhi the Man, (II) Gandhi on Religion and Ethics, and (III) Gandhi on Politics and Economics. Although the Mahatma would almost surely have objected to the separation of his life and message into categories of this type, the fact is that the modern reader usually comes equipped with conceptual lenses that make it necessary to adopt this approach. Perhaps this is, in itself, an indictment of modernity and the pervasive tendency most of us have to study Gandhi on our terms, instead of his. In any event, the editors of this volume have chosen to adopt the conventions of scholarly dissection, confident in the knowledge that many of the papers we have included present compelling arguments for integrating Gandhi's ideas, actions and symbols into a single, dynamic concept of Truth.

Note

1. 'Gandhi: the other side of the balance sheet', in Krolik and Cannon (eds.), *Gandhi in the Postmodern Age* (Golden, Col.: Colorado School of Mines Press, 1984) p. 15.

1

Gandhi's Relevance Today

James W. Gould

The assassin foolishly believes he can kill a powerful idea by killing the person who utters it. He finds some truth in this delusion when a Gandhi or a Martin Luther King is killed because many false prophets eagerly declare that the reform is ended, and even good people despair that the spirit of reform can be sustained or that resurrection can come. Even during the life of the reformer, character assassins will try to destroy the idea by calumniating the reformer, and the slander goes on after death as the faults and peccadilloes of the 'saint' are revealed. But it only affirms a man's humanity if we know that King may have loved a good time and fine clothes, or that Gandhi tested his self-restraint by sleeping with young women and carried his health cures to dangerous extremes. What really matters is that the idea which the reformer gave utterance and tried to practice is still a powerful force that speaks to our time.

TRUTHFORCE

The most revolutionary idea of our twentieth century is the truth of nonviolence. As Gandhi asserted, the idea is 'as old as the hills', going back to Mahavira, Buddha and Christ, developed by the martyrs of Islam and Christianity, given moving expression by Tolstoy and loving practice by William Lloyd Garrison, women suffragists and boycotters of many lands. But it was Gandhi's 'experiments with Truth' in the beginning of this century that first proved that nonviolence could be used on a large scale to redirect society towards a more humane course, with a minimum loss of life and property, and thus make reform lasting. It is not surprising that there is continued resistance to the truth of nonviolence, and even vehement denial of that truth, for violence has been entrenched in culture for a long time, and much of the present structure of society still depends upon force.

Yet the amazing event is the rapid spread of the politics of nonviolence since the assassination of Gandhi 40 years ago. One would least expect it in war-steeped Europe, but by 1952 in Italy Danilo Dolci was using the principle to liberate the poor in Mafia-bound Sicily. That Gandhi's Truthforce was not a one-time miracle of a saint is shown by the creativity of Dolci in inventing the reverse strike, doing a positive public service (repairing a road) which the government prohibited, at Partinico in 1956.

The next year, still less than a decade after Gandhi's assassination, Lanza del Vasto used a Gandhian fast to protest against the French war in Algeria. Shortly thereafter he directed nonviolent action against the military takeover of poor shepherds' pastures, conducted one of the earliest European protests against nuclear power (1958), and directed the attention of the Catholic Church to nonviolence by a personal appeal to Pope John XXIII.

By the 1970s there was not a country in Europe that did not have some nonviolent movement, whether the drive for environmental protection, which spread rapidly, or against conscription and nuclear war in Western Europe, or human rights assertions in Eastern Europe. All of these movements linked hands across national boundaries, learning new tactics and creating a new solidarity of common humanity. Recent peace encampments against the Pershing and Cruise missiles have extended from southern Sicily to Scotland, and link the Green Party in the German Bundestag to environmentalists of every land, in an ecumenical peace movement of Catholics, Protestants and Jews which is truly an international cause that includes people of all ages and classes, consciously following nonviolence, and training in its use.

In the United States the expansion of nonviolent politics is no less amazing. It is easy to forget that only 25 years ago most people, Christians included, would have despaired to see an effective nonviolence campaign in the United States, given the deep entrenchment of violence and prejudice in American society. Religious societies such as the Quakers who had both inspired Gandhi and supported him continued their quiet protests and vigils and distributed information about nonviolence. They were joined by associations promoting the spiritual basis of nonviolence preached by Gandhi, such as the Fellowship of Reconciliation (1917), and secular groups like the War Resisters League (1923). They disseminated Gandhian ideas and trained others in nonviolent techniques under leaders like A. J. Muste and Allan Hunter. In the mid-1950s nonviolent protest campaigns came with increasing frequency and support: against civil defense shelters (1955), atomic testing (1958), chemical warfare (1959), intercontinental missiles (1959), sit-ins against discrimination (1960) and freedom rides (1961). Martin Luther King, like Gandhi, gave nonviolence the character and publicity of a mass movement, and demonstrated that the connection between social injustice and militarism had important political implications.

The lessons learned in the civil rights movement were soon transferred to the campaign against the Vietnam War, resulting in the largest nonviolent protests in American history (1971), which were the most important factor in bringing about peace in 1975, the first war in history ended by nonviolent means. As important as that victory was the fact that the antiwar movement learned to coordinate the efforts of groups with diverse aims, to decentralize decision-making and not to depend upon leaders – who could be assassinated. The leading groups deliberately sought democratic decision-making processes, and thus helped to spread the learning and commitment to nonviolence.

Thus, when the war ended, new nonviolent groups sprang up all over the country using Gandhian techniques to oppose draft registration, building of nuclear plants like Seabrook and San Onofre, research laboratories like Livermore and Rocky Flats, shipyards at Groton and Bellingham, and assembly plants in Amarillo. Finally, the Nuclear Freeze Campaign which culminated in the huge rally of nearly one million people in Central Park on June 12 1982, has continued with lobbying in Washington D.C., declaration of nuclear-free zones and support for mass marches for jobs and justice such as the one held in the national capital on August 24 1983. The grassroots nature of this movement, its spread to every part of the country, and its widening appeal to many professionals and politicians shows that Gandhi's ideas of nonviolence have not only been absorbed by millions, but that they have become part of peoples' lives through living experience of the effectiveness of nonviolent action.

The same spread and deepening of nonviolent action is occurring on all the other continents. Twenty years ago in Latin America little was heard of nonviolence, and most observers would have predicted a poor future. Yet the progress is marked by the recognition of two Nobel Peace Prize laureates, Adolfo Perez Esquivel in 1980 for his nonviolent human rights protests in Argentina, and Alfonso Garcia Robles in 1982 for his diplomatic achievement of a nuclear-free continent. We now have continent-wide conferences on nonviolence. Several leaders of the Catholic Church, such as Bishop Helder Camara of Brazil, have promoted nonviolent ideas, and the assassination of Archbishop Romero of El Salvador in 1980 is widely regarded as a martyrdom for his advocacy of nonviolence. Most important is that nonviolence is being taken up by formerly silent groups such as Indians, rural peasants and urban poor. The successful protests in 1983 against illegal detentions supported by the Chilean supreme court is another example of the increasing use of nonviolent protest in Latin America.

In Africa, where Gandhi first experimented with nonviolence and helped found the African National Congress, the idea has had unusual support from government leaders, notably Kenneth Kaunda of Zambia and Julius Nyerere of Tanzania. In the war-ridden Middle East, Anwar Sadat, whose memoirs tell of his youthful admiration of Gandhi, was murdered in part for his extraordinary offer of peace to Israel. There is a growing use of nonviolent protests in the occupied West Bank by Peace Now, supported by intellectuals such as Hebrew University professor Daniel Amit.

In Asia, Japan is remarkable for having a nonviolent organization which has taken the Gandhian title of Sarvodaya, and there is also a strong revival of nonviolence among Buddhist sects, some led by persons inspired by Gandhi, such as the venerable Nichidatsu Fujii. In Korea an indigenous nonviolent movement has led the protests for democracy and human rights, including a fast by former President Kim Young Sam in 1983. Nonviolence in Sri Lanka promoted by the Sarvodaya movement, and developed under Ariyaratne and Upali Senanayake is carried on by the Non-Violent Action Group led by K. Jeevagathas.

In India itself the assassins early wrote off any survival of nonviolent politics, which have had a most remarkable life for an idea that was supposed to be dead. A new generation of university students fed up with the prevailing corruption invited Gandhi's disciple J. P. Narayan to train them in nonviolent methods for a campaign that led to the totally nonviolent overthrow of the Indira Gandhi government in 1977 and its replacement with a Gandhian premier, Morarji Desai. Although the Janata-led government was short-lived it provides a model of nonviolent policies and statecraft, as well as the problems of compromise and retention of power. The Mahatma's most ardent Muslim follower, Abdul Ghaffar Khan continued to practice nonviolence in Pakistan after partition, but has spent most of his life in jail. That nonviolence is not dead in Pakistan either is shown by the civil disobedience against the Zia-ul-Haq regime in 1983.

On every continent there is growth of nonviolent action. For example, Australians sent the sailboat *The Pacific Peacemaker* in 1981 to join with New Zealanders to continue protests against nuclear tests in the Pacific Ocean, and to support the growing Nuclear Free Pacific movement of islanders.

At the world level there has also been an expansion of nonviolent politics. United Nations officials have been influenced by nonviolent ideas to an extent unknown in the League of Nations, particularly in the diplomacy of its third Secretary General, U Thant (1961–1971) and high officers like Ralph Bunche and Robert Muller. The founding of the UN University for Peace in Costa Rica owes much to the Gandhian orientation of its proposer, President Rodrigo Carazo (1978). The most striking development in world political thought has been the emergence of the discipline of Peace Research which begins by assuming peace is a goal, and often sets nonviolence as an explicit means. Future studies has been similarly influenced by nonviolence, particularly when adopted as a specific value, as was done by the World Order Models Project. Out of peace research has grown the intensive study of nonviolent civilian-based defense by Wing Commander Stephen King-Hall, Boserup and Mack, Adam Roberts and other scholarship which has attracted the favorable attention of military professionals.[1] An example of the growing importance of such studies is the award of the Wallach Prize to Professor Gene Sharp's study, 'Making Abolition of War a Realistic Goal'.

Summing up, we have seen a remarkable geographical and theoretical expansion of nonviolent political action since the death of Gandhi 40 years ago. It has spread to every part of the world, is known to and used by larger numbers of people of every social class, and constantly develops new forms of expression. The vitality of the concept is so striking that it may prove to be the most revolutionary idea of the twentieth century.

'BUDDHIST ECONOMICS'

Thus far we have presented the most obvious and effective influence of Gandhi on the modern world, the growth of nonviolent political action. However, other aspects of Gandhi's thought are gaining importance too. For much of Gandhi's generation his ideas of reverence for nature and conservation of resources seemed contrary to the dynamic of growth that had dominated the West since the Renaissance. Gandhi had emphasized opposite values to those of the consumer society: the reduction of individual wants, the return to direct production of foodstuffs and clothing, and self-sufficiency rather than growing dependency. As the limits of growth and the inherent scarcity of resources broke upon the world of the 1960s, the Gandhian idea of restraint suddenly made sense. One of the most effective expressions of this view was presented by the former head of the British Coal Board, E. F. Schumacher.[2] What he called 'Buddhist Economics' was clearly Gandhian economics of loving care for the earth rather than its exploitation, striving for self-reliance rather than external dependency, application of appropriate, i.e. low-level, easily repaired and inexpensive, technology like Gandhi's spinning wheel, and concern for the welfare of the peasant and preservation of rural society rather than its neglect in favor of urban industrialization.

This shift of attitude has been resisted by the dominant social paradigm, in the India of Nehru as much as the developed world, but the change has been obvious. It can be seen in the growth of nonviolent communes, including some specifically Gandhian ones of the Community of the Ark in France, the United States and Argentina, or in the voluntary simplicity of Arthur Harvey's apple picking in New Hampshire.[3] Vegetarianism, for which Gandhi first got intellectual support from the West, is now spreading, aided by Gandhi's example and arguments.

In India itself the organization which Gandhi founded for the welfare of all, the Sarvodaya movement, has grown under the direction of his favorite *satyagrahi*, Vinoba Bhave. Going beyond his master's discoveries, Bhave found a nonviolent means of land reform to obtain gifts of 4.5 million acres of land between 1951 and 1958. Bhave and others have given reality to Gandhi's dream of a peace brigade based upon local service, the Shanti Sena, and have achieved the peaceful surrender of thousands of rural bandits who fled from and preyed upon rural poverty. Robert Trumbull recently reported that India has hundreds of volunteer projects in rural development, among them the Roys' village school and craft centers in Rajastan, the Bhais' work for tribal education and health, 100,000 villages where *khadi*, the home-spun cloth promoted by Gandhi is produced, and 2,000 volunteer groups promoting village welfare in Gandhi's home state of Gujarat alone. The Quaker Marjorie Sykes has carried on a successful Gandhian rural development center in the Nilgiri Hills. Heifer International has assisted Gandhi's goal of improving cows by aiding cattle breeding for Operation Flood which helps 1.3 million producers of milk in 40,000 village cooperatives.

Outside of India, Gandhian ecological ideas have had increasing popularity and use. In Sri Lanka, Ariyaratne began rural development projects promoted by the Gandhian Sarvodaya movement in 1957, which continued with tank-cleaning and weeding campaigns that have extended Gandhian ideas under Senanayake. American university students have participated in these projects as part of the semester abroad program of the Food, Land and Power Program of Pomona College, bringing back important first-hand experience of the reality of Gandhian solutions for the problems of Third World development.

With the rapid growth of the ecological perspective of economics, recognizing the reality of limited resources and the fragility of the ecosphere, as well as concern for the welfare of the rural majority of humankind, the Buddhist economics of Gandhi makes more and more sense.

SOCIAL JUSTICE AND HUMAN RIGHTS

The successful adoption of Gandhi's technique of nonviolence for political reform has obscured the extent to which he applied it to achieve social justice. Starting with racial discrimination in his first campaign of 1908, he promoted womens' rights (1909 onwards), industrial labor rights in the Ahmedabad strike of 1918, rural land reform in Champaran (1917), Kheda (1918) and Bardoli (1922, 1928); he campaigned against religious discrimination (Vykom temple access, 1924); against liquor sales (1930); for concern and care for the poor (1930); and for Untouchables (1931), to name only the major campaigns.

One of the first extensions of Gandhian nonviolent agitation for human rights was his friend Rev. Charles F. Andrews' campaign for the abolition of indentured labor in Fiji by 1920. Gandhi gave direct encouragement to American Blacks to use nonviolence for equal rights, and the leaders of CORE freedom rides and SNCC sit-ins were influenced by Gandhian ideas and techniques. Martin Luther King's 'pilgrimage to nonviolence' tells of his intellectual introduction to Gandhi at Boston University, then of his adoption of the practice when he got to Montgomery in 1955. King's assassination in 1968 brought the usual premature obituaries for nonviolence, but the influence among Black Americans has deepened as Coretta Scott King established a permanent center for nonviolent training in Atlanta, and widened as experienced followers of King carried the technique to the impoverished ghettoes of the West and North. One of the most impressive is Operation PUSH for Humanity led by Rev. Jesse Jackson which has extended rights agitation to problems of employment and education. Voter registration has continued in the South, contributing to a real sense of ability to remedy economic problems as Blacks gain offices in legislatures and governments.

Nonviolent action for social reform was taken up by Cesar Chavez in 1965 under the inspiration of Gandhi, using fasting, picketing and boycotts successfully to achieve a major reform of farm labor conditions in California. While skeptics were eagerly writing off nonviolent social reform, a new campaign to help Mid-Western field workers was begun in 1982 by Baldemar Valasquez in the Gandhian spirit. The Catholic Worker movement has supported nonviolent reforms, and adopted some aspects of Gandhian thought to agitate and extend the rights of the urban poor of America. Most American social rights movements, from Greenpeace to Gay Rights, have profited from Gandhian ideas and extended their application. Of course inspiration for such action comes from many other sources, both religious and secular, but Gandhi's particular emphasis upon the fundamental right to life which nonviolence protects has given many social reform campaigns of the twentieth century a far more peaceful character than the strikes, boycotts and protests of the previous era, and has consequently achieved more permanent reform.

EQUALITY OF RELIGIONS

Gandhi's extremely tolerant religious views now seem increasingly in accord with world trends of the century. To him the cardinal virtue of religious tolerance was based upon the intrinsic value of the equality of all religions. He felt that human limitations permit one to see only part of the whole, and that it was one's 'duty, to blend into our faith every acceptable feature of other faiths.' [*Yeravda Mandir*, Ch. x]. This would not weaken our own faith, but give it greater strength, as he personally discovered in becoming a better Hindu. This anticipates much of the ecumenical spirit that has arisen among Christians in the mid-twentieth century, going beyond mere tolerance of other faiths to an appreciation of their insights, and beyond that to seeking the common features of all religions. The encouraging trend is of course resisted by traditional narrow bigotry, both in Western intolerance and in the Indian fanaticism that killed Gandhi. But we now find traditionally hostile Christians reaching out not only to each other, but to long-persecuted Jews, to persistently misunderstood Muslims, and to all religions of the world, as in the World Conference on Religion and Peace. None of this appears to have weakened anyone's faith, but rather turned it from superficial differences to the deeper meaning of religious faith.

Another aspect of Gandhi's religious thought that is becoming more relevant is the link between faith and politics. When the century opened, the four-hundred-year-long secularization of politics in the West was affecting India. But Gandhi had found effective political action through religion, one which insisted upon tolerance and nonviolence. Thus, 'those who say that religion has nothing to do with politics do not know what religion means'. [*Autobiography*, 'Farewell']. Breaking the false dichotomy between ethics and action, Gandhi demonstrated that all of life's activities, including effective politics, can be governed by a religious spirit. This comes hard to a cynical and brutalized Machiavellian power politics or to Kautilyan India, but we find more and more altruistic statesmen like Dag Hammarskjold, U Nu of Burma, Anwar Sadat of Egypt, and Borge of Nicaragua, as well as countless ethical politicians in every land.

THE PHILOSOPHY OF TRUTH

We are witnessing the growing importance of Gandhi's philosophy of Truth. Gandhi, of course, made no pretense to be a philosopher, and his modesty in this may make us overlook the tribute of Radhakrishnan, India's most important philosopher, who held a chair at Oxford, that 'Gandhi was a revolutionary thinker' [*Mahatma Gandhi*, p. 1]. Both Karl Jaspers and Albert Schweitzer also reckoned Gandhi as an important philosopher. The most systematic exposition of his thought is in *From Yeravda Mandir*, written from the prison of that name where he was incarcerated after the great Salt March of 1930. This begins logically with his metaphysical foundation, 'Truth is God.' Truth is the supreme reality of the universe, and the end of all existence.

From this base Gandhi systematically derived his ethics: the means to Truth must be nonviolence or love. This eternal law of love/nonviolence, two sides of a coin, is 'the supreme duty' of all. From Truth is derived all the ethical principles of Gandhi's life and the observances of the community *ashram*: self-control, nonstealing, poverty, bread labor, humility, adherence to Truth, service of all, and self-sacrifice.

Gandhi completed his philosophical system with a sound psychology of individual action. As a *karma yogin*, or active seeker of God through 'experiments with Truth', Gandhi integrated theory with practice. Thus, the search for Truth must begin with self-control: reining of one's natural desires, control of one's thought, and ultimately renunciation of all attachment. For this Gandhi used a new term, *Anasakti Yoga*, or the gospel of detachment. This surely meant no indifference to the world and its suffering, but a devotion to the service of humanity by a deliberate renunciation of personal desire and possession, in a sole devotion to God, or Truth. Gandhi's psychology developed specific ways to overcome fear through love, subduing pride with humility, linking ethics to action by the use of vows, acceptance of personal sacrifice to serve the common good, practical steps to self-reliance and self-help, and most important, the essential dedication to noninjury, for which he coined the term *satyagraha*, or Truthforce.

With a well-integrated metaphysics, ethics and psychology Gandhi presented a systematic and complete philosophy that accorded with the reality that he had found in practice, and that others could also test. Gandhi claimed no uniqueness for this system, and asserted that it was expressed in the basic tenets of every great world faith: Islam, Judaism, Buddhism, Christianity, as well as his own Hinduism. Whether these faiths and the other major cultures of the world would accept Gandhi's unifying principles may be doubted, but we owe much to Gandhi in showing that every system started with the reality of Truth or God, called for an ethics of love, and showed the devotee the way to Truth by personal devotion and renunciation of selfish desire.

Notes

1. See Stephen King-Hall, *Defence in the Nuclear Age* (Nyack, NY: Fellowship Publications, 1959); Anders Boserup and Andrew Mack, *War Without Weapons: Non-violence in National Defense* (New York: Schocken Books, 1975); Adam Roberts (ed.), *The Strategy of Civilian Defence* (London: Penguin, 1969).
2. See E. F. Schumacher, *Small is Beautiful* (London: Abacus, 1974).
3. Arthur Harvey, the leading American supplier of Gandhi's writings and books on nonviolence, maintains a Gandhian lifestyle, training in apple picking. For information, contact Arthur Harvey, Canton, ME. 04221.

Part I
Gandhi the Man

Introduction to Part I

John Hick

The idea for this book arose from a colloquium held at The Claremont Graduate School in 1984 entitled 'Mahatma Gandhi and his Significance for Today'. The emphasis of the colloquium fell upon the latter half of the title and stressed the relevance of Gandhi's ideas to the problems of our contemporary world. This is undoubtedly what Gandhi himself would have wished. He did not seek personal adulation, and would not have desired it retrospectively; but he did insistently challenge the world with a revolutionary idea – not new but lived out by him in a new way – which could profoundly affect human life, and he was deeply concerned that it be allowed to make its impact upon peoples' minds and hearts. He believed that nonviolence is a truth whose time has come, and that it only needs to be heard and to be seen at work in the lives of those who have accepted it, to win a response.

But even though our eyes are on the world around us, it is impossible to forget the man Mohandas K. Gandhi. For he was certainly one of the outstanding human beings of this or perhaps of any century. His life enlarges our understanding of the human potential and is thus a source of hope for many. It was above all a life of continuous inner growth. Gandhi was not born, but became a *mahatma* – a 'great soul'. He was not created as such by the media but recognized by the untutored perception of millions of ordinary people, the peasants of India. What they recognized in him was a man of towering moral integrity and authority who was not concerned for himself but for them, because he was concerned for what he called Truth. The ordinary Indian villagers felt that the Mahatma was on their side, on the side of humanity, against the oppressive powers of foreign imperialism, economic exploitation, caste barriers, racial and religious discrimination.

It was thus Gandhi's gradual transcendence of ego, his near attainment of a universal, rather than a self-centered, outlook that constituted him a saint. If one expects a saint to be perfect, then Gandhi was (as Mark Juergensmeyer points out) a flawed saint; and indeed in this sense no doubt all saints have been flawed saints. Certainly Gandhi made mistakes, even 'Himalayan blunders', which he did not conceal either from himself or from others. (Though whether his judgment concerning the separate franchise for the 'Untouchables', to which Juergensmeyer refers, was a mistake, is open to debate. Gandhi saw the proposed separate franchise for the outcastes as a continuation of the long-standing British policy of 'divide and rule'.) Yet, despite his mistakes, Gandhi was so singlemindedly, so effectively, and so infectiously dedicated to the achievement of inner and outer liberation that his life and thought, in their inseparable unity, give substance to the perennial human hope for a better future. In his paper titled 'Gandhi in South Africa' James Hunt reminds us that although there are said to be more than four hundred biographies of Gandhi, there is, nevertheless, a dearth of well-researched studies of particular phases of his life. Hunt provides an invaluable bibliographical resource concerning Gandhi's twenty years in South Africa, indicating both the successful work done on this and the large gaps waiting to be filled. Also in the area of Gandhi's biography, Arvind Sharma, in 'Gandhi and Celibacy', shows interestingly how the unity of Gandhi's life and thought was expressed in his vow of celibacy. He took this vow of *brahmacharya* at the same time that he began his life of public service and the vow, like that of a celibate priest, was an aspect of his total self-dedication to a cause greater than himself. He saw his moral power to influence the masses as dependent upon his own mental and bodily discipline. Even his experiment in old age, testing his brahmacharya by sleeping close to a young girl, at the time of his attempt to halt the bloody outbreak of Hindu–Muslim violence, seems to have been a testing in his personal life of the moral power that he needed in his public life.

This unity of life and thought is well expressed by Paul Mundschenk in his paper on satyagraha as a search for inner dignity rather than for political power. Gandhi was not working simply for Indian self-government. This he helped to achieve. But he was also working for something much deeper – the inner liberation and self-government of each Indian man and woman; and in this he failed, as all other great religious leaders throughout the world have failed. Human beings continue to be largely self-centered and human society to be largely unjust.

But the truth of nonviolence was not killed by the bullets that killed Gandhi, and indeed his approach to life seems more manifestly relevant to the world's problems today than it did, except in India itself, in his own time. Ahimsa is an integral concept which affects the whole of life, holding profound challenge and profound promise for a world caught in the multiple dangers of the threat of nuclear war, of conflict between rich and poor, White and Black, North and South, and of the irresponsible depletion of the earth's natural resources. The paradox now is that in India, despite the Mahatma's revered status as the Father of the Nation, his distinctive ideas have had comparatively little influence since his death, whereas in other areas of the Third World there has recently been a marked growth of interest in the Gandhian approach to a wide range of problems. As one who travels extensively in the Third World, and who is himself the former President of a developing country (Costa Rica), Rodrigo Carazo reported to the colloquium on this widespread new turning to Gandhi. It has to do not only with de-escalating the arms race, but also with focusing attention upon the needs of the poorest rather than the richest, and of the villages rather than the Westernized cities; the development of appropriate technologies which will conserve resources whilst spreading employment as widely as possible; economic policies whose basic value is not money but human welfare; and educational and consciousness-raising development for all.

In such ways the man and the message are still speaking to us today.

2
The Heart of Satyagraha: A Quest for Inner Dignity, not Political Power

Paul Mundschenk

Mohandas Karamchand Gandhi, the Mahatma, called a meeting of the Congress workers of the Bardoli District for Friday, February 10 1922. The entire country seemed poised on the threshold of resolute action: they were about to begin a campaign of civil disobedience by refusing to pay taxes, a campaign which was to be launched in Bardoli and which many felt had the potential of crippling the mighty British Raj, and thereby winning *swaraj*, or self-rule, for the Indian people. It was the final phase of the non-cooperation movement begun early in 1921, and Gandhi himself had forecast the consequences of the Bardoli campaign with these words: 'When the Swaraj flag floats victoriously at Bardoli, then the people of the district next to Bardoli ... should seek to plant the flag of Swaraj in their midst. Thus in district after district, in regular succession, throughout the length and breadth of India, shall the Swaraj flag be hoisted.'[1] There were even those within the government who felt that this campaign could not be handled, that 'Bardoli was checkmate', as one civil servant put it.[2]

In Bardoli, then, the very air was electric with the excitement of anticipation, but the Mahatma was far from exhilarated. He was restless and unsettled, but clearly in no mood to lead his troops of moral warriors off to battle the satanic forces of the Raj. Thus he brought the meeting to a close by telling the gathered faithful:

> I regard those who have assembled here as some of the best workers in the country. In fact, I can see the condition of India at the present time truly reflected by this small assembly. What I have heard now confirms me in the belief that most of those who

are present here have failed to understand the message of nonviolence. This convinces me that the country at large has not at all accepted the teaching of nonviolence. I must, therefore, immediately stop the movement for civil disobedience.[3]

What was going on here? What had he heard at the meeting that led Gandhi to call off the Bardoli campaign, and leave thousands of jailed Congress workers – including Jawaharlal Nehru – seething with anger? The answer, in short, is simple: just as he said, the people had failed to understand the message and teaching of nonviolence, i.e. the manifest meaning of *satyagraha*, the power of Truth as he understood it. Hence, he was compelled to call a halt to a movement that might even have crippled colonial rule, for the sole attainment of political power itself was not the Mahatma's primary concern. To be sure, the goal of satyagraha was swaraj, self-rule, and, as a mass movement, people quite naturally understood it to mean the end of British dominion and the control of the government by Indians. But Gandhi's vision of swaraj included much more than the sparse measure of sovereignty assigned to power politics. He labored for the Indian soul, not merely her visible polity.

Gandhi called off the campaign because he himself finally realized what his goals genuinely were. That realization and the full range of its implications came slowly to Gandhi over a period of about three or four years. During that time he came to see with greater and greater clarity that the masses of Indian people had not even begun to integrate the meaning of swaraj and nonviolence into the unfolding of their everyday lives. Just five days before he called off the Bardoli campaign, a mob in Chauri Chaura, a town some 800 miles from Bardoli, had rioted and burned the city hall, killing several constables who were trapped inside. On the surface, it appeared that Gandhi terminated the pending civil disobedience in Bardoli because of the riot in Chauri Chaura. Indeed, at the meeting on February 10 he had asked every one present how they felt about going ahead with the campaign, given the Chauri Chaura tragedy. (All but three of those present said to go on with it.) Furthermore, in an article published in *Young India* six days later entitled 'The Crime of Chauri Chaura', Gandhi's first words were 'God has been abundantly kind to me'.[4] (God had inscrutable ways of being kind to Gandhi.) He went on to explain that this was the third time God had warned him that his impending course of action was wrong. (The first was his 'Himalayan blunder' of 1919, and the second the Bombay riots of November 17 1921.) Yet we would be wrong to link the two events causally and conclude that if Chauri Chaura had not exploded, the Bardoli campaign would have gone on as planned. Gandhi felt he had been mistaken in pushing for external change before the requisite internal realignments had been made. Hence, when Chauri Chaura blew up, he humiliated himself, accepted the blame for the violence, fasted, and felt good again, even as he was carted off to jail.

TRANSFORMATION

The process of Gandhi's inner transformation involved two distinct changes in his thinking and one truly decisive event. We will begin with a brief look at the circumstances in South Africa that led to the emergence of the term *satyagraha* itself.

The story of the 1906 'Black Act' in the Transvaal is well known. The government proposed an ordinance that would require all Indians to register with the authorities and to carry a certificate at all times, on penalty of imprisonment or deportation. The Indian community responded with a movement that Gandhi at first called 'passive resistance', but this phrase caused some confusion. When a small prize was offered for the best designation for the new struggle, the word *sadagraha* meaning 'firmness in a good cause', was suggested. Gandhi responded by saying:

> I liked the word, but it did not fully represent the whole idea I wished it to connote. I therefore corrected it to 'Satyagraha.' Truth (Satya) implies love, and firmness (Agraha) serves as a synonym for force. I thus began to call the Indian movement 'Satyagraha,' that is to say, the Force which is born of Truth and Love and nonviolence, and gave up the use of the phrase 'passive resistance' in connection with it ...[5]

Few would dispute that dramatic acts of love or of devotion to truth do, in fact, have the capacity to touch those centers of the human heart where high thoughts and noble deeds germinate and sometimes come to fruition. There really is a kind of power juxtaposed to *satya*, to Truth and Love. For Gandhi, however, that

The Heart of Satyagraha

power was real, concrete, and utterly irresistible. What's more, he felt that whatever the circumstance, the course of action that most closely expresses Truth itself is discernible, and that if one were to act in accordance with it in any given situation, one's opponent would be made to see and acknowledge Truth. At that point, because of Truth's power, the opponent would be converted and would join in the appropriate action.

Initially, these convictions were combined in Gandhi with a generally positive view of the British and their Empire. Even during his early satyagraha campaigns in India (in Champaran, Ahmedabad, and Kheda), Gandhi believed that the British Empire was based on sound moral principles and that the intentions of the men ruling India were by and large for the good of the Indian people. Errors were made, of course, but Gandhi felt that India had benefitted from contact with the British, and though he spoke of swaraj even in those days, he had no desire to see India leave the Empire. It was for this reason that he worked with such enthusiasm during the recruitment drive in 1918, even though he had little success. The Rowlatt Act shook him, but he still believed in British constitutionalism. He also felt that the 'British' in the government accepted their own standards, that they could and would be made to see their own errors, and would therefore one day confer Dominion status upon India of their own accord.

Then came Amritsar – the massacre at Jallianwalla Bagh on April 13 1919 – the one decisive event in Gandhi's inner transformation, the incident that triggered the first fundamental change in his basic perception of the British in India and what he should do about the bare fact of the colonial situation. Under the clear light of fire from General Dyer's rifles, Gandhi came to a new understanding of British paternalism, and the reason the British were there. He branded the whole system with the strongest term he knew: satanic. The Hunter Commission, which whitewashed Dyer's act, strengthened his new understanding, and Gandhi would never again view the British with the same sense of love and trust. Yet he would always remain unembittered toward the British as individuals. He knew they would never leave of their own accord, yet the kinds of activities that are natural to a drive for political power were abhorrent to him. He wanted the British out, but he didn't want to force them out in the traditional manner. He would find another way – a way aimed principally at the Indians themselves – which would rely solely on action in accordance with the Truth, for in Gandhi's mind no other course of events would be appropriate.

At the very outset, then, Gandhi confronted certain dilemmas which he would never overcome with complete satisfaction. He was against the British, but not British people; he hated the British system of government, but not those individuals who ran it, who composed it. He depersonalized the System, abhorring it, but sparing those who, in reality, created and sustained it. He was aware that the government, as a system, was somehow invulnerable to the converting force of satyagraha, yet he would allow no other tactic in working for its (the government's) demise. In short, Gandhi set out to fight to the death a system composed of people, without harming the people.

He thus came up with a plan to gain independence, to free Indians from colonial rule as no people had ever sought freedom before. His tool, as always, was satyagraha, but his objective was no longer to convert the invulnerable Raj. Rather, Gandhi would pursue the complete moral regeneration of the Indian people; he would mold them into a spiritual giant against whom the degenerate Empire would not have a chance. India would simply stand up straight, shrug her shoulders, and the morally-impoverished Raj would roll from her back. At this juncture, then, after Amritsar, Gandhi still employed satyagraha as a means toward political independence, but Truth's power would now be directed towards the conversion of Indians, not Britons.

Gandhi's vision found expression in a positive program with specific steps leading toward specific goals, all in the service of cultivating self-respect among the people and strengthening the moral fiber of the nation as a whole. Express objectives included getting the spinning wheel into every home and putting an end to the use of foreign cloth, the abolition of untouchability among Hindus, and placing the Congress into every village in India.

Gandhi worked out a long-range scheme in which the Indian people would progress through four stages toward the implementation of measures that would bring about swaraj. The first stage was more or less symbolic: the surrendering of all honors and titles bestowed upon Indians by the British. The second stage included the resignation of all civil servants and all lawyers in the service of the Raj. This was to be carried out slowly, in piecemeal fashion, for Gandhi did not envision a sudden disruption of Indian society.

In addition, all students would be withdrawn from government-sponsored schools, and put into national schools which would be taught in the vernacular. After this, the only ones remaining in the service of the Raj would be called upon to end their cooperation as well; i.e., the police and members of the armed forces would step down. This was to be the third stage, which Gandhi saw as occurring somewhere in the remote future. The final act of non-cooperation – a tax strike – lay in the still-more-distant future.

The transformation that was taking place in India, beginning with the Khilafat agitation during late 1919 and early 1920, lacked the nationwide dedication to a real and profound spiritual regeneration as the necessary and sufficient step to swaraj. There were some, of course, whose lives were to become reflections of the Gandhian spirit, but these would always be in a tiny minority. Gandhi predicted that swaraj could be attained within a year if the response to his program was sufficiently strong. He emphasized the conditional, the 'if', but he should never have placed moral transformation in a time frame. In December 1920, Congress finally authorized the non-cooperation movement with swaraj as the objective. 'Swaraj within a year' became the slogan, the flag around which the thousands of volunteer workers would rally. It also spelled out the inevitable doom of the movement. Gandhi was able to bring the change in Indian thinking just so far; 'Swaraj within a year' killed it, for a nationwide conversion to Gandhian morality might conceivably be approximated to a small degree within a generation, say, but nothing substantial could possibly come to fruition in one year. Hence, the year that was to bring swaraj to all the people brought, in its place, a deeper understanding to Gandhi himself of the meaning and applicability of the heart of the satyagraha.

The end of the non-cooperation movement, then, was inevitable. Its timing depended solely on how long it would take Gandhi to realize what was really going on, and, hence, the story is a sad tale to tell. Misgivings cropped up early, but even the Mahatma had the power to rationalize, which seems to be the lot of us all. The year 1921 must have been an amazing year to watch what was happening in India, for occasionally, at least, Gandhi seemed to think the people were pushing full steam ahead toward moral regeneration, but the vast majority of Indians who were involved at all were simply getting more and more excited about expelling the British from Indian soil. In the end, his vision would clear.

Along the way toward this clarity, however, Gandhi said and did some remarkable things. He never tired of reiterating that his program was constructive, that it was directed towards curing the ills of Hindu society, bringing Hindus and Muslims together, and building spiritual strength among both communities. He even disclaimed being against the British. On May 5 1920, he had written: 'the (non-cooperation) movement is not anti-English. It is not even anti-government'.[6] He added that 'I serve the Empire by refusing to partake in its wrong',[7] and cited historical examples of Britons who had done the same thing before him. The British felt Gandhi was being about as straightforward as a fox, and while they were wrong in believing him devious, one can easily understand their view.

The problem of Gandhi's being misunderstood by both Indians and the British may be traced in part to his own lack of skill in presenting his ideas clearly and forcefully. His article in *Young India* entitled 'The Doctrine of the Sword', for example, was written with the express intent of convincing skeptics that nonviolence is infinitely preferable to violence; but it gained immortality because it contains Gandhi's famous statement that he would prefer violence to cowardice. In fact, this article exemplifies the kind of Gandhian thinking that led to widespread misunderstanding and confusion.[8] In an attempt to show the strength and 'manliness' of the basic posture of non-cooperation, he first asserts that 'forgiveness is more manly than punishment'. What follows is an argument which begins by pointing out that 'abstinence is forgiveness only when there is the power to punish', as a mouse can hardly be said to forgive a cat for killing it. Gandhi then says that he understands those who yearn for the punishment of General Dyer ('They would tear him to pieces if they could', he says), but, suddenly, as if he realized that he was portraying the British as the cat and India as the mouse, he changes the analogy, telling his readers: 'I do not believe India to be helpless. I do not believe myself to be a helpless creature. Only I want to use India's and my strength for a better purpose.' So, now we have the assertion that only those with the power to punish can forgive, and that many Indians would like to punish Dyer but can't. The logical result of this is that 'therefore India lacks power', but Gandhi doesn't say that. Instead we get a brief statement that India and Gandhi both have strength. But there was more. Gandhi points out that 'strength does not come from physical capacity', for he seems to have realized that he implied India was without physical power.

He adds that strength is a matter of will, and he documents India's strength with these words: 'We in India may in a moment realize that one hundred thousand Englishmen need not frighten three hundred million human beings.' We are overwhelmed by the irony of Gandhi's appeal to the sheer strength of numbers in convincing his people that they commanded the true strength found only in *spiritual* force, and he then goes on to beg the question: 'A definite forgiveness would therefore mean a definite recognition of our strength. With enlightened forgiveness must come a mighty wave of strength in us.' In other words, India is strong, therefore we should forgive; if we forgive, then we will be strong.

Here and in other places where he appeals to spiritual strength, Gandhi also tells his readers what they want to hear – namely, in essence, 'let's get rid of the British'. In the article in question, he says: 'India considers herself to be powerless and paralyzed before the machine guns, tanks, and airplanes of the English. And she takes up non-cooperation out of her weakness. It must still serve the same purpose, namely, bring her delivery from the crushing weight of British injustice . . .'

Statements such as the above meant that Gandhi himself sowed some of the seeds which bloomed into large-scale misunderstanding of the movement's objectives. As implied earlier, the use of the term *swaraj* was enough to guarantee that the vast majority of those working under Gandhi's leadership would assume their goal was control of the government by Indians. Bhargava defines swaraj as 'self-government, home-rule, autonomy, independence'.[9] Gandhi said it was 'self-realization; the capacity of the people to get rid of their helplessness; the ability to regard every inhabitant of India as our own brother or sister; abandonment of the fear of death'.[10] At another time, he was looser yet: he said simply that it was undefinable. Years later, in retrospect, Jawaharlal Nehru could write about the uncertainty of Gandhi's thought with apparent fondness: 'It was obvious that to most of our leaders swaraj meant something much less than independence. Gandhi was delightfully vague on the subject, and he did not encourage clear thinking about it either.'[11] When Gandhi called off the non-cooperation movement in 1922, however, Nehru was sitting in jail. When he received the news, he burned with rage – not yet having felt the delight in Gandhi's vagueness.

A few more examples will help to illuminate Gandhi's inner journey during 1921. At the meeting of the All-India Congress

Committee on March 31, Gandhi introduced four resolutions which were all passed. He emphasized the need to register more members in the Congress, to expand the program of introducing the spinning wheel into the villages, and to continue to stick to the principle of nonviolence. But in one resolution he also included the statement that 'The Committee is of the opinion that the country is not yet disciplined, organized and ripe for the taking up of civil disobedience.'[12] Shades of things to come.

As the year progressed, Gandhi continued to talk about swaraj in sweeping, spiritual terms. He emphasized *swadeshi* – the use of hand-woven *khadi* and the boycott of foreign cloth – as of utmost importance. A huge bonfire of foreign cloth at a public meeting in Bombay led Gandhi to call the day 'sacred', but his friend Charlie Andrews was distressed by what he understood to be little more than people venting their hatred of the foreigner. Gandhi answered that the Indians were only burning their taste for foreign fineries which they did not need, and that therefore the motive was to punish themselves, not the foreigners: 'The idea of burning springs not from hate but from repentance of our past sins.'[13]

In time, there came events which forced Gandhi to become more realistic about the progress of his constructive program, and he began to understand the real extent to which the people had responded to his reforms. By October, the government began to move in and arrest many of those involved in the movement, and the Congress leaders who remained free were itching for direct action: after all, the end of the year in which swaraj was to have been won was drawing near. On November 5, the All-India Congress Committee authorized every province to undertake civil disobedience by its own choice, and Gandhi announced he would make an experimental start with a tax strike in Bardoli. Then the Prince of Wales landed, Bombay blew up, and Gandhi uttered the appropriate words: 'The swaraj I have witnessed in the last two days has stunk in my nostrils.'[14] What he had witnessed was an embodiment of the paradox that by that time permeated the movement: properly attired in home-spun khadi, his army of non-violence, his cadre of disciplined satyagrahi, filled the Bombay streets with uncontrolled fury and rioting.

Gandhi began to comprehend the fullness of what had happened in the past year. In January, Tagore made a public statement in which he mentioned that although he, too, believed in *ahimsa*, it had to spring truly from the people themselves, and could not be forced, as a technique, upon millions who did not feel it.[15] Gandhi probably knew Tagore was correct, but, at the Bardoli Conference in which the decision was made to go ahead with the tax strike, Gandhi sought to reassure himself one last time that perhaps everything would turn out all right. He posed five questions, and all present thereupon firmly answered that they: (1) regarded Hindu–Muslim–Christian–Parsi friendship as a sacred duty; (2) believed that nonviolence was the only method that could bring swaraj; (3) believed that swaraj could not be reached without adopting swadeshi, and even resolved that they would not use khadi made outside the Bardoli district; (4) believed that untouchability was contrary to *dharma*, and affirmed that they were ready to let untouchable children sit with their own children in national schools; and (5) were ready to lose all and go to jail, without getting angry, even if all their property were seized and they were reduced to beggary.[16] All having thus professed virtual sainthood, Gandhi went ahead and approved the impending tax strike.

Finally, days later, Chauri Chaura exploded and pushed the Mahatma to call the meeting with which we began this chapter. In a letter to Jawaharlal Nehru, Gandhi later poured out his feelings. He said:

> I received letters from both Hindus and Mohammadans ... telling me that our people were becoming aggressive, defiant, and threatening, and were not nonviolent in demeanor. Thirty-six thousand volunteers were enlisted in Gorakhpur, not 100 of whom conformed to the Congress pledge. I assure you that if the thing had not been suspended we would have been leading not a nonviolent struggle but essentially a violent struggle ... The cause will prosper by this retreat. The movement had unconsciously drifted from the right path. We have come back to our moorings, and we can again go straight ahead.[17]

It is doubtful the movement could ever have gone 'straight ahead' in the manner Gandhi envisioned, but that issue is academic. With the Bardoli affair, Gandhi expressly understood satyagraha to be a tool for the cultivation and nurturing of dignity within the individual – one that could not be used to convert an opponent, as he had learned from the British, or be counted on to raise the collective moral consciousness of the Indian masses. In an ironic sort of way, he had violated one of the basic teachings of his beloved Bhagavad Gita, for he had practiced satyagraha as a means toward an end. In the Gita, Arjuna is repeatedly admonished by Krishna to 'set thy heart upon thy work, but never on its reward' (2:47; Mascaro translation). Gandhi had not heeded that command, was disappointed with the fruits of his action, and had come up with a series of bizarre rationalizations which further infected and polluted his inner being. He would himself forever feel compelled to live according to Truth as he understood it, and therein lies the implication for anyone involved in a Gandhian movement today: satyagraha, at its heart, is an effective means to nurture one's own inner life, one's own spiritual journey. To hope for broader influence is only human, but no more is to be expected.

Notes

1. Mohandas K. Gandhi. Cited in Geoffrey Ashe, *Gandhi: A Study in Revolution* (London: Heinemann, 1968) pp. 228–9.
2. From an unknown member of the British government. Cited in ibid., p. 228.
3. Gandhi, 'Speech to Congress Workers, Bardoli', February 10 1922. *The Collected Works of Mahatma Gandhi* (New Delhi: The Publications Division, Ministry of Information and Broadcasting, Government of India: vol. xvii, 1965; vol. xviii, 1965; vol. xix, 1966; vol. xx 1966; vol. xxi, 1966; vol. xxii, 1966), vol. xxii, p. 377. Hereafter referred to as *Works*.
4. In *Young India*, February 16 1922. *Works*, vol. xxii, p. 417.
5. Gandhi, *Satyagraha in South Africa* (Madras Ganesan, 1928) p. 170.
6. Ibid.
7. Ibid.
8. Gandhi, 'The Doctrine of the Sword', *Young India*, August 4 1920; *Works*, vol. xviii, pp. 131–4. All the quotes in the following discussion are taken from this article.
9. R. C. Pathak (compiler), *Bhargava's Standard Illustrated Dictionary, Hindi–English*, p. 1129.
10. Gandhi, cited in Ashe, *Gandhi: A Study in Revolution*, p. 210.
11. Jawaharlal Nehru. Quoted in Rajani Palme Dutt, 'Gandhi and the Nationalist Movement: A Marxist View', in Martin Deming Lewis (ed.), *Gandhi: Maker of Modern India* (Boston: D. C. Heath and Company, 1965) p. 31.
12. Gandhi (drafter), 'Resolutions at the AICC Meeting, Bozwada', March 31 1921. *The Hindu*, April 1 1921. *Works*, vol. xix, p. 497.
13. Gandhi, 'A Protest Against Burning', *Young India*, September 15 1921; *Works*, vol. xxi, p. 102.
14. Gandhi, 'Appeal to Bombay Citizens', *Young India*, November 24 1921; *Works*, vol. xxi, p. 466.

15. Rabindranath Tagore, cited in Ashe, *Gandhi: A Study in Revolution*, p. 227.
16. Gandhi, 'Speech at Bardoli Taluka Conference', January 29 1922, *Navajivan*, February 2 1922; *Works*, vol. XXII, p. 294.
17. Gandhi, 'Letter to Jawaharlal Nehru', February 19 1922. In Nehru, *A Bunch of Old Letters* (Bombay: Asia Publishing House, 1958); *Works*, vol. XXII, p. 436.

3
Shoring Up the Saint: Some Suggestions for Improving Satyagraha

Mark Juergensmeyer

No one should be expected to be perfect, not even Gandhi, and from time to time he had occasion to rebel against such lofty expectations. Gandhi is on record more than once as having renounced the title of saint that his followers persistently thrust upon him. 'To clothe me with sainthood is too early even if it is possible', Gandhi said, adding that 'I myself do not feel a saint in any shape or form.'[1]

Despite these protestations, however, a myth of the Mahatma has emerged in which Gandhi looms larger than life. The saintly qualities imputed to Gandhi are frequently those related to his legendary control over personal passions, possessions, relationships, and social forces. Together they create a mighty image of moral power.[2]

Many of the legends are, in fact, quite true, and there is much in Gandhi's character and ideals to admire. But Gandhi is so recent a figure and so closely scrutinized an actor that the realities of his life protrude through the myth. Unlike the hagiography of the more traditional and distant saints, the stories of modern saints are constantly challenged by the records of journalists and historians, and by the abundant, sometimes incriminating, memorabilia that such figures often leave behind.[3]

In Gandhi's case, many of the inconsistencies between fact and legend are of little consequence. Historians report that he was stubborn, that he slighted his family, and that he pandered to admirers from the West. And there are rumors that his passions were not so carefully under control as he would have liked them to be.[4]

Some of Gandhi's human failings are of more troubling concern, however. These are the ones that affect the legitimacy of the Gandhian enterprise by causing us to question whether Gandhi's ideas can be made to work. These shortcomings are the patterns in Gandhi's behavior that suggest that difficulties might be encountered in applying Gandhian theory. If Gandhi himself could not implement his own ideals, one might ask, how can we?

Gandhi is susceptible to those sorts of questions because he was an activist as well as a thinker, and his most enduring legacies – his image and his ideas – are intimately bound to one another. The legendary figure of the saintly Mahatma battling the foes of injustice is an image that graphically demonstrates many of the principles for which he stood, including the striking notion that political and spiritual values can, at their best, be intertwined. The remembered Gandhi projects a picture of that ideal, someone who is simultaneously active and reflective – a 'sage in revolt'.[5] At the same time, his ideas – especially the seminal one of *satyagraha* – are meant to be guides to life, and to be incarnate in images such as his.

Even those of us who attempt to present his ideas in an abstract way, as universally applicable principles, must contend with the way that Gandhi applied them in his own life.[6] This need to test the ideas against the actions is probably more urgent for Gandhi's thought than it is, say, for the theories of Marx or Freud. We would be less disappointed, I suspect, if Marx were to deny that he was a Marxist (as he is once said to have done) than if Gandhi were shown to be un-Gandhian.[7] The reason, of course, is that Gandhi's ideas were so personal. Gandhi's life was intimately tied to his thought, and as Joan Bondurant has shown, one can often understand the latter by closely observing the former.[8] So it is especially incumbent on those of us who admire the Gandhian concepts to understand instances in which Gandhi acted in ways inconsistent with his own principles, and to see what can be done to reconcile the differences.

Let us take what is perhaps the most significant of Gandhi's concepts, satyagraha, and see to what degree Gandhi followed its tenets in one of his best-known encounters – the one that precipitated his 'epic fast'. We will ask what problems might have existed in Gandhi's actions, which of these might have been attributable to flaws in the concept, and how these conceptual matters might be improved in ways that are consistent with, and supportive of, the whole edifice of Gandhian theory.

THE CONCEPT OF SATYAGRAHA

Gandhi was not a philosopher or a theorist. His writings, however, are full of ideas, inchoate and unsystematic though they may be. His economic, political, and ethical insights all point towards a fundamental conviction about human nature: that it is capable of achieving genuine morality and can move toward an ideal society. Fundamental to these ideas, and to the whole structure of his thought, is *satyagraha*, the term Gandhi created out of two Sanskrit words, *satya*, 'Truth', and *agraha*, a word that means 'holding firm to', but which Gandhi often translated as 'force'.[9] He also described satyagraha as a movement,[10] indicating that the term was meant to be applied not to some static situation, or to an ontological state, but to a form of action. It is action to be done in the context of conflict, which is why satyagraha is often described as a method of fighting.

Satyagraha is also often characterized as a method of conflict resolution, but it is in the first instance not so much a method of resolving fights as one of waging them. An easy resolution to a fight – especially one that was premature, unjust, or arbitrary – would not have pleased Gandhi, nor would the cessation of hostility at a superficial level if some deeper disharmony continued to fester. Gandhi placed no premium on quiescence as such, and often seemed to encourage engagement, especially when silence would imply consent to an ongoing form of injustice.

Considering that he is often praised as a pacifist, it is noteworthy, then, that Gandhi's main theoretical contribution is a concept of struggle rather than of social order or inner peace. Perhaps a concept of conflict was important to Gandhi because he entered politics fighting. He was first drawn into the political arena because he wanted to challenge unjust authorities – first in South Africa, then in India – not because he wanted to implement a vision of ideal political order. Yet his continuing emphasis on satyagraha suggests that he viewed conflict as more than a matter of individual scuffles. For Gandhi, conflict appeared to be an enduring characteristic of society. Like Hobbes and Marx, he saw this persistent state of conflict as the greatest challenge facing socially responsible individuals and institutions.

What makes Gandhi different from these and many other thinkers is his insistence that conflict itself can be moral. He felt that the process of fighting, as well as its goals, can be virtuous. The difference between an unethical conflict and an ethical one is whether the fight involves Truth (*satya*) or 'untruth' (destructive actions and negative motives). Truthful fighting is critically different from any other kind, for it requires the fighters to suppress their own narrow positions in favor of something more inclusive, a principle to which all parties in a dispute would presumably assent, and through which all would gain.

A corollary to this concept of truthful fighting is the notion that the means of fighting should embody the same truthful state that it aims to bring into being. As Gandhi put it, 'the means are to the ends as the seed is to the tree'.[11] Gandhi contradicts the frequently held notion that any means can be justified if the ends are noble enough. In Gandhi's view, the method of fighting is as important as the goal; the means must be as moral as the end.

Moral fighting should be supportive rather than destructive, and it is from this premise that the well-known Gandhian insistence on nonviolence springs. Gandhi even defines satyagraha in nonviolent terms, as 'the force born of Truth and love or non-violence'.[12] In Gandhi's lexicon, nonviolence means not only restraint from using physical force but also the renunciation of any form of coercion. He admonished his followers even for saying 'shame, shame' to their opponents,[13] and decried any act that limited 'the freedom of the opponent'.[14]

Satyagraha, then, is a way of engaging in conflict that employs methods of fighting that are consistent with a harmonious resolution. It relies on the force of moral suasion, and abhors any form of coercion. To see whether Gandhi himself implemented such policies, let us look at the dramatic moment in Gandhi's own life when his commitment to a certain cause for what he regarded as Truth led to an 'epic fast'. It was a critical event in the development of India's policies toward Untouchables, and a turning point in Gandhi's own life. But was it satyagraha?

THE EPIC FAST

Early on the morning of September 20 1932, Gandhi wrote to Tagore that he was about to 'enter the fiery gate'[15] – an apt metaphor for what was to become an inflammatory event, the undertaking of a fast against the new British policy of establishing separate electorates for Untouchables. Gandhi had taken recourse to fasting before – including a 21-day fast in Delhi in 1924 – but never had he embarked on a fast with such dramatic publicity and such seriousness of purpose. This fast was to be 'unto death', as he ominously termed it, a warning as ultimate for a pacifist as a militant fighter's threat to shoot on sight. 'Nothing like it has been witnessed or heard of before', Gandhi's secretary breathlessly reported in a book-length account of the fast written several weeks later, 'and now that the crisis is over it has left a world taken unawares still wondering at the miracle.'[16] The event 'threw the country into a state of alarm, consternation and confusion', a Congress party historian proclaimed several years afterward.[17]

Considering the hyperbole and the publicity it received, the fast itself was not much of a feat. It lasted only six days – not long enough to pose a serious threat to the Mahatma's life, but long enough for the wrath of the politically active Untouchables to rise against him. Their ire was stirred not only by Gandhi's dogmatic support of a position they thought to be inimical to their interests, but by the audacity he displayed in claiming to speak on their behalf.[18] Gandhi regarded the completion of the fast as a victory for them, a 'message of freedom' which he hoped would 'penetrate every untouchable home'.[19] The message apparently did not penetrate the home of Dr B. R. Ambedkar, the representative of the Untouchables at the Round Table Conference, who was supporting the idea of separate electorates for his people.[20] Nor was it heard by the many other Untouchables who protested about Gandhi's position at the time, including some who embarked on their own fasts in opposition to his.[21]

The political drama of Gandhi's fast had begun the year before in London when the Round Table Conference raised but did not entirely deal with the matter of representation of minorities – especially Muslims and Untouchables – in the Indian Parliament. The British favored a scheme of communal representation, an approach applauded by the minority leaders themselves. The Indian nationalists were vehemently opposed, for the political costs were potentially staggering. In many areas of the country, such as the Punjab, the Untouchables held the balance of political power between Hindus and Muslims, and for them to be excluded from the Hindu camp would seriously have diminished the political clout of organized Hindus,[22] and eroded Congress's claims to speak for a united Indian society. So the stakes were high, and the British government's decision on August 17 1932 was in some ways an artful concession: it provided for two kinds of Untouchable representation, one to be elected by Untouchables themselves, and the other to be chosen by the general electorate but with reserved seats for candidates from lower castes. But even though the British policy seemed to be conciliatory, Gandhi would have none of it.

His vehemence on this point went beyond all political considerations. Nehru at the time 'felt angry with him at his religious and sentimental approach to a political question', as he put it in his autobiography.[23] Gandhi described his commitment to the fast as a 'call from God',[24] and parallels were drawn between his struggles and those in the *Mahabharata*. Much of the response to the fast, then and now, has been within religious circles, and the impact on Gandhi's own spiritual life was enormous: the fast was a turning point away from political and towards social involvement, especially social action regarding the removal of untouchability. It became, thereafter, a sort of obsession with him, and some have traced his declining political influence within the nationalist movement to that 'conversion' to anti-untouchability, as one biographer put it,[25] at the time of the epic fast.

WAS THE FAST SATYAGRAHA?

Did Gandhi's devotion to the ideals for which he fasted force him to compromise his ideals of moral struggle? In many ways Gandhi's behavior in this incident was consistent with satyagraha: his actions were centered on a principle, he held fast to it, and he used methods for advancing that principle that were nonviolent.

There were problems with this otherwise satisfying example of moral conflict, however. To begin with, the principle for which Gandhi fought was only one side of the Truth. Gandhi supported a truthful principle, all right – that Hindu society should be unified and harmonious – but neglected to see that Ambedkar and the other Untouchable leaders were fighting for a truthful principle of their own: that harmony could come only when the Untouchables expressed their freedom and dignity as a separate community within the Hindu fold. By ignoring Ambedkar and refusing to acknowledge the validity of his point of view, Gandhi appeared to be short-sighted in formulating his assessment of the truth that lay behind the conflict.

Gandhi's lack of respect for Ambedkar's position was unfortunate, not only because he failed to honor the Untouchable leader as a person, but also because he failed to recognize the morality of Ambedkar's mission. Although the Untouchable leader may have appeared to have been a separatist, by insisting on the right of distinct representation for his people Ambedkar's aim was to bring them, through those means, into the mainstream of Indian life. Ambedkar was embarking on something of a satyagraha of his own. But it was a satyagraha Gandhi was never able to see.

The dogmatism with which Gandhi asserted his own view of the truth was compounded, moreover, by the inflexibility implied by his use of a fast to support that view. Fasting as such is not antithetical to satyagraha – it may be regarded as a form of self-purification, or an attempt to take the suffering of a conflict upon oneself. But fasting 'unto death' is another matter. As soon as one embellishes the act with a dire prognosis for its outcome, what was a spiritual practice becomes a threat. I know of no way in which such a stance can be justified by Gandhian ethical logic – even if it is undertaken by Gandhi himself. It seems to me that the threat of killing oneself can be nothing else but coercion, for it severely limits the choices of the opponent; it encourages him or her to capitulate to the faster's position whether there is an agreement on principle or not. The threat of killing is, therefore, a violent act in Gandhian terms. This is obviously the case if the threat is carried to its morbid conclusion. But even if it is not, the threat violates the Gandhian injunction against desiring to harm, in this case desiring to harm oneself.

Moreover, once one has adopted a tactic of fasting 'unto death' there is no graceful retreat from one's position, save victory or a face-saving accommodation. The threat has the effect of hardening one's position unalterably, and this violates another fundamental tenet of Gandhian ethics, to remain always open to new versions of the truth. Gandhi's own rigidity in the case of the epic fast prevented him from embracing Ambedkar as a comrade, and made him deaf to what a Gandhian might otherwise have described as the truthful aspects of Ambedkar's own creative solution to the situation.

The nadir in Gandhi's use of fasting for coercive purposes is described by Pyarelal when, in the final stages of negotiating the pact with Ambedkar that ended the fast, there was a minor difference over whether the negotiated arrangement would be allowed to go for ten years before being reconsidered in a referendum, or whether it should go for only five. Pyarelal claims that Gandhi stated: 'I am adamant on this point. I may be a despicable person, but when Truth speaks through me I am invincible.' And then Pyarelal recalls that Gandhi used a tone of finality 'not unfamiliar to so many', and quite prepared to use his fasting as political leverage, said, 'there you are. Five years or my life'.[26]

These words do not sound as if they come from the kindly, generous Gandhi of our imaginations. They illustrate what should not surprise us – that our Gandhian idol, like most idols, has feet of clay. But they also show that satyagraha, as Gandhi had developed it by 1932, had some problems in its implementation, and perhaps some inherent contradictions.

SOME SUGGESTIONS FOR SATYAGRAHA

Interpreted in its simplest form, the theory of satyagraha seems to allow for stubbornness and coerciveness such as Gandhi's. After all, the notion of 'holding fast to Truth' implies that there is a single truth to be discerned in a conflict; one side has it, and the other does not. In the case of the epic fast, Gandhi clearly felt that he held claim to the truth; but then, so did Ambedkar.

Gandhi's blindness to Ambedkar's position may have been partially due to the exigencies of the situation. Gandhi felt he needed to act, and that he had to stick with whatever version of the truth was available at the time. But this points up a contradictory aspect of satyagraha: the fact that it is a form of analysis as well as action. The tasks of satyagraha require one to reflect on the nature of a conflict and envision a harmonious alternative to it, at the same time one is engaged in struggle with an opponent. Needless to say, the demands of engagement can interfere with the detachment necessary for reflection.

Nothing, however, is supposed to come between a Gandhian fighter and his or her allegiance to nonviolence. And perhaps nothing would challenge our saintly image of Gandhi more than to imagine him engaging in a violent act. Yet, if one is to accept his own insistence that coercion is a form of violence, Gandhi's threat to fast 'unto death' was indeed such an act. The difficulty here is not just Gandhi's own aggressive personality, but another contradiction in Gandhian theory: satyagraha requires one to be forceful without being coercive. Where can the line be drawn?

These issues are interrelated, but let us look at each of them in turn. My object will be to see how the difficulties might be resolved in ways that are consonant with the whole of Gandhian thought.

Begin with a search for Truth

It seems to me that the logic of satyagraha requires the practitioners of it to begin the procedure with a search for Truth, and not assume that they know it intuitively. I am so convinced of the logical necessity of this first step that in my primer of satyagraha, *Fighting With Gandhi*, I spend much of the first section on describing it, and showing how to go about the search for Truth in a way that is consonant with Gandhian ideals.[27] In Gandhi's own use of the term, however, this first stage is seldom mentioned – perhaps it is assumed. Instead, Gandhi emphasizes the necessity of fighting for Truth, and using Truth in one's means as well as in one's goal.

Why, then, do I consider the search for Truth to be a logical necessity? My answer is based on fundamental Gandhian ideas. It seems to me that if we accept the moral metaphysics implied in Gandhi's definition of Truth – that Truth is an ultimate moral reality – then this reality must lie in some measure behind virtually any moral position, as flawed and inchoate as that position may be presented. This means that the whole truth is greater than any one person's perception of it, a point of view that Gandhi seems to affirm in his statement about the inadequacies of humanly devised moral codes,[28] and his observation that we all have different 'angles of vision' through which we perceive the same Truth.[29]

If we accept this notion, we can never, at the outset of a fight, assume that we have the truth; rather, discerning it must be the first aim of our encounter with the other side. Joan Bondurant has described the first step for any *satyagrahi* as an analysis, in which 'he must clarify his understanding of his own position'.[30] I would add to that the necessity of a satyagrahi understanding the position of his or her opponent as well. Only in that way can the fight be 'Truth-creating', as Bondurant claims that it can be,[31] for only when the partial truth of one side is added to the partial truth viewed by the other can a larger vision of Truth be perceived. And only a view of Truth broader than our own initial perception of it is worth fighting for.

Yet the fact remains that Gandhi himself seldom talked about how one should go about the search for Truth, and the case of the epic fast shows that his inattention to this crucial aspect of satyagraha may have limited his own effectiveness in using it. If he had been less dogmatic, the cause of Truth might have been better served.

If we take seriously the notion that satyagraha is an 'experiment with Truth',[32] as well as the defense of it, we will be able to see Gandhi's approach as a fluid response to conflict situations, rather than a mechanical one. Such a notion has philosophical, as well as practical, significance. It seems to me that satyagraha, in its wider sense, signifies a style of ethics that is not rule-bound but exploratory in nature, and relies more on the character of the ethical quest than in guidelines for moral and political action.

Continue the Truth-search while fighting

Since the search for Truth involves an encounter – albeit an encounter of ideas – it may appear in the form of a struggle. This means that a Gandhian fight can be waged on two levels: the conflict between two views of truth, and the contention of power that (ideally) will allow the more truthful side to win out.

The two levels of fighting may be waged simultaneously. This means that my comment about the search for Truth being a stage in the Gandhian fight may have been a bit incomplete: it should be the first stage in a conflict, all right, but it should continue throughout the encounter, as a dimension of the struggle.

This notion of satyagraha as a dual form of fighting was implicit in Gandhi's ideas – 'a persistent element', Bondurant claims;[33] but it was not an idea that Gandhi fully developed or expounded on at length. And in the case of the epic fast it is noticeably absent from his conduct as well, for there the fight seems to be waged solely on the level of a confrontation of power. But even though Gandhi seldom included the confrontation of ideas in his discussion of satyagraha, I think that this way of thinking extends logically from his notion of Truth and the role it plays in a Gandhian fight. Moreover, Gandhi's discussion of the Bhagavad Gita indicates that he thought of struggle ultimately in cosmic terms, as a war between Truth and untruth where 'the field of battle is in our own body'.[34] This, I think, supports the notion that Gandhian fighting always has a deeper level, a struggle for Truth, even in the midst of a struggle for power on behalf of a truthful cause.

When Gene Sharp describes satyagraha as based upon 'a theory of power', therefore, he is only partly right.[35] In addition to providing a means for mobilizing strength nonviolently (largely through non-cooperation),[36] satyagraha also provides the arena in which truth can be pursued in a dialectical manner, as Joan Bondurant puts it.[37]

If this is the case, satyagraha should be thought of not only as a political strategy but as an epistemological concept. It is a way of knowing, by pitting opposing perceptions of it together. Satyagraha, then, should be described not only as an approach to conflict but as a process of discovering an emerging Truth. The Sanskrit term for truth, *satya*, is based on a verb, so it is appropriate to think of it in fluid terms; not something one must determine before being engaged in the fight, but something that emerges in the process of fighting.

Clarify what coercion is permissible

Even though we defined satyagraha as fundamentally opposed to coercion, we found Gandhi's use of fasting 'unto death' to be indeed coercive. How can this apparent contradiction be reconciled?

Joan Bondurant would show no surprise over Gandhi's behavior, for in her view he was often coercive, and justly so. She allows for a measure of coercion in satyagraha, especially in the later stages of a campaign, in order to make a truthful position win out; but this is allowed only after the more civil attempts at moral suasion have been exhausted.[38] Even so, she claims, the coercion that is allowed in these later stages must be of a nonviolent character. Borrowing from the ideas of Clarence Marsh Case, Bondurant describes a concept of nonviolent coercion – one in which coercion is the indirect result of the action, and not the purpose of it; suffering is accepted by the nonviolent coercer as well as by the opponent; and the coercion is used in a constructive spirit.[39]

Yet this is somehow unconvincing. For not only have 'a few followers of Gandhi' protested against the view that satyagraha is 'always persuasive and never coercive', as Bondurant would have us believe,[40] but Gandhi himself – again and again, in myriad ways – prohibited, as he put it, 'the use of violence in any shape or form'.[41] And he made it clear that the shape and form of violence included anything that limited the free will of the opponent.[42]

Moreover, if Gandhi's prescription against coercion is to be abandoned, it seems to me that the worst moment to do so would be the 'later stages' of a fight, when positions harden, and devices of persuasion escalate to a potentially dangerous degree. Gandhi's own use of fasting at the later stages of negotiation in the epic fast incident is an unfortunate example of the perils inherent in using coercion at this stage.

Rather, it seems to me, if coercion can be justified at all in a Gandhian fight, it can be justified only at the beginning – pre-satyagraha, so to speak – rather than at the end. In *Fighting With Gandhi*, I argue for an amendment to Gandhian theory that would allow for a certain form of coercion in unusual situations where satyagraha could not proceed otherwise: in instances, for example, when an unruly opponent must be bridled and restrained in order for a reasonable encounter to take place. Such coercion would give the nonviolent fighter the leverage of power to then wage a nonviolent fight effectively. Utilizing a distinction made by Case, and also by Kirby Page, I call such coercion 'detentive', as opposed to the destructive kind which aims at incapacitating an opponent. Detentive coercion, by contrast, aims only at restraining an opponent's violence.[43]

What difference does the timing of coercion make – whether it is before or during the later stages of a Gandhian fight? Isn't the significant question whether coercion is permissible at all? Yes, and that is why I argue that coercion is essentially outside the rules of satyagraha, and justified only if it makes satyagraha possible.

It seems to me that what is at issue here is not just the matter of satyagraha as a technique, but as a form of moral order. It is as if two ways of conceiving social relationships are at stake: one based on dominance and singular control, and the other based on cooperation and mutual consent. The latter is a hopeful ideal, to be sure, but in embracing it Gandhi also begins with a realistic assessment of the human condition – one mired in conflict. The ingeniousness of the concept of satyagraha is that it takes that situation of conflict and attempts to impose upon it a radically different notion of social reality. The success of these attempts, it seems to me, lies in the integrity of the attempts themselves, for much of the power of satyagraha comes from the attractiveness of its vision of a compelling alternative. Coercion has no role in that vision, and the use of it – as Gandhi's use of it in the epic fast demonstrates – largely undercuts whatever appeal the vision might have had. But the use of coercion at the outset – in order to stop violence that is in progress – is a different matter, for without it satyagraha might have no room to grow. A conflict may require some of the techniques of the old reality to allow for a moment of calm where the new reality of the social world of peaceful conflict resolution can enter.

SAINT OR SAINTLY ACTION?

This way of thinking about satyagraha – as the imposition of a new social reality – brings us back in a curious way to the matter of saintliness and the kind of moral image that Gandhi projects. For what makes a saint a saint is not just the honorable virtues he or she exhibits but the vision of a remarkably different way to live that the saint projects. The images of saintly figures are appealing precisely because they are not lists of moral rules or techniques for actions; they are portrayals of persons. As whole beings, these figures convey an image of a moral character that is not of our ordinary, morally messy world. They are harbingers of a new reality.

If that is the case, then the saintly element in Gandhi is satyagraha, not so much the man. It is his approach – his style of living – characterized by satyagraha that introduces a new moral reality, one to which Gandhi's own personal virtues or lack of them are subordinate. For that reason his own moral failings, such as those traits of dogmatism and coerciveness seen in the episode of the epic fast, may be seen as that, failings of the sort to which we are all heir. Gandhi's actions ultimately are judged not by the standard of his image, but by the standard of the saintliness of satyagraha – that vision of a new reality of social relationships which judges and inspires us all.

Notes

1. *Young India*, January 20 1927.
2. These ideas are touched upon in my article, 'Doing Ethics in a Plural World', in Earl E. Shelp (ed.), *Theology and Bioethics* (Dordrecht and Boston: D. Reidel, 1984); and are explored more fully in my essay, 'St. Gandhi', in J. S. Hawley (ed.), *Saints and Virtues* (Berkeley: University of California Press, 1986).
3. There are ninety volumes in *The Collected Works of Mahatma Gandhi* (New Delhi: The Publications Division, Ministry of Information and Broadcasting, Government of India, 1958 to 1984).
4. The release of Richard Attenborough's *Gandhi* was the occasion for a revival of many of these old accusations. For a particularly strident example, see Richard Grenier, 'The Gandhi Nobody Knows', in *Commentary*, 75:3 (March 1983). The fascination with the sexual secrets of heroes seems to be a familiar theme: John F. Kennedy and Martin Luther King, Jr., have also recently been subjects of these prurient interests. it is as if we somehow want to be assured that these virtuous few are not relieved of the burdens with which most of us are saddled, including the most insistent: the familiar, uncontrollable urges of sexual desire.
5. The phrase is that of Pran Chopra, *The Sage in Revolt: A Remembrance*, assisted by Manoranjan Mohanty (New Delhi: Gandhi Peace Foundation, 1972).
6. Gandhi's ideas have been presented in systematic, generally applicable form in Joan Bondurant's *Conquest of Violence: The Gandhian Philosophy of Conflict* (Princeton: Princeton University Press, 1958 – reprint, Berkeley and Los Angeles: University of California Press, 1967); Raghavan Iyer, *The Moral and Political Thought of Gandhi* (New York: Oxford University Press, 1973); and my own *Fighting With Gandhi* (New York and San Francisco: Harper and Row, 1984 – reissued in 1985 under the title *Fighting Fair: A Nonviolent Strategy for Resolving Everyday Conflict*).
7. Saul Padover, *Karl Marx, An Intimate Biography* (New York: McGraw-Hill, 1978) pp. 410–28.
8. Bondurant, *Conquest of Violence*.
9. Gandhi, *Satyagraha in South Africa* (Ahmedabad: Navajivan Trust, 1961 [orig. 1928]) p. 172.
10. 'Statement to the Hunter Commission', in Gandhi's journal, *Young India*, November 5 1919.
11. *Young India*, July 17 1924.
12. *Young India*, November 5 1919.
13. *Young India*, February 9 1921.
14. *Young India*, August 25 1920.
15. Letter to Rabindranath Tagore, September 20 1932, in *The Collected Works of Mahatma Gandhi*, vol. LI, item 149, p. 101.
16. Pyarelal, *The Epic Fast* (Ahmedabad: Mohanlal Maganlal Bhatt, 1932) p. 4.
17. B. Pattabhi Sitaramayya, *The History of the Indian National Congress*, vol. 1, 1885–1935 (Bombay: Padma Publishers, 1935) p. 533.

18. Pyarelal, *Epic Fast*, p. 7.
19. 'Statement to the Press', September 26 1932, *Collected Works*, vol. LI, item 218, p. 144.
20. For Ambedkar's point of view, see his *What Congress and Gandhi Have Done to the Untouchables* (Bombay: Thackur, 1945).
21. For an account of a counter-fast against Gandhi that occurred in the Punjab, see Chapter 12, 'Mangoo Ram vs. Gandhi', in my *Religion as Social Vision: The Movement Against Untouchability in 20th Century Punjab* (Berkeley and Los Angeles: University of California Press, 1982).
22. In the central district of the Punjab, for example, the population was almost evenly quartered among Muslims, Sikhs, upper caste Hindus and Untouchables. For an account of the political ramifications of this demographic situation, see Chapter 2 of my *Religion as Social Vision*.
23. Quoted in Geoffrey Ashe, *Gandhi* (New York: Stein & Day, 1968) p. 317.
24. Letter to C. F. Andrews, September 30 1932, *Collected Works*, vol. LI, item 235, p. 154.
25. Geoffrey Ashe, *Gandhi* (New York: Stein & Day, 1968) Chapter 15.
26. Pyarelal, *Epic Fast*, p. 71.
27. *Fighting With Gandhi*, pp. 3–64; see especially Chapter 3.
28. Gandhi, *Ethical Religion* (Madras, India: Ganesan Press, 1930 [orig. 1922]) p. 35.
29. *Young India*, September 23 1926.
30. Bondurant, *Conquest of Violence*, p. 194.
31. Ibid., p. 193.
32. The phrase is the title given to Gandhi's autobiography.
33. Bondurant, *Conquest of Violence*, p. 193.
34. *Young India*, November 12 1925.
35. Gene Sharp, *The Politics of Nonviolent Action, Part One: Power and Struggle* (Boston: Porter Sargent Publishers, 1973) p. 83.
36. See *Fighting With Gandhi*, Chapter 7.
37. Bondurant, *Conquest of Violence*, Chapter 6.
38. Ibid., p. 11.
39. Ibid., pp. 9–10.
40. Ibid., p 9.
41. *Young India*, November 5 1919.
42. *Fighting With Gandhi*, pp. 27–30.
43. Ibid., pp. 151–5.

4

Gandhi and Celibacy

Arvind Sharma

Much has been written by Mahatma Gandhi on celibacy,[1] and much has been written on Mahatma Gandhi's celibacy.[2] Those who are not bewildered by Mahatma Gandhi's preoccupation with celibacy[3] adopt several approaches to the question, either singly or in combination. It seems useful to begin by identifying some of these approaches. There is the psycho-analytical approach which traces Gandhian preoccupation with celibacy to guilt feelings he had about being with his wife, and not by his father's side, when his father died.[4] There is the contraceptive approach, which is concerned with celibacy as a form of family-planning, an aspect which came into prominence as a result of Margaret Sanger's encounter with Mahatma Gandhi.[5] It is also possible to adopt a dietetic approach to the issue, as Mahatma Gandhi himself sometimes did.[6] Or one may adopt a bio-mystical approach as is often done in Hindu writings which suggest, by a curious biochemical alchemy, the conversion of the vital fluid into *tejas* or spiritual potency.[7] Moving further along the same road, one may approach the issue of celibacy, more comprehensively and more subtly, as essentially a spiritual one, as one of Brahma-faring or leading a life which leads to the realization of God.[8] Further along the same road a religious approach may be adopted – which connects celibacy with Tantrika practices *à la* Ramarkrishna.[9]

These approaches have been tried. A few which appear to be hitherto untried may also be mentioned. A cultural approach to the issue could be developed, perhaps along two lines. Intra-culturally one could ask, not only to what extent were Mahatma Gandhi's views influenced, if not conditioned, by his Hindu background, but more penetratingly perhaps: to what extent Mahatma Gandhi's charisma is to be attributed to the subliminal appeal his vow of celibacy may have had in a Hindu ethos. Cross-culturally one could ask: would such a vow make any impression on a Muslim?

One could ask: would the vow of celibacy impress a Confucian, if one now exists? Would it even make an impression in the Western world as it loses whatever Christian value-orientation it had in favor of celibacy and enters into a sort of post-Christian era? One could, on the other hand, adopt a personal or biographical – one might even say a biological or clinical – approach and detail Mahatma Gandhi's near-sexual experiences after the adoption of the celibate vow under the curious title: 'The sexual life of a celibate'.

LINKING PUBLIC AND PRIVATE LIFE

In the presentation which now follows, to which the above remarks constitute an introduction, none of these approaches has been adopted. Rather, an attempt has been made to adopt what may be called a psycho-historical approach of a certain type. The rest of this chapter will try to detect the connection, if any, between Mahatma Gandhi's private life as represented by his efforts to adopt, maintain and test, if necessary, his celibate vows, and the public events in which, as a leader, he was involved. That a person's private life bears *some* relation to his public life – both in the case of prophets[10] and ordinary mortals – is perhaps undeniable, but what now needs to be asserted is that in the case of Mahatma Gandhi the relationship may be a specially close one. It is clear that Mahatma Gandhi did not see his life as one in which the personal and political aspects were unrelated. Not only were they interrelated – he said they were indivisible. Towards the conclusion of his autobiography he remarks:

> To see the universal and all-pervading Spirit of Truth face to face one must be able to love the meanest of creation as oneself. And a man who aspires after that cannot afford to keep out of any field of life. That is why my devotion to Truth has drawn me into the field of politics; and I can say without the slightest hesitation, and yet in all humility, that those who say that religion has nothing to do with politics do not know what religion means.[11]

Not only that, Mahatma Gandhi saw the personal and spiritual as primary and the public and political as secondary. Thus he writes in the Introduction to his autobiography:

What I want to achieve – what I have been striving and pining to achieve these thirty years – is self-realization, to see God face to face, to attain *Moksha*. I live and move and have my being in pursuit of this goal. All that I do by way of speaking and writing, and all my ventures in the political field, are directed to this same end.[12]

As a matter of fact, one of the reasons for his autobiographical enterprise seemed to lie in this fact. For he observes, in the Introduction to the autobiography, that 'My experiments in the political field are well known, not only in India, but to a certain extent in the "civilized" world. For me they have not much value.'[13] What he did value were his 'experiments in the spiritual field' which he was now going to share with a wider audience through his autobiography or *The Story of My Experiments with Truth*.

Not only did Mahatma Gandhi regard life as an indivisible whole, and not only did he openly acknowledge the relatedness of the personal and the public and the primacy, at least to him, of the former over the latter; he also goes on to state, in no uncertain terms, that it is from 'my experiments in the spiritual field from which I have derived *such power as I possess for working in the political field*'.[14]

It is clear, then, that for Mahatma Gandhi his public life reflected his private life; success in public life reflected success in private life and failure in public life reflected failure in private life. This attitude may be described as one of reflexive causation. Since for Mahatma Gandhi religion was central, and for him religion was synonymous with morality,[15] this view may be described as one of reflexive moral causation. As within, so without. If Mahatma Gandhi thought along these lines and if one of the main concerns in his inner life was that of celibacy, then it seems logical to suggest that his trials and tests in this field would have not merely a chronological but also a psychological connection with his public life, one of the main arenas of which was political. It is now being suggested, in other words, that it may be possible to bring his experiments in celibacy at least in relation to, if not in line with, certain political events.

TAKING THE VOW

The initial point of contact is provided by the circumstances in which Mahatma Gandhi adopted the vow of celibacy. Mahatma Gandhi informs us that 'After full discussion and mature deliberation I took the vow in 1906',[16] although 'The more or less successful practice of self-control had been going on since 1901.'[17] It is interesting to observe that the assumption of the vow of celibacy coincides with the transition of Mahatma Gandhi's public life from working with the British Government, as represented by his volunteering for medical work in the Zulu war, to working against it, as represented by his agitation against the Asiatic Registration Act of 1907. Indeed, 'On returning from service to the Zulus, and after acquainting Kasturbai with his celibacy vow, he had rushed off to Johannesburg, in answer to a summons from the Indian community.'

At this point we may pause to ask: What made Mahatma Gandhi adopt the vow of celibacy? Louis Fischer writes:

> It is difficult to plumb Gandhi's motives; it was difficult even for him to know them. Gandhi believed his celibacy was 'a response to the calls of public duty'. On the other hand, 'My main object was to escape having more children'.[18]

> But why avoid additional children? Phoenix Farm was one big joint family into which Gandhi invited many adults and children. Their care was a common responsibility and expense. More of his own would not have increased the burden.[19]

Although Louis Fischer does not seem to think that more children would have come in the way of public duty, Mahatma Gandhi seems to have thought so. He describes the situation thus while referring to the assumption of the vow:

> The final resolution could only be made as late as 1906. Satyagraha had not then been started. I had not the least notion of its coming. I was practicing in Johannesburg at the time of the Zulu 'Rebellion' in Natal, which came soon after the Boer War. I felt that I must offer my services to the Natal Government on that occasion. The offer was accepted. But the work set me furiously thinking in the direction of self-control, and according to my

wont I discussed my thoughts with my co-workers. It became my conviction that procreation and the consequent care of children were inconsistent with public service. I had to break up my household at Johannesburg to be able to serve during the 'Rebellion'. Within one month of offering my services, I had to give up the house I had so carefully furnished. I took my wife and children to Phoenix and led the Indian ambulance corps attached to the Natal forces. During the difficult marches that had then to be performed, the idea flashed upon me that if I wanted to devote myself to the service of the community in this manner, I must relinquish the desire for children and wealth and live the life of a *vanaprastha* – of one retired from household cares.[20]

It is clear that while several factors may be involved in the assumption of the vow, the 'trigger' was provided by the call to public service. Thus Mahatma Gandhi took the vow of celibacy and entered political life virtually simultaneously.

EXPERIMENTS

If at the beginning of his political career we observe a coincidence between his assumption of the celibate vow and his embarking on a life of political activity, towards the end of his career one may see a connection between the political circumstances with which he was confronted and his experiments in celibacy. These experiments, which consisted of sleeping in the same bed with a member of the opposite sex, were not a novelty, though 'For a long time these experiments were not widely known. The English found out when a policeman happened to call at night. However, they judged it unwise to release his scandalized report.' 'It was the pilgrimage in Noakhali' towards the end of 1946, 'that brought a crisis', as described by Geoffrey Ashe:[21]

His experiments had begun moving toward a climax with the advent of Manu, his cousin's granddaughter. Kasturbai was nursed by the girl, and entrusted her to Bapu's care. He wrote her a letter saying: 'I have been father to many but to you I am a mother'. Though nineteen years old, she averred that she had never felt any sexual impulse. Not unnaturally a query arose in his mind as to whether this assertion was true, and what it implied if it was. But a young woman with the right kind of innocence might be a promising *brahmachari* herself.... Within a year or so of Kasturbai's death, uneasiness was spreading to friends who were not in his closest circle.

When she wanted to go to Noakhali, where he was almost without other companions except Professor Bose himself, he weighed the issues carefully. This would be the ultimate trial. But it would come in the course of duty, not through his own devising. If he could perfect his own *brahmacharya*, and if Manu possessed the cool and crystalline balance he dared to hope for, all would be well. Public opinion had no terrors for him. She could join him at Srirampur, he said, so long as she was completely frank and co-operative. But if he detected any ambiguity in her, she would have to leave. Manu replied that to her he really was more like a mother than a male guardian. In Noakhali she attended to his travelling kit, and aided the mission in such ways as she could: he looked after her with the deepest solicitude; and they slept in the same bed.[22]

While Gandhi and Manu were at Haimchar, in February 1947, the major scandal broke. Anguished outcries went up from his disciples. Some deserted him. When he aired the topic at prayer meetings, and sent the transcript of his remarks to *Harijan*, two members of the staff resigned rather than print it. He wrote to Kripalani asking him to take soundings among the Congress leaders. Kripalani found time, in the death-throes of the British Raj, to compose a long and somewhat embarrassed answer. Gandhi was unrepentant. He told inquirers that he held 'radical views of *brahmacharya*,' and urged them to study the Tantra cult. Several objectors were won over. Ghaffar Khan, who had come to labor among fellow-Muslims in riot zones, watched the couple with his cloudless heroic eyes and was persuaded and touched. The ancient wonder-worker had invented a new human relationship. The intimacy which ought to have been repellent was not.

It is important to consider at this point that this was the period when Mahatma Gandhi seemed to be losing control in the political field. The plain fact is that the 'tragedy of partition hung over

Gandhi's head from the time he was freed from jail in 1944 to the day of his death in 1948'. Talks with the Qaid-e-Azam Jinnah broke down in September 1944, and the cause of Hindu–Muslim unity received a setback; this was followed by the failure of the Cabinet Mission in 1945, which he regarded as the best British offer to date, and there was the ugly fact of communal rioting which flared up sharply in 1946. Not only was Mahatma Gandhi unable to control the Muslim League led by Qaid-e-Azam, he was losing control over the Congress, an organization he had brought into national prominence, and also of the people – if the adverse mail he was receiving was any index of their attitude. On the doctrine of reflexive moral causation, he would be inclined to connect this failure with suspicions that he was not in full control of himself. Hence the need to test his vow of celibacy.

CONCLUSION

To conclude: by a kind of mystical or moral logic, Mahatma Gandhi believed that such power as he possessed for working in the political field derived from the spiritual field. His experiments in this field centered in a major way on maintaining the vow of celibacy. When he sensed a loss of power to control events in the political field, he seems to have tended to associate it with a loss of sexual self-control and this may have led him to test his vow of celibacy.[23]

This is the conclusion, but not the end of the chapter. The chapter may be brought to a close on an ironic, if not tragic, note. After his experiments with Manu, Mahatma Gandhi concluded in May 1946 that 'Sixty years of striving have at last enabled me to realize the ideal of Truth and purity which I have ever set before myself.'[24] In August 1947 the Indian subcontinent achieved Independence – something he had always fought for; but it was partitioned as well – something he had always fought against. At the moment of his spiritual triumph he was still powerless to control events in the political field even though he had proved to himself his total self-control in the spiritual field.[25]

Notes

1. Jagdish Saran Sharma, *Mahatma Gandhi: A Descriptive Bibliography* (Delhi: S. Chand & Co., 1968) p. 121, etc.

2. Almost every Gandhian biography takes it into account, not to mention special studies.
3. See Judith M. Brown, *Gandhi's Rise to Power* (Cambridge University Press, 1972) p. 43.
4. M. K. Gandhi, *The Story of My Experiments with Truth* (Washington DC: Public Affairs Press, 1948) Part I, Ch. IX. Also see Erick H. Erikson, *Gandhi's Truth or the Origin of Militant Non-violence* (New York: Norton, 1969) *passim*.
5. Jagdish Saran Sharma, *Mahatma Gandhi*, p. 119.
6. M. K. Gandhi, *My Experiments with Truth*, Part IV, Ch. VIII.
7. Geoffrey Ashe, *Gandhi: A Study in Revolution* (New Delhi: Asia Publishing House, 1968) p. 351.
8. See Marie B. Byles, 'Brahmacharya = purity = Gandhi's way', *Gandhi Marq*, vol. 20 no. 1 (Jan. 1976) pp. 46–51.
9. See Geoffrey Ashe, *Gandhi: A Study in Revolution*, pp. 246–7; Pyarelal, *Mahatma Gandhi – the Last Phase*, vol. I (Ahmedabad: Navajivan Publishing House, 1958) p. 589, etc.
10. 'If Amos was the prophet of the righteousness of God, then a younger contemprary of his, Hosea, must be called the prophet of God's love. Unlike Amos, Hosea was a native of the North and enough accustomed to the social conditions there to be less appalled by them; his deepest concern was, therefore, not moral but religious. The state of the text of his prophecies leaves us in some doubt as to the exact circumstances of his personal life. It seems probable, however, that he married a woman who was unfaithful to him and left him; he could not acknowledge her children as his own; yet, after years of infidelity on her part, he was able to take her back into his home, reclaimed and regenerated. As Hosea contemplated his domestic trials, he began to see a similarity between his inner history and the experience of Yahweh with Israel. Yahweh, too, suffered on account of the unfaithfulness of his people. Unfaithful they were in more than one way. Too blind to see that the political and social doom overhanging them was the inevitable result of abandoning the true God, they were seeking to forestall disaster by the political device of running after "foreign lovers", one party courting Damascus, another Egypt, a third climbing to the throne through alliance with Assyria. Religiously, they were wooing alien gods and futile native baals, their unholy religious paramours' (John B. Noss, *Man's Religions* (New York: Macmillan, 1967) p. 520).
11. M. K. Gandhi, *My Experiments with Truth*, p. 615.
12. Ibid., p. 5.
13. Ibid., p. 4.
14. Ibid., p. 4, emphasis added.
15. Ibid., p. 207.
16. Ibid., p. 257.
17. Ibid., p. 257.
18. Louis Fischer, *The Life of Mahatma Gandhi* (New York: Harper Brothers, 1950) p. 74. Geoffrey Ashe remarks: 'He was well aware that Hinduism taught the virtue of *brahmacharya* ... But no religious

Gandhi and Celibacy 59

teaching set him in motion along that line. Nor was he impelled, as some have supposed, by guilt over his father's death. His characteristically prosaic motive was to avoid having any more children' (op. cit., p. 92). This leaves the misleading impression that he used celibacy *merely* as a form of birth control if it is not realized that he wanted no more children in order to engage freely in public service.

19. Ibid., pp. 72–3.
20. M. K. Gandhi, *My Experiments with Truth*, p. 254.
21. That they slept in the same bed does not mean that he slept with her in the colloquial sense, rather that they literally slept in the same bed.
22. Geoffrey Ashe, *Gandhi: A Study in Revolution*, pp. 369–70.
23. In this context, the Chauri Chaura incident is perhaps not without some significance. The events associated with this incident took place in February 1922. On February 1, Mahatma Gandhi announced his intention of calling for mass civil disobedience in Bardoli subdivision, in the Bombay Presidency. On February 5, however, violence broke out at the village of Chauri Chaura in the United Provinces and on February 12, plans for civil disobedience were called off 'citing violence at Chauri Chaura' – see Martin Dening Lewis, (ed.), *Gandhi: Maker of Modern India* (Boston: D. C. Heath & Co., 1965) p. x.

In November 1925 Mahatma Gandhi 'resumed a project he had twice tackled and twice shelved without getting it under way. This was the writing of his autobiography' (Geoffrey Ashe, *Gandhi: A Study in Revolution*, pp. 316–19). Earlier on, passages from the Introduction to the *Autobiography* were quoted. It is helpful to cite one of them again even at the risk of repetition to make the next point:

> My experiments in the political field are now known, not only in India, but to a certain extent to the 'civilized' world. For me, they have not much value ... But I should certainly like to narrate my experiments in the spiritual field which are known only to myself, and from which I have derived such power as I possess for working in the political field ...

The point to my mind is that according to Geoffrey Ashe:

> The passage must be read in the light of his comments on Chauri Chaura. He then said that he needed to undergo personal cleansing, so as to make himself a worthy leader. But the connection between that process and leadership became tenuous and esoteric. Purification meant working harder at *brahmacharya*, at self-control ...
>
> When he faced his moral self, as the telling of the story required, his spirits tended to wilt. All was far from well. He closed the introduction darkly.

> I must exclaim with Surdas:
> 'Where is there a wretch
> So wicked and loathsome as I?'
> I have forsaken my Maker,
> So faithless have I been . . .

The passions that afflicted him were not solely carnal. He accused himself of pride, for instance. But many passages in the *Autobiography*, and his choice of words in them, make it plain that sexual unrest was mounting rather than declining. There is medical testimony that he remained physically youthful to the last. Also, on account of the nature of his program, the presence and pressure of women round him grew steadily more obtrusive. In May 1924 he told the readers of *Navajivan* about his 'bad dreams', and he reverted to these a year later.

In other words, when Mahatma Gandhi saw himself as losing political control over political events, as in the case of Chauri Chaura, by applying reflexive moral causation to the situation he seems to have deduced that the roots of that loss of political control lay in his loss of self-control as represented by his failure to maintain perfect celibacy.

24. Quoted by Geoffrey Ashe, *Gandhi: A Study in Revolution*, p. 371.
25. Just as Lord Krishna, for all his divinity, could not prevent his Yadu clansmen from indulging in internecine strife, Mahatma Gandhi, for all his humanity, could not prevent Hindus and Muslims from killing one another.

5
Gandhi in South Africa
James D. Hunt

Serious biographical research on Mohandas K. Gandhi remains in a fairly primitive condition. Louis Fischer's *The Life of Mahatma Gandhi* (New York: Harper Brothers, 1950) was as thoroughly documented as a first biography can be when written by a fine reporter and political journalist. Since then there have been only a handful of biographical studies which make extensive critical use of primary source documents. None of them have been whole-life biographies, for very good reasons.

Among the best of the partial studies are Chandran Devanesen's 1961 Harvard dissertation, *The Making of the Mahatma* (Madras, 1969), Pyarelal's *Mahatma Gandhi: I. The Early Phase* (Ahmedabad, 1965), *II. The Discovery of Satyagraha* (Bombay, 1980), and *III. The Birth of Satyagraha* (Ahmedabad, 1986), Judith Brown's *Gandhi's Rise to Power* (Cambridge, 1972), and *Gandhi and Civil Disobedience* (Cambridge, 1976). In view of the total number of Gandhi biographies – said to be over four hundred – it is apparent that this list of critical studies is brief indeed. I am happy to say that I will be making some additions in the course of this chapter.

If we look for detailed monographic studies of well-defined aspects of Gandhi's life and career we find a similarly depressing prospect, for these are likewise few, especially for the early period. Full-length biographies have been the favored genre; there seems to be a compulsion to tell the sacred drama in its entirety, as in Richard Attenborough's film (1982). None of these biographies has a proper foundation in critical monographic studies. They are condemned to repeat the same ritualized and mythologized versions of familiar incidents, with perhaps a new detail here and there and a sprightly bit of debunking to indicate that the author has originality. The film does them all one better by inflating the old myths into powerful new images that are in some instances not only mistaken but perverse.

All that may be said about the poor quality of biographical

studies of Gandhi applies with greater force to his early history, by which I mean not merely his childhood but his first 44 years, more than half of his life span. The first 22 years are the subject of a study being developed by Stephen N. Hay,[1] and I will give no attention to these. I am interested entirely in his second 22 years, the period of his young manhood in South Africa from 1893 to 1914.

The principal elements in Gandhi's South African story come from the two autobiographies, *The Story of My Experiments with Truth* (Ahmedabad, 1927, 1929) and *Satyagraha in South Africa* (Ahmedabad, 1928). The scenes are familiar: the unsuccessful young lawyer is called to South Africa to help settle a lawsuit; there he immediately encounters racism and has a moment of decision during a chilly night in the Maritzburg station. In Pretoria he encounters kindly Christians and also discrimination, and settles the lawsuit with a compromise. As he is about to return home he discovers a threat to Indian rights in Natal and is persuaded to remain and fight it. He establishes a community defense organization and settles down as an attorney and advocate for Indian rights. On bringing his family to Durban in 1897 Whites attempt to murder him, but he refuses to press charges. During the Boer War he organizes an Indian ambulance corps and takes it to the front lines. After the war he returns to India but at the end of 1902 is called back because of new threats to the rights of Indians, this time in the Transvaal. He settles in Johannesburg, has many English friends, chiefly vegetarians, does life-saving work in a plague epidemic, and establishes a newspaper. Later he reads Ruskin and moves his paper to a farm at Phoenix. In 1906 he provides an ambulance corps in the Zulu rebellion, and decides on the vow of celibacy (*Brahmacharya*). At the Empire Theatre on September 11 1907, the Indians vow to go to jail rather than submit to the new registration law. Shortly after the arrests begin, Gandhi is released in connection with a compromise settlement, and Indians attempt to murder him. The struggle renews as Indians burn their passes, and Gandhi is again jailed. He establishes a second rural retreat, Tolstoy Farm, where he carries on experiments in diet and education. In 1913 he launches large-scale civil disobedience, with over two thousand Indians crossing the border in a great march toward Johannesburg. The Viceroy of India and others are moved to intervene, and General Smuts agrees to the Indian Relief Bill, enabling Gandhi to go home and seek his country's freedom through *satyagraha*.

These events form the core of the Gandhi saga and are repeated in every biography. A few other stories are added, sometimes totally new ones. In the film, for example, one of the most memorable scenes shows the young Gandhi beaten by the police as he attempts to burn passes. Not only was he never, in his whole life, beaten by the police – indeed his relations with them were most respectful – but the scene suggests that Gandhi foolishly rushed into defiant challenge of the law before doing his careful legal work. It therefore distorts his character. Later he is shown frightening horses in a scene which has no basis in history or nature. The printed media are generally more modest in their additions to historical truth, but they are rarely any more helpful in penetrating the myths.

The first two accounts of Gandhi's life appeared in 1909, when he was 40. Both were by intimate friends in Johannesburg. The Rev. Joseph Doke, a Baptist pastor with an unusual interest in the social questions of his city, sought out the Indian leader when the first arrests were taking place to find out the other side of the story. He decided to interview Gandhi and write a character sketch so as to introduce his personality to the English public. From these interviews came the first biography, which Gandhi himself saw through the press.[2] A second sketch was prepared the same year by his aide Henry S. Polak, to be published in India.[3] Three years later, another friend. Dr Pranjivan Mehta published a sequel to these, bringing the story of the South African struggle up to date and including observations from his visit to Tolstoy Farm.[4] From these beginnings grew the Gandhi story and, we might add, the Gandhi myth, which was greatly enriched by Romain Rolland in his *Mahatma Gandhi: The Man Who Became One With The Universal Being* (1924).[5] At about this time Gandhi himself, having shaken India in the civil disobedience campaign of 1920–22, was enjoying his rest in His Majesty's Hotel and employed it to begin the chapters of 'Satyagraha in South Africa',[6] followed by *The Story of My Experiments with Truth*.[7] In the years when he dominated the political landscape of India, little else was published on his South African years. The sole significant exception was a small volume of memoirs by an English woman who had lived in his household, Millie Polak's *Mr. Gandhi – The Man*,[8] still one of the most intimate glimpses of his personal life during this period, by a loving friend who kept her independence of judgment.

Though little may have been written about Gandhi, the history of South Africa was being written and rewritten. Much of this historiography was of a very high quality, and some dealt with the Indian community, which was surveyed by G. H. Calpin in 1949[9] and by Mabel Palmer in 1957.[10] But in this history, as in South African history generally, there has been a missing element, a fact which has recently been pointed out by Shula Marks, who notes 'the absence of any major thrust into this historiography from below, from the Africans themselves'. She goes on to observe that 'although liberal historians were concerned with the position of the Black in South African history, it was still largely as the object of policies and practices of White South Africans . . .'.[11] The same may be truly said of the Asiatic community.

A major limitation of almost all studies on Gandhi and his work in South Africa is the near-total absence of the Indian community as a significant actor in the drama. All which have reached furthest into this subject have concentrated primarily on the actions of Government in relation to Gandhi and the Indians. Some of the reasons for this are not hard to find. The special position of the Indians in South Africa was determined largely by government action, and attempts to modify this position necessarily meant altering the policy of governments. All this generated a vast quantity of records: correspondence, reports, parliamentary papers, news stories, magazine articles, and afterwards memoirs of the participants. Furthermore, this trove of material has another especially attractive feature: much of it is available outside of South Africa. Many of the documents can be examined in London and New Delhi.

An example of this genre, and a superior one, is Puballan Pillay's *British Indians in the Transvaal*.[12] In this volume we learn very little about the British Indians other than that they form the basis of a problem or 'question', despite the fact that Puballan Doraswami Pillay was born and educated in South Africa. The title of his original University of London thesis is more precise: 'The Imperial Government and the British Indians in the Transvaal'. It is in fact an excellent book and provides the best narrative of the Indian 'question' in the Transvaal between 1885 and 1906. Moreover, its thorough documentation has been a blessing to scholars, opening up many avenues in the Public Record Office at Kew and the Pretoria archives, for instance.

Another and less satisfactory example is Robert Huttenback's

Gandhi in South Africa,[13] which reveals some of the riches of the South African archives and has been fruitful in that respect, but which is better described by its subtitle, 'British Imperialism and the Indian Question, 1860–1914'. I will say that in following up on documents cited or briefly quoted in this study, much important light has been shed on Gandhi's political action, but I found more useful than the book the microfilm rolls of the documents on which it was based, and I found more insight in the author's various articles on South Africa in the context of British Imperial history.

A third example, this time based on the documentary resources of the National Archives of India, is Iqbal Narain's *The Politics of Racialism*,[14] which shows how much a diligent worker can learn of South African government policy by reading the Viceroy's files in Delhi.

A similar instance may be seen in the work of Pyarelal Nayer, who pioneered in the exploration of the early Gandhi and carried his story up to 1906 before his death in October, 1982. Utilizing Gandhi's correspondence files, press clippings, communications with surviving companions, and increasingly public documents as he moved into the politically active phase, Pyarelal created a portrait full of detail on the public life of Gandhi, and on the background of persons and events. Much of this seemed far removed from Gandhi as a person. His first volume contained an 81-page chapter on Tolstoy, while his last volume, published in 1986, has four chapters on the struggles between Lord Milner in Africa and Lord Curzon in India over the supply of Indian labor; in this Gandhi hardly appears, though there is some striking evidence here of how seriously his writings were being taken at high levels even in 1904. Pyarelal was a Victorian in his theory of history. Like Rev. Doke, Gandhi's first biographer, he sought the key to history in character, and in his studies of South Africa was more interested in the personal qualities of Gandhi's antagonists, as revealed through their actions, than in other forms of analysis. Indeed, it may be said that Pyarelal was hardly interested in analyzing Gandhi at all. He identified with him and wanted to discover with whom and with what Gandhi had to contend. His work is still the fundamental secondary source for the study of the early Gandhi, though contemporary researchers will be asking quite different questions.

The reliance on official records and the emphasis on 'the Asiatic question' in South Africa has had several unfortunate effects which need to be recognized if we are to have an adequate biography of the young Gandhi. The steady focus on governmental action has resulted not merely in the neglect of the Indian community but also in the distortion of its history by looking only at Gandhi as the chief actor. It is certainly true that he was the most prominent figure on the scene from 1894 until 1914, but he was not the only one. In addition to distorting the history of the community by observing only one actor, we have a reduced portrait of Gandhi, since we have no way of knowing the stature of the people among whom he moved and who were the chief participants in the struggle of which he was often the leader. It cannot be adequate to dismiss other Indian leaders simply as opponents of Gandhi who failed to recognize his wisdom or as obstructionists who tried to thwart his high purposes out of selfish or ignoble aims. They should be allowed to tell their own story.

A second consequence of the emphasis on government is the neglect of non-governmental interest in Gandhi and the Indian situation among Whites in South Africa and elsewhere. Gandhi was rare in having a large circle of White friends and allies, but the nature of these persons and groups, and of his relation to them, has barely been mentioned. The role of the church, the press, theosophists and vegetarians,[15] social reformers of all sorts, needs to be examined, and also the social location of his British allies.

A third neglected area is the social milieu of the South African communities among which Gandhi and the Indians found themselves, in which enormous changes were occurring, including the transformation from an agricultural frontier society to industrialism, social class formation, and most critically for the Indians the transformation of race relations from those appropriate to a rural society to those required by capitalist development, the patterns of which were being defined in the years of Gandhi's residence there. Policies toward Indians have too often been studied in isolation from what was called 'the Native question', which was of far greater consequence to the society as a whole. It profoundly affected the way the Indians were treated, and defined the options which were open to Gandhi and the Indians.

I realize that the program suggested here for improving the quality of biographical studies in the South African period of Gandhi's life may be disappointing to some, as it seems to concentrate on external relations, and does not enter into the inner spirit of the man, or begin with his philosophy. To the extent that philosophy arises out of the material conditions of life, I hold that this program will greatly increase our ability to understand the development of his philosophy and to judge the effectiveness of satyagraha in its first trials. His philosophy must of course be studied primarily as an expression of the Indian tradition, but his program for the revivification of that tradition cannot be understood except through a thorough examination of his experience in the West, of which the most important part was in South Africa.

With respect to this agenda, a principal purpose of this chapter is to report on a most hopeful new development in the study of Gandhi's life and role in South Africa, namely, the emergence of Indian South African scholars. Through them this community has become more articulate in telling its own story, and is reflecting a new valuation of its own heritage. These scholars, it will be apparent to all, are not only in a position to utilize local resources to an extent never before realized, but also to interpret these findings with a far greater recognition of the nature of the Indian community and the relationships and struggles within it.

Amongst this group, perhaps the pioneer was Pranshankar S. Joshi, not an academic but an activist who played a prominent role in Indian affairs since his arrival in South Africa in 1920; his books include *The Tyranny of Colour* (1942), *The Struggle for Equality* (1951), and most recently *Mahatma Gandhi in South Africa* (1980).[16] His are the works of a dedicated advocate who is a talented journalist.

Among the academic scholars, the dean of them all must be Dr Fatima Meer of the University of Natal, who has not only produced a number of important sociological studies of the Indian community, but has suffered imprisonment and a banning order for her work with the Institute for Black Research and other forms of political activism. Her volume *A Portrait of Indian South Africans*[17] contains not only description, economic and sociological analysis, and cultural information, but important historical sections as well. A member of a prominent Muslim family, Dr Meer has criticized the neglect of those Indians who found Gandhi's program incorrect in some regards. In an interview in 1977, she told me that other Indian leaders had been neglected by scholars, for example the labor leader Albert Christopher, who was responsible for the important strike of Durban municipal workers in 1913 which helped create the crisis leading to the Indians Relief Act of 1914. She was of the view that Gandhi took only an incidental interest in working-class Indians. Though he would help individuals in distress he did not raise issues that accented their economic interests. Dr Meer sees Gandhi as essentially conservative, in the sense that he avoided revolutionary confrontation, preferring the method of satyagraha in which one stays close to persons in power in order to effect a change of heart. Its purpose she understood to be to awaken a sense of responsibility among the powerful, who would act as trustees for the poor. In the end, Gandhi accomplished nothing for South African Indians either politically or economically, which is not, she emphasized, to deny that he had a massive effect. In the face of injustice, he insisted that something should be done, offering a model not of acceptance but of action in the face of oppression, thus generating a new sense of power and dignity. Her own respect and admiration for Gandhi is evident in a short biography for young people, *Apprenticeship of a Mahatma*, published in 1970 by the Phoenix Settlement Trust.[18]

Of the academic historians, the most prominent is Dr Bridglal Pachai, recently of Dalhousie University. His master's thesis, 'The History of "Indian Opinion", 1903–1914',[19] was one of the first carefully documented monographic studies of any aspect of the early career of Gandhi. Then he published *The International Aspects of the South African Indian Question, 1860–1971*,[20] before moving to Malawi and devoting his efforts to the history of that country. Returning to South African questions as he moved to Canada, he edited an excellent survey volume, *South Africa's Indians: The Evolution of a Minority*,[21] examining contemporary political, economic and cultural issues with the help of 14 South African scholars, both Indian and White.

The work of Dr Puballan Pillay, who is also now in Canada, has already been cited. Mention should also be made of Essop Pahad's Sussex dissertation on the post-Gandhi era, 'The Development of Indian Political Movements in South Africa, 1924–1946'.[22]

In 1974, Frene Ginwala, a South African Indian with training in the law and a career in journalism, completed a D.Phil. thesis at Oxford, 'Class, Consciousness and Control – Indian South Africans. 1860–1946. A member of the African National Congress and an exile, she was not able to return to the country for research and therefore worked in London and in the National Archives of India, aided to some extent by friends in South Africa. The subject of her thesis was not Gandhi but the Indian population. Using Marxist categories of analysis she raised important new questions concerning Gandhi's role, and his relation to economic classes. By this means she is able to shed new light on familiar incidents, such as the Durban demonstration against Indian immigration in 1897, in which Gandhi was nearly killed. The usual presentation of the event as White opposition to Indian traders and to the return of Gandhi confuses the occasion with the cause, she maintained, pointing out that most of the demonstrators were clearly of the White working class who were being threatened by the recent practice of substituting cheap Indian indentured labor in semi-skilled jobs hitherto performed by Whites.

Dr Ginwala distinguished several interest groups in the Indian population: the indentured laborers, the large traders who were established before the beginning of discriminatory legislation, whom she called the 'bourgeoisie', and the mainly non-trading free Indians, mostly former indentureds, the 'petty-bourgeois'. Gandhi was largely associated with the bourgeoisie. The Natal Indian Congress which he created required the huge membership fee of at least 3 pounds sterling and conducted its proceedings in Gujarati, the language of the merchants and of Gandhi. However, in her analysis of the first passive resistance campaign of 1906–8, Ginwala shows that there occurred significant withdrawal by the bourgeoisie and an increasing participation by hawkers of the petty-bourgeois class. In later phases, new issues of substance to the merchants, such as the restrictions of trade under the Gold Law, were not taken up by Gandhi. In Natal, the petty-bourgeois began to develop new organizations to represent their interests, including the Colonial-Born Indian Association, the Natal Patriotic Union, and a rival newspaper, the *African Chronicle*.

Divergent class interests were evident in the final satyagraha effort in 1913. The decision to resume passive resistance was taken in the Transvaal, and it was to be on the question of immigration rights, a matter of concern to both sections of the bourgeoisie. The Natal 3 pounds sterling tax was not an issue. When Gandhi later decided to involve indentured laborers in his struggle, the leadership of the Natal Indian Congress opposed the plan. Gandhi and his friends then bolted and formed the Natal Indian Association, with many petty-bourgeois members who shared with the indentured laborers the burden of the annual tax. Gandhi, she then avers, was caught by surprise by the mass response of the workers to the tax issue, which had symbolized perpetual indenture for them.

Dr Ginwala felt that what needed explanation was not the extent of Gandhi's manifestation of his position with the bourgeois class, but his transition from it. Since her subject was the class struggle within the community she did not attempt an answer to this question, but her thesis broke new ground for the analysis of Gandhi's role by putting the focus for the first time on the Indian community itself, and by identifying those segments which were allied to Gandhi, those which left him, those who were later in his camp, and those which were largely untouched. For the first time a political analysis of his work became possible.[23]

Much of the thrust of this line of study which takes seriously the South African Indian community, has been drawn together and powerfully synthesized by Maureen J. Swan in her D.Phil. thesis, submitted to St Antony's College, Oxford in 1980 under the name of Maureen J. Tayal, a study which will, I believe, form the foundation not only of future political analysis of this period of Gandhi's life, but also analysis of the development of his ethical philosophy. This thesis has since been published as *Gandhi: The South African Experience* (Johannesburg, 1985).

Working with South African archives, Dr Swan made good use of several previously unused or poorly used primary sources, including the files of the Protector of Immigrants for Natal, the Colonial Secretary of Natal, the logs of ships calling at Durban, the files of the Union Departments of Justice and Defense, and the *African Chronicle*, among others. She used these to explore and to understand the divisions within the Indian community and to identify groups left outside of Indian politics. Centering on Gandhi, she examined the roles he played in this contest and gave critical attention to the passive resistance campaign – its various phases and transformations, the participants, the extent of its success or failure and the reasons for these.

Like Ginwala, Swan sought to identify the Indian political community in Natal and the Transvaal,[24] which she divided into the 'Old Elite' and the 'New Elite'. She provided names and descriptions of representative members of both elites, their institutions, and their political interests in both colonies. She has some particularly interesting material on the political activity of the elites before the advent of Gandhi. In Natal, much of the leadership was given by Gandhi's employer, Dada Abdulla, who was hampered by the lack of time a businessman could give to community defense work, as well as by the need for legal counsel. What better agent could there be for carrying on this work than a young Indian lawyer eager to establish himself in practice and who was fluent both in English and Gujarati? Swan found Gandhi's account of his entry into Natal politics 'highly romanticized', and holds that he was retained not to lead the merchants but to be their representative to continue political activity which they had already begun, and she shows how the Natal Indian Congress and later *Indian Opinion* served their ends, and provides an interesting analysis of the organization and methods of the Congress.

In 1901 Gandhi left South Africa and returned home. Little information exists on the reasons for this decision. Swan suggests that after some initial activity, Natal Indian politics stagnated, and Gandhi went in search of a new political arena which would offer him opportunities that were lacking in Africa. However, he failed to turn his South African experience into a vehicle for entering Indian political life, and therefore welcomed the call to return to South Africa, at which time he established himself in Johannesburg. There he built a new political vehicle, the British Indian Association, to serve the commercial elite, and conducted a successful practice, the chief activity of which centered on the permits and licences required for trade. Swan considers his political activity for the first three or four years ineffective, and his analysis of the reasons for this incorrect. He believed, she says, that the cause of political weakness was moral inability to work for the welfare of the wider community. It was for this reason that he welcomed the vow of non-registration taken at the Empire Theatre.

As passive resistance began, Gandhi was 'a politican of the elite groping inexpertly for the means to become the leader of a mass movement' (p. 144), she said, and observed how in the learning process involved in overcoming the weaknesses in the movement one can find the dynamics which changed him from a hired representative to a leader with a constituency, and at the same time clarified his moral doctrines. As he did so, his constituency shrank, and he became increasingly inactive in public affairs, but after 1912 he developed a new strategy for a successful culmination of the passive resistance struggle, which was necessary if he was to realize his personal goal of entry into Indian political life at home. He devised new goals which appealed to the 'Old Elite', the 'New Elite' and the 'masses', but which stopped short of demanding what the government had long refused to concede. In the process, Swan asserts, 'Gandhi drove the Transvaal resistance movement virtually into the ground before he began to make the moral and political adjustments which were necessary to ensure its sucess' (p. 271).

Swan finds that Gandhi's leadership role in South African politics 'has been consistently over-rated' (p. 270), and that the title of 'leader' is inappropriate for him before 1906, and must be qualified for the period following; and that his primary commitment was to moral autonomy rather than to community goals. One need not agree with all of Dr Swan's observations or conclusions to recognize that here is a strong new voice in Gandhian studies, full of new insights and provocative conclusions. It is beautifully researched and well argued, and raises a host of questions that are long overdue. It should presage a new era in the study of Gandhi in South Africa. The author is proceeding with a study of South African Indian politics after the Gandhi era.

The interest of Indian South Africans in exploring and defining their own history shows no signs of abating. At the University of Durban-Westville, despite the exclusion of Indian history from the curriculum, two Indian lecturers in History have taken an active role. Dr Surendra Bhana, who was trained in the United States with a thesis on another colonial subject, Puerto Rico, has recently given attention to Indian subjects, including the history of Tolstoy Farm, the origins of *Indian Opinion*, and together with a colleague has recently published a survey of the historiography of passive resistance among Indian South Africans, to which this chapter is greatly indebted.[25] The colleague, Miss Uma Duphelia (now Mrs Mesthrie), a descendant of Gandhi, is writing a thesis on the representatives of the government of India in South Africa in the post-Gandhi era. An attorney in Durban, Mr Hassim Seedat, as an amateur historian, published a long series in the local Indian newspaper on community history, and has recently turned to more academic history. In a thesis in progress for Rhodes University, he is examining an idea broached by Drs Meer and Swan, among others, that Gandhi, after initiating passive resistance with the merchant community, increasingly turned away from such politics and withdrew into a private spiritual search.

Researchers such as these have begun to explore previously neglected archives to which they have comparatively easy access and unique capabilities for their interpretation. The Natal records in Pietermaritzburg and the local records in Durban have hardly been touched. Recently they have uncovered court records which show Gandhi appearing in case after case on behalf of Indian clients, offering the possibility of a whole new picture of his legal work. Old Natal police records, including informers' reports on the meetings of the Natal Indian Congress and other bodies can, when used with due respect for the conditions of their creation, provide a world of new information on the workings of these organizations. This would help to fill a gap created in part by the seizure of organizational records by the state security agencies of the Republic. Another archival source which can help us understand the composition of the Indian community is the elaborate shipping records, which in the case of the indentured laborers contains demographic information which can be subject to computer study.

The University of Durban-Westville, in spite of conditions created by segregation, has initiated its own contribution to community history by establishing a Documentation Centre for South African Indian history, with Dr C. G. Henning as Director and Mr B. Naidoo as Deputy Director. The Centre, in addition to collecting materials for social and cultural history, is microfilming all the early Indian newspapers which, as I discovered to my horror in 1977, seem to exist only in unique copies at the Natal Archives. The *Colonial Indian News* (1901–03) and *Indian Views* (1914–44) have already been microfilmed, and *African Chronicle* (beginning 1908) will follow. Another project for which I had long hoped is the translation into English of the Gujarati articles in *Indian Opinion*, which is now complete for the first three years of publication.[26]

We may hope that one result of all this will be a richer portrait of the indentured laborers and their descendants, who form the vast majority of the population. Although the subject of Gandhi's concern and his efforts in individual cases, he did not take up their economic interests until the final phase. The studies of Swan and Ginwala show that it was the emergence of a new elite of the children of previously indentured parents which was essential for effecting this new alliance. Despite the beginnings which have been made by Hugh Tinker in exploring the system of indenture (and Gandhi's role in bringing it to an end),[27] and Swan's study of the causes of their political inertia,[28] much needs to be done in understanding this community and exploring Gandhi's relations with it.[29] Incidentally, one benefit which may perhaps come as members of the community explore their own history is the restoration of their true names. Many significant participants are now known to the world only by the simplified or anglicized names used in Gandhi's autobiographies.

The satyagraha struggle created and orchestrated by Gandhi was a wonderfully complex event which generated effects not only on the local scene, but in the capital cities of Pretoria, London, and Calcutta, with occasional peaks of mass action and long sustained periods of low-level activity in which he concentrated on the development of his communal centers, Phoenix and Tolstoy Farm. It is through the study of this complex event that I believe we have our best route into the construction of a full critical biography of the young Gandhi. A mere psychological study would be completely inadequate, to say nothing of its impossibility without a study of his environment and his political action. With the increasing fullness and subtlety in studies of the Indian community we are in the midst of what may be compared to a paradigm shift in our understanding of the origins of satyagraha. At the same time, despite the existing studies of Gandhi's struggle with the government, and indeed as a consequence of the concentration on such relations, priority should be given to certain other aspects of the South African scene, specifically Gandhi's White friends and supporters, and the relationship between the Indian struggle and the Black struggle. To these two topics I will devote the remainder of this chapter.

It has been long recognized that Christians were very important in Gandhi's religious formation, but hardly any attention has been given to the fact that Christianity has many variants, and Gandhi came into close relations with certain kinds of Christians and not with others.[30] In South Africa he had the closest personal relations with certain Protestant evangelicals, and these were of two different sorts. Best known of these encounters is his friendhip with members of the South Africa General Mission, a faith group strongly influenced by the Keswick movement in England. He met them in his first days in Pretoria and maintained close relationships with missionaries of this group for more than a decade. A recent dissertation by James Kallam has for the first time examined the history of this Mission and the personalities of some of its leading figures.[31] Dr Margaret Chatterjee in her recent book, *Gandhi's Religious Thought*, has recognized the influence of Nonconformist formulations in Gandhi's religious expressions, including the concept of guidance by the holy spirit, in which is a call for action, a vehicle of insight, and a source of strength, as well as the lingering influence of such evangelical terminology as the God/Satan dichotomy, and his love of certain hymns.[32] This deserves further study, but there is another experience with evangelical Christianity which has been overlooked, and it occurred at the crucial moment of his first ventures in civil disobedience. A group of reform-minded, politically active, Nonconformist clergy in Johannesburg openly sided with Gandhi and the Indian cause over a period of years. They included the Baptist pastor Joseph Doke, who made his home a hospital for the injured Gandhi, and wrote his first biography; and there were others. They brought to Gandhi a model of the religious leader as a social reformer and a certain amount of experience not only in civic reform but in passive resistance also. They brought their knowledge of the English passive resistance movement against the 1902 Education Act conducted by the evangelical churches, chiefly Baptist, Congregational and Primitive Methodist. This campaign, which reached the height of its effort in 1905, saw several thousand clergy, lay readers, and municipal officials suffering distraint of goods or imprisonment for tax refusal. Evangelical Christianity contributed not only to Gandhi's personal piety, but also to his vision of a socially transforming religion.[33]

With respect to the sources of contemporary experience in passive resistance, attention should also be given to Gandhi's study of the campaign of the Women's Social and Political Union, commonly called the 'suffragettes', which originally was nonviolent and saw prison as a badge of honor. Gandhi was in London to observe their actions, and interviewed Mrs Pankhurst and other leaders.[34] Another topic in the origins of satyagraha which deserves exploration is the membership and program of Gandhi's rural communities, Phoenix and Tolstoy Farm. R. M. Thompson, an Australian, has completed for Bombay University a thesis on Gandhi's ashrams, working largely from Indian sources;[35] however, little else of a serious nature has been done. Dr Surendra Bhana has published a paper on Tolstoy Farm, incorporating interviews with aged former students of Gandhi's school,[36] and the rebuilt farmhouse is now being preserved by an Indian trust. Phoenix is still a living settlement, and now finds itself in the midst of a vast new Phoenix Indian Township being constructed by the Durban corporation. Much needs to be done in plotting out the evolution of Gandhi's ideas of an ashram, and the changing purposes and economic structure of these pioneer communities, including the examination of other communities which may have played a role as models for them, such as the Tolstoyan colonies and the 'simple life' movement in England, to which Gandhi and the Phoenixites paid much attention in the early years of the experiment. The letters and memoirs of those who took part in these experiments have not yet been seriously examined for the insight they can give us into the nature of life in these communities. Albert West, the printer, wrote a short memoir, and Millie Polak's book has already been mentioned in another connection. Prabhudas Gandhi, a nephew who was a child at Phoenix, has written a most valuable memoir in Gujarati which is available in English only in abridged form.[37] A large body of correspondence between Gandhi and his intimate companion Herman Kallenbach was purchased at auction for the National Archives of India in December 1986, and a smaller part of this correspondence, sold in London in 1972, has recently been acquired by the Durban Local History Museum; taken together, these provide a most personal account of Gandhi's later years in South Africa. I also note that no research has been done on the career of Henry Polak, Gandhi's closest political associate in this period. I mention these only to suggest that if Gandhi studies in some areas have not developed, it is by no means because of the lack of available material.

Another promising subject should be Gandhi's career as a lawyer, from which he withdrew in 1911 and which he later abandoned. T. K. Mahadevan has recently shed light on the first law case, the one which drew Gandhi to South Africa. Though his research needs to be put in context and read cautiously, due to his dubious use of what he calls 'processed' quotations, he shows that the fire of ambition was burning in the young Gandhi from the moment of his arrival in Africa, and that he carefully prepared not to return home but to establish himself there.[38] The autobiography is less than candid on this point. Mahadevan did not have available the perspective of Swan, which would show that as Gandhi strove to remain the merchants strove to keep him, not as their leader, but as the most effective agent for continuing the political protests they had already begun. The rich Natal court records of Gandhi's cases, together with others which could without doubt be found in the Transvaal, should provide the basis for a new account of his legal career.

I have become increasingly aware of the power and effectiveness of his legal work in the period immediately before the publication of the Registration Bill of 1906, which he called the 'Black Ordinance' and made the occasion of his first mass civil disobedience. In a series of appeals to the higher courts, some in deliberately initiated test cases, Gandhi had been able to secure the overturning of important sections of the anti-Indian ordinances, and to expose the weakness of race and class legislation when brought to the light of British justice. As late as the Spring of 1906, he announced his intention to initiate test cases on five more points of law. I have often wondered what it was about the Registration Act which made it the 'Black Ordinance', when on the face of it it appears to be similar to many other anti-Indian actions. There are, I found, some important differences, but in addition one factor which led Gandhi to civil disobedience at this point must have been the consistent manner in which the integrity of the courts, which he could use so well, was subverted by government subterfuge or new actions of a blatantly racist nature so as to void the hard-won victory. The exploration of Gandhi's legal success and its nullification will yield a new understanding of his turn to extral-legal protest.

It is the larger matter of the relation of 'the Indian question' to formation of modern South African society which is my final subject. The economic and social history of the early twentieth century is a field whose contemporary vigor promises significant impetus for the study of South African Indian history and for comprehending the milieu in which Gandhi operated. For instance, Charles van Onselen's two volumes of *Studies in the Social and Economic History of the Witwatersrand, 1886–1914* provide a richly textured account of the working-class sections of Johannesburg among which the Indians dwelt.[39] Though he pays no attention to the Asiatics in these volumes, he suggests the need for a study of what he calls the inter-racial 'slum yards' of the western side of the city, which I hope will be forthcoming. Meanwhile he has provided glimpses of the social engineering of the Milner administration which, on principles not unlike those of the Fabian socialists, transformed the town from a rough mining camp to a modern industrial city.[40] The plan called for breaking up the old center-city working-class districts, among which was the Indian location. Gandhi reports its destruction in 1904 as a result of the outbreak of plague. For him and the Indians the disease seemed only the excuse to implement a consistent anti-Indian policy, which is no doubt true, but van Onselen makes it possible to see the move as an aspect of a different plan also, and it will be possible to show, I believe, that Gandhi did not object to this plan in principle – only that it was being worked consistently and unnecessarily to place the Indians at the maximum disadvantage. Such studies as this, and others that may follow under the leadership of van Onselen and Brenda Bozzoli of the University of Witwatersrand, may in addition provide a more complete picture of the social location of the anti-Indian groups in Transvaal society which continually forced the government into taking more extreme discriminatory measures.[41]

The major social transformation in South Africa in Gandhi's time was the creation of the modern system of racial segregation which, as John Cell has recently shown, was fundamentally different from the racial patterns in the agricultural society of the old Transvaal.[42] Its creation was, not by chance, simultaneous with the passage of 'Jim Crow' legislation in the American South. As this process is examined, attention should be given to the question of the relation of evolving Indian policy to evolving 'Native' policy. The Indians, Gandhi included, tried continually to get themselves excluded from classification with the Blacks in such matters as housing, trading rights, transportation, prison accommodations and the carrying of passes, among other matters, while at the same time disclaiming any demand for full White privileges. In this way Gandhi, along with many liberal-minded social reformers of his day, accepted and promoted aspects of the segregation doctrine, in so far as he called for a social status for Indians that was different from that of the Whites and the Blacks. Not surprisingly, he has been termed racist in this respect and criticized for his failure to take up a common cause with other non-White elements against racism. Dr Swan's book makes this point strongly. She also suggests that Gandhi's Phoenix settlement owed an unacknowledged debt to the inspiration of John L. Dube, the founder of the African National Congress, whose school and newspaper press were located only a few miles from the settlement. No one has seriously examined Gandhi's relations with urbanized and educated Blacks, and with the leaders of the Colored community. To see if an effective alliance among such groups were possible, and for what purposes, we would need to know more about the history of the times as seen from the Black perspective. Gandhi himself argues, of course, that satyagraha would provide a means by which any group might free itself, and there were many Blacks and Whites who, some with hope and some with fear, thought this might be true. Of all the questions concerning Gandhi, the relation between Blacks and Indians has the greatest importance for the future of Indian South Africans.

What may emerge from these new studies will be a new portrait of Gandhi and a new assessment of his role. He will be shown not always to have led, but often to have responded to the initiatives of others; and other Indian leaders and other views of the development of the Indian community will be seen as contending with his, and not always wrongly. He will be shown as failing to effect an alleviation of the chronic disabilities of non-Whites in the South African situation, despite certain successes. None of this, I believe, can possibly diminish Gandhi. His place in the story is assured, though our understanding of it may have to be modifed. In this connection I am reminded of I. Bernard Cohen's remarks on Galileo's place in the history of science. Cohen wrote that Galileo's originality was in fact different from what Galileo had proclaimed. No longer need we believe that there had been no progress in understanding motion since Aristotle. Recent investigations have uncovered a tradition of criticism of Aristotle which paved the way for him, and Cohen concluded: 'By making precise exactly what Galileo owed to his predecessors, we may delineate more accurately his own heroic proportions. In this way, furthermore, we may make the life story of Galileo more real, because we are aware that in the advance of the sciences each man builds on the work of his predecessors.'[43]

Notes

1. Portions of Dr Hay's work may be seen in 'Between Two Worlds: Gandhi's First Impressions of British Culture', *Modern Asian Studies*, 3, 305–19 (1969); and 'Gandhi's First Five Years', in Donald Capps, *et al.* (eds.), *Encounter with Erikson* (Missoula, Montana, 1977) pp. 67–112.
2. Joseph J. Doke, *M. K. Gandhi: An Indian Patriot in South Africa* (London, 1909; reprinted: Varanasi, 1956; Delhi, 1967).
3. Henry S. L. Polak, *M. K. Gandhi: A Sketch of His Life and Work* (Madras, 1910). See also Polak, Brailsford, and Pethick-Lawrence, *Mahatma Gandhi* (London, 1949).
4. 'Metha, Dr P. J.' (Pranjivan J. Mehta). *M. K. Gandhi and the South African Indian Problem* (Madras, n.d. [1912?]). This rare volume is difficult to find due to the misprinting of the author's name on the title page.
5. Paris, 1923. English translation, London and New York, 1924.
6. Published in *Navajivan* and *Young India*, 1922–25, and as a book in 1928.

7. Published in *Navajivan* and *Young India*, 1925–29, and as a book in 1927 and 1929.
8. London, 1931.
9. *Indians in South Africa* (Pietermaritzburg, 1949).
10. *The History of the Indians in Natal* (Natal Regional Survey, vol. 10).
11. Shula Marks, 'Towards a People's History of South Africa? Recent Developments in the Historiography of South Africa', in Raphael Samuel (ed.), *People's History and Social Theory* (London, 1981) pp. 297–308, esp. pp. 299ff.
12. London, 1976.
13. Ithaca, 1971.
14. Delhi, 1962.
15. James D. Hunt, 'Gandhi and the Theosophists', in V. T. Patil (ed.), *Studies on Gandhi* (New Delhi, 1983) pp. 163–76.
16. Privately printed at Rajkpt. Gujarat.
17. Durban, 1969.
18. Phoenix, Natal, 1970.
19. *Archives Yearbook for South African History*, 1961. The origins of this newspaper have been newly examined in *Gandhi's Editor: The Letters of M. H. Nazar, 1902–3* (New Delhi: 1988), edited by Surendra Bhana and James D. Hunt.
20. Cape Town, 1971.
21. Washington, 1978. See also his pre-publication summary, 'Indians in South Africa', in I. J. Bahadur Singh (ed.), *The Other India* (New Delhi, 1979) pp. 154–67.
22. Ph.D. thesis, University of Sussex, 1972.
23. For a summary and extension of this analysis see her 'Indian South Africans'. Minority Rights Group Report No. 34 (London, 1977).
24. She also examined the reasons for the political inactivity of the majority of Natal Indians in the early years in 'Indian Indentured Labour in Natal, 1890–1911', *The Indian Economic and Social History Review*, xiv, 4 (1977).
25. Surendra Bhana and Uma Duphelia, 'Passive Resistance Among Indian South Africans', South Africa Historical Society Conference, July 1–3, 1981.
26. 'Indian Archive', *South African Panorama*, 28, 1 (January, 1983) pp. 30–3.
27. Hugh Tinker, *A New System of Slavery: The Export of Indian Labour Overseas, 1830–1920* (London, 1974).
28. See note 24 above.
29. The available materials may be surveyed with the help of J. J. C. Greyling and J. Miskin, (compilers), *Bibliography on Indians in South Africa* (University of Durban-Westville, 1976), and Susan J. Kovalsky, *Mahatma Gandhi and His Political Influence in South Africa, 1893–1914*, a selective bibliography (University of the Witwatersrand, 1971).
30. James D. Hunt, 'Gandhi and the British Religions', presented to the American Academy of Religion, St Louis, MO, October 29 1976.
31. James G. Kallam, 'A History of the Africa Evangelical Fellowship

From its Inception to 1917' (Ph.D. Thesis, New York University, 1978).
32. London, 1983; see especially pp. 96–9.
33. See D. W. Bebbington, *The Nonconformist Conscience: Chapel and Politics 1870–1914* (London, 1982). I have presented my evidence in two unpublished papers: 'The Political Activist Clergyman: A Role Model for Gandhi?' at Collegium, An Association for Liberal Religious Studies, October 1983; 'British Nonconformity and the Young Mr. Gandhi', American Academy of Religion, Southeastern Section, March 1984.
34. James D. Hunt, 'Suffragettes and Satyagraha', *Indo-British Review* (Madras) IX, 1 (1981), 65–77; and my *Gandhi in London* (New Delhi, 1978) *passim*.
35. 'Gandhi and His Ashrams: an Inquiry into the Social Dynamics of Nonviolence.' See his publications, 'Gandhi at Sevagram: "India in a Village".' *Gandhi Marg*, 20 November 1980, pp. 431–52, and 'The Humanization of Community: a Historical Perspective.' *Gandhi Marg*, 32, November 1981, pp. 443–59.
36. 'The Tolstoy Farm: Gandhi's Experiment in "Cooperative Commonwealth"', in Bhana and Pachay, *A Documentary History of Indian South Africans* (Cape Town: David Philip Publishers).
37. *My Childhood with Gandhi*. In Gujarati, 1948; English translation, Ahmedabad, 1957.
38. *The Year of the Phoenix: Gandhi's First Year in South Africa, 1893–1894* (New Delhi and Chicago, 1982).
39. Vol. 1, *New Babylon*, and vol. 2, *New Nineveh* (London, 1982).
40. See also Shula Marks and Stanley Trapido, 'Lord Milner and the South African State', *History Workshop*, 8 (1979) pp. 50–73, esp. p. 55.
41. The process has been well described in Robert A. Huttenback's *Racism and Empire* (Ithaca, 1976).
42. *The Highest Stage of White Supremacy: The Origins of Segregation in South Africa and the American South* (Cambridge and New York, 1982).
43. *The Birth of a New Physics* (New York, 1960) p. 111.

Part II
Gandhi on Religion and Ethics

Introduction to Part II
John Hick

Gandhi taught that Truth is God. This very naturally puzzles the philosophically educated Westerner, who is likely to think of the truth as the sum of all true propositions. This is not, however, at all what Gandhi had in mind. The key word for him was *satya*, Truth – the term that he invented, *satyagraha*, meaning the power of Truth. The heart of *satya*, Truth, is *sat*, reality, the real, the true, the ultimate. Indeed, Gandhi treated *satya* and *sat* as synonymous. [*From Yeravda Mandir*, Chap. 1]. Thus in his dictum that Truth is God, Gandhi was freeing the idea of God from particular images of the ultimate in the form of Vishnu or Shiva or Allah or the Heavenly Father, etc., and was saying that God is *sat*, the Real. So far this is a familiar idea within the Hindu tradition: the Gods are all manifestations of the one ultimate reality, called Brahman. But, as Rex Ambler so interestingly shows in his chapter, 'Gandhi's Concept of Truth', Gandhi went beyond this traditional understanding with a startling originality which has had immense consequences. The opposite of *sat* 'reality' is *maya* 'illusion'. According to the Hindu (and Buddhist) tradition, the world of our ordinary ego-centred perception, together with its pervasive values and concerns, is distorted, illusory, concealing reality from us. Gandhi's new insight was that this illusion of maya, which dominates ordinary human life, has a powerful social-economic-political dimension. It includes the structure of false ideas, valuations, attitudes in virtue of which human beings despise, exploit and ill-treat one another because of color, caste, class or religion. And so when Gandhi, the young lawyer, left alone on the railway station at Pietermaritzburg after being expelled from a first-class compartment as a non-White, vowed to oppose color discrimination, he was not merely reacting against an insult to himself – this, as he said, was not very important – but against a powerful and pervasive web of thinking which he saw to be profoundly false and harmful. He, like millions of others, was not being seen as a fellow human being but as a 'non-White' – a 'nigger', a 'coolie', a 'non-person'. This misperception was an aspect of maya; and the function of Truthforce, satyagraha, was to overcome this moral falsehood which poisons the human community. For if maya has a social dimension, so does satya, Truth, reality. And so it was that Gandhi looked for God in the face of the poor, the outcast, the downtrodden, and experienced the presence of God/Truth/Reality in the creation of human community and the bringing about of human freedom. As maya is manifest in injustice and prejudice, so satya is manifest in justice won by love.

This understanding of Gandhi's use of *satya* is read by Ambler more from Gandhi's life than from his words. Gandhi was not a philosopher. Nor, as Kees Bolle reminds us in 'Gandhi's Interpretation of the *Baghavad Gita*', was he either a sanskrit scholar or an historically accurate interpreter of the *Gita*. He appropriated this great Hindu scripture in terms of a kind of 'internationalized romanticism', reading into it at least as much as he read out of it. But in the central matter of recognizing the social and political aspects of the Truth which religion seeks to realize in human beings, Gandhi was at the forefront of a major development within his Hindu tradition. Raghavan Iyer, in his chapter, 'Gandhi on Civilization and Religion', interestingly identifies this as a 'radical reinterpretation of Hindu values in the light of the message of the Buddha', which 'was a constructive, though belated, response to the ethical impact of the early Buddhist Reformation on decadent India'.

If Ambler is right and Gandhi was indeed seeing a political dimension in the contrasting notions of maya and satya, he was in the late nineteenth and early twentieth centuries discovering as a Hindu what Christianity was discovering at about the same time in its social gospel movement and, subsequently, in dialogue with Marxism and in the development of liberation theologies.

In this respect Gandhi had a larger vision of Truth than most of his Hindu contemporaries. In another respect he also had a larger vision of Truth than most of his Christian contemporaries. For this was still the period – which may be said to have substantially ended only with World War II – of the missionary expansion of Christianity from the West into the world that the West had colonized. It was assumed by the great majority of Christians that the Hindus, Muslims, Sikhs and Jains of India must be converted to Christianity if they were not to forfeit salvation. As Margaret Chatterjee shows in her chapter on 'Gandhi and Christianity', Gandhi had a dual response to his encounters with the Christian movement. On the one hand he was deeply impressed by and attracted to the person and teachings of Jesus. On the other hand he was repelled by much of institutional Christianity with its dogmatic narrowness and its smug validation of imperialistic oppression. What appealed to him in the Jesus of the New Testament was his teaching of a nonviolent love which reflects the nature of the divine Reality. This was what Gandhi had learned from his own Jain and Hindu background, and it was this that he taught as satyagraha. Gandhi could be called, and sometimes called himself, a Christian in the sense that he acknowledged Jesus as a great teacher of Truth, and in the sense also that he accepted Christians as his brothers and sisters. In comparable senses he likewise called himself a Jew, a Muslim, a Sikh, a Jain, and a Buddhist. From his point of view it was possible to exist within all of these different traditions. For he did not see them primarily as mutually exclusive socio-religious tribes, but as something more like overlapping fields of spiritual force; so that one can live within the influence of several of them at once. But this is not, of course, the traditional Christian view of other religions. That traditional view, much less questioned in Gandhi's time than today, was that a Christian is one who has not only responded in his life to the claim of the Truth mediated by Jesus, but who also professes a particular system of church doctrine which must minimally include Jesus being the Second person of a divine Trinity, and his unique atoning death alone making possible human salvation. None of these credal beliefs impressed Gandhi as being true in the all-important sense in which the claim of nonviolent love is true; and he did not profess them. From a traditionally orthodox point of view, then, he was outside the Christian fold. But from the point of view of a Christian for whom Christianity is one way of responding to the ultimate Reality that Gandhi called Truth, he can be recognized as a fellow servant of the Truth, and indeed as one of the greatest such servants known to us, rightly (despite his own demurring) called a mahatma.

To say that Truth is God is also to open the way to an understanding of the different religious traditions as brothers rather than as foes. For, as Elton Hall shows in 'Gandhi's Religious Universalism', Gandhi distinguished between, on the one hand, the varying concepts or images of God held within the different traditions, and, on the other hand, God the Truth, beyond our human imaginings. The religions have their different visions of Truth, and each has developed its own special organic system of ideas and practices related to its vision; but within each of these God can be served to the fullness of our ability, and within each tradition our ability to serve God can itself grow without limit. And so Gandhi rejected the idea that there is one and only one 'true religion', all others being (perhaps in varying degrees) false. It did not matter to him whether someone who was his brother or sister in the service of Truth had drawn their inspiration from Hinduism, or Christianity, or Islam ... He therefore deprecated attempts to convert others to one's own faith; and, accordingly, he did not want his many Christian friends to become Hindus. He held – surely rightly – that the religious tradition which has formed one from childhood must normally be best fitted to meet one's spiritual needs and to provide for one's spiritual growth. Only in exceptional instances did he recommend conversion from one religion to another. Occasionally, however, there were such instances. I know an Indian Christian of Brahmin family who became a Christian as a young student. His family sent him to Gandhi, hoping that the Mahatma would dissuade him from this, to them, terrible step. Gandhi talked at length with the young man, questioning him carefully, and finally concluded that conversion to Christianity would be appropriate in his case, and advised him to proceed, giving him his blessing.

In this pluralistic understanding of religion, Gandhi was far ahead of his time. Indeed, he is still far ahead of our own time, a generation after his death. Nevertheless, the kind of approach that Gandhi promulgated now finds favor with an increasing proportion of those thinkers, within all traditions, who are deeply concerned with the issue of religious pluralism. An increasing amount of the literature now reflects attitudes which are basically in harmony with Gandhi's.

But references to Gandhi's thought, and to his ideas, are always liable to be misleading if they become detached from his life in the specific contexts of South Africa and India. For what has made Gandhi's ideas such a powerful field of force, spreading through the world and becoming more widely influential today than when he was alive, is the fact that they were incarnated in his life. He did not advocate any principle or policy which he was not already living out. There was no gap between theory and practice such as weakens the impact of so much moral exhortation. This fact is itself significant for moral reflection, as Steven Smith shows in his paper on 'Gandhi's Moral Philosophy'. For many moral philosophers are today tending away from the meta-ethical theorizing of recent decades to look again at the concrete forms of the moral life and at specific current ethical issues. Case studies are proving rewarding. And Gandhi's life can provide a rich resource for this approach. An examination of his life and thought, and of the ethical crises which were the growth points of his moral insight, can be highly illuminating.

6
Gandhi's Concept of Truth
Rex Ambler

We learn from his Introduction to *The Story of My Experiments with Truth* that Gandhi's search for Truth was a search for personal liberation. He had not really intended to write an autobiography, he tells us, only to tell the story of his numerous experiments with Truth, but 'as my life consists of nothing but those experiments, it is true that the story will take the shape of an autobiography'.[1] That this Truth was and had been his main concern in life he reaffirms later in the Introduction, despite the fact that his account will 'include experiments with non-violence, celibacy and other principles of conduct believed to be distinct from Truth. But for me, Truth is the sovereign principle, which includes numerous other principles ... I worship God as Truth only. I have not yet found him, but I am seeking after him.'[2] It is also evident from this that Truth had for him the kind of ultimacy that can only be ascribed to the ultimate reality, what he also describes in the capitalized 'Absolute Truth'. Yet two paragraphs earlier he had depicted his life's struggle in a quite different language, with different implications: 'What I want to achieve – what I have been striving and pining to achieve these thirty years (he was writing in 1925) – is self-realization, to see God face to face, to attain *Moksha*.'[3] Evidently, his discovery of Truth would involve in some way a liberation from the self, *moksha*, which was in turn, paradoxically, a realization of the self. On another occasion he put it more succinctly: 'Truth is the same thing as *moksha*.'[4]

Following the *Gita*, which he took as his guide in these profounder matters, he believed the pursuit of Truth required 'selflessness';[5] he would often interpret the *Gita* as recommending a life of 'selfless action', that is, action that was indifferent to the personal gain (or pain) that might accrue from it. At the same time he was not in the least reluctant to confess a selfish interest in the quest for Truth: 'Quite selfishly, as I wish to live in peace in the midst of a bellowing storm howling round me, I have been experimenting with myself and my friends by introducing religion into politics.'[6] The tension between selfish and selfless concerns here is resolved, I believe, by relating them to the overriding Truth which he hoped to realize, and to the two aspects of the self which figure in the *Gita* and more generally in the philosophical tradition. When he expresses a desire for self-realization he is thinking of his *true* self which is ultimately identical with the one true reality of life as a whole, with Truth itself. When he longs to be free of the self he is thinking of the false self which is identified with the human body and, therefore, cuts him off both from reality in general and from his own deeper reality. He gives an example of this falsity in an account of one of his experiments, including a rare reference to the philosophical doctrine of maya, illusion.

His wife, he tells us, was offered the privilege of a second-class bathroom, and although it would have gone against the principles they both espoused, he 'connived at the impropriety'. He then, characteristically, blames himself for the mistake. 'This, I know, does not become a votary of Truth. Not that my wife was eager to use the bathroom, but a husband's partiality for his wife got the better of his partiality for Truth. The face of Truth is hidden behind the golden veil of maya, says the Upanishad.'[7] The quotation was from the *Isawasya Upanishad*, which became a favorite of Gandhi's and was used regularly in his ashram at morning prayers. The full verse reads,

> The face of reality is surrounded by the golden veil.
> O Provider of the world, unveil the refulgent face,
> That the Truth seeker can have a glimpse
> Of the light of reality.[8]

The beauty of the golden veil is nothing compared to the beautiful face it conceals, but it is enticing nonetheless. Much of Gandhi's own struggle was against the enticements of natural affection and desire, which, though not evil in themselves, obscured his vision of reality and weakened his resolve to realize the Truth in his life.

In all this, Gandhi's search for Truth, and his corresponding concept of Truth, were traditionally Hindu.[9] But the search for Truth took an unusual turn, and the understanding of Truth he acquired as a result was something remarkably fresh and original.

It seems to have begun with the discovery that the self from which he wanted to be delivered was in part at least *imposed* upon him by other human beings and that such an imposition had, therefore, to be *resisted* if he was completely to realize himself. His experience at Pietermaritzburg on his first arrival in South Africa was crucial here. He referred to it himself as the most creative passage of his life,[10] and we can see why from his account of it in *Satyagraha in South Africa* and the 'autobiography'. He was humiliated, like so many Indians and Black Africans before him, by being turned off a train for riding in the 'Whites only' compartment. But he responded, unlike others, by resolving *not* to accept the identity being violently foisted on him. His own account of the incident, however, focuses less on the immorality or indignity of the action than on the false perception that made it possible. Sitting on the cold platform that night, 'I began to think of my duty. Should I fight for my rights or go back to India . . . ? It would be cowardice to run back to India without fulfilling my obligation. The hardship to which I was subjected was superficial – only a symptom of the deep disease of colour prejudice. I should try, if possible, to root out the disease and suffer hardships in the process. Redress for wrongs I should seek only to the extent that would be necessary for the removal of the colour prejudice.'[11]

The wrongs were secondary. It was the 'prejudice' that mattered. Even the 'hardship' was 'superficial'. Fundamentally, for the young and not so confident Gandhi, this crisis was a matter of Truth, *his* truth first of all, but also, by implication, the truth of other human beings who were infected by the 'disease' of prejudice. But this discovery and the resolve that went with it led in turn to another tension which I think proved to be one of the sources of Gandhi's creativity. He had really come to the paradoxical conclusion that in order to be liberated from the self he had to assert it – and that paradox could not so easily be resolved by a philosophical distinction between empirical self (associated with the human body) and the deeper divine self. The self to be asserted was also a bodily self, a concrete individual.

The resolution came in a manner that proved to be characteristic of Gandhi's whole life, namely, in the practical mode of personal or collective action.

He had sufficient experience from his student days in England, from his knowledge of liberal reformers like Henry Salt and Charles Bradlaugh, to know that false social attitudes could be changed by organized campaigning. And he seems to have perceived in that crucial moment at Pietermaritzburg that the source of his suffering and humiliation was not only a false attitude, but a widely spread and deeply rooted *social* attitude that was responsible for a great deal of suffering among Colored and Black people generally. It would not, therefore, be 'selfish' of him to seek to oppose this prejudice and try to uproot it. On the contrary, he began to sense a 'duty' to do so. He was perceiving the false identity of maya as in part a social imposition which could and, therefore should, be opposed through social action. The perception became much clearer to him later when he wrote, for example, that 'on the political field, the struggle on behalf of the people mostly consists in opposing error in the shape of unjust laws'.[12]

The corollary of this is that Truth also has a social dimension. This is to say that the truth by which and in which people could find their true identity was partly at least a truth about their common humanity which was being denied by existing social structures. Gandhi's talk about Truth, when it related to specific instances, usually revolves around the idea of the *oneness* of things, especially of human beings, the idea of 'the essential unity of God and man and for that matter all that lives',[13] that 'all mankind in essence are alike'.[14] The great illusion, the social maya, as we may call it, is that human beings are fundamentally different from one another, and that some are inherently superior to others and are, thereby, entitled to dominate them. Gandhi found this divisive and oppressive attitude in South African racism, in British imperialism (from the early 1920s, at any rate), in Hindu–Muslim antagonism, and perhaps most hurtfully in 'the scourge of untouchability'. His life's work was largely devoted to the exposure of that illusion and the realization of the hidden Truth of human oneness. That is why his personal search for Truth so often assumed the form of a social insistence on Truth, that is, a social struggle to achieve at least a minimal expression of human unity. And that is why the struggles themselves, which involved nonviolent means that were consonant with the ends he hoped to achieve, were so appropriately described by him as satyagraha, literally, 'adherence to Truth'.

On the more personal level, it is evident that the changes in his life-style towards greater simplicity and the assumption of an almost peasant way of life were attempts to put this Truth into practice, i.e. 'experiments in Truth'. He was trying to realize his identity in God by identifying himself with the masses of the people who were in one way or another having their identities denied. That in its turn became a source of power and charisma in his leadership as the masses began to see him as a man of God. On the other hand, Gandhi came to see the masses as themselves a mediation of God and resolved to serve God in and through them, the God whom he called *Daridranarayana*, 'the God of the poor', adopting a phrase of Vivekenanda. 'To see the universal and all-pervading Spirit of Truth face to face', Gandhi wrote as the conclusion to his *Story of My Experiments*, 'one must be able to love the meanest of creation as oneself.'[15] There is an echo of St Francis here, for those in the Christian tradition, and an uncomfortable reminder, to me at least, of how far religion in the West has strayed from a concern for the poor. Perhaps this is one of the first points of relevance in Gandhi's concept of Truth.

To the extent that Gandhi sought and served Truth in humanity he could be described as a humanist.[16] But it would be wrong to leave the account there if it were to leave the impression that Gandhi was merely struggling for an ideal, with perhaps little sense of the realistic possibilities before him. He is often talked of as an idealist in this sense, someone who puts human values above political expediency or felt human needs. But this, as I see it, is to miss what is perhaps the most important feature of Gandhi's Truth, that is, that in some sense it already exists and is only waiting to be realized in actual experience. It exists in people, in everybody, and not only as the ground of their common identity as I described it before, but also as the source of their own realization of it. 'There is an inmost center of us all, where Truth abides in fullness. Every wrong-doer knows within himself that he is doing wrong.'[17] It is a daring and startling claim, for it implies that Truth exists even in those people whom Gandhi himself, for example, might feel bound to oppose in the name of Truth; and moreover, that it exists in their consciousness, however dimly, and if only in the negative form of being aware of doing wrong. Gandhi was not thinking merely of conscience, as we shall see later on, but he was making a connection of some sort between conscience and the presence of Truth in its 'fullness'.

This matter may be clarified by reference to another text where Gandhi is suggesting that although 'God' is difficult to define, everyone knows what Truth is: 'The definition of Truth is deposited in every human heart. Truth is that which you believe to be true at this moment, and that is your God. If a man worships this relative truth, he is sure to attain the Absolute Truth, i.e., God, in the course of time.'[18] He is appealing to the most basic form of human awareness, and suggesting that that in itself is enough to guide a person towards the fullest realization of Truth. 'I have been taught from my childhood, and I have tested the Truth by experience, that primary virtues of mankind are possible of cultivation by the meanest of the species. It is that undoubted universal possibility that distinguishes the human from the rest of God's creation.'[19] But how can he make inferences for humankind as a whole on the basis of his own experience? By discovering that for all his own achievements he is fundamentally no different from anyone else, which is precisely the 'Truth' on which his own life was based. He follows that statement I quoted earlier about all mankind as 'in essence ... alike' by asserting, 'What is therefore possible for me, is possible for everybody.'[20] We may suspect Gandhi of being over-optimistic here, and there are indications that towards the end of his life he came to think so himself. But these doubts do not, I think, affect the fundamental claim that in so far as each person has a capacity for truthfulness he or she is dimly aware of that ultimate Truth in which he or she would find self-realization.[21] He is not, after all, making a school-masterish point about everyone being able to reach a certain standard if only they make the effort. He was well aware of the vast differences in the degrees of awareness and moral resourcefulness. But he wished to assert nonetheless that there was an 'undoubted universal possibility' of realizing Truth, whatever the difficulties of its realization.

I think one of the reasons Gandhi found it important to emphasize this was that the Indian masses tended to despair of their own capacities and were all too ready to submit to the authority of fate, or *karma*, or British rule, or even the Mahatma himself. He saw the universal availability of Truth as a source of personal liberation and independence, which would in turn provide the basis for a genuine liberation and independence for India.

At any rate it was important to Gandhi himself, for however meager this potentiality may have been, it was enough to give him a special confidence in the power of ordinary people to lay claim to the truth of their own humanity. Put negatively, it was enough to ensure that people could not be completely taken in by the illusions and lies foisted on them by those who wished to dominate them. 'The Truth would out', in the widest possible sense. This was the basis for his remarkable claims for the power of Truth in contrast to the power of brute force. And when he spoke of the power of Truth he was not thinking, as we might in the modern West, about the power of the pen or of the press. He was thinking more of Tolstoy's claim – in the book that greatly affected Gandhi, *The Kingdom of God is Within You* – 'There is one and only one thing in life in which it is granted man to be free and over which he has full control – all else being beyond his power. That one thing is to perceive the Truth and profess it.'[22]

To perceive Truth and profess it was more a matter of courage than of intelligence – here again the moral quality of Truth becomes apparent. Raghavan Iyer is surely correct in saying that 'The crucial thing for Gandhi, as for Kant, is not to teach people what is right ... but to get them to do what they know they ought to do. In this way, Gandhi tended to assimilate all the virtues to that of moral courage.'[23] And for Gandhi there was always enough perceivable Truth to be acting on. He was quite willing, in principle at least, to engage the whole nation of India in a satyagraha campaign as a 'profession of Truth', although most people would have had only the dimmest idea of the truth they were fighting for. Yet he also saw these campaigns as educational, in that commitment to truth on a particular issue, and particularly some suffering in the course of that commitment, made people much more aware of the larger issues in which they were involved. He described his first campaigns in India as 'object-lessons'; and Vinoba Bhave, as one of the few people to have pursued satyagraha in that spirit, described it as a form of 'dialogue' which, if it finds people not willing to listen, 'provokes thinking'.[24]

In the social and political forms that truth-seeking assumed under Gandhi's leadership there was a spiral process in which initial insights led to collective action which in turn led to greater insight. For example, a vague insight or suspicion about the oneness of humanity might lead to a campaign against a divisive government law. The experience of struggling and suffering together, possibly sharing a jail with Indians they would otherwise have little or nothing to do with, would create a new bond of fellow-feeling.[25] This in turn would strengthen the nonviolent struggle, which, if successful, would create yet another bond with the opponents, thereby opening up a deeper insight into Truth. In Gandhi's whole career the Salt Tax campaign, with the historic march to Dandi Beach, was probably the finest example of this process. It demonstrated perhaps more effectively than any other campaign what Gandhi meant by 'the power of Truth'.

His attitude to Truth, we have to conclude, goes beyond a humanist idealism and becomes a confident faith in the universal, if partially veiled, reality of Truth and its power to disclose itself through ordinary people perceiving and professing it.

There was a problem, however. Collective social action was being guided by individual and internal awareness. What if people felt differently about the issues concerned? This was not such a problem when the issue in question involved everyone in the same way, or when Gandhi was allowed to act on behalf of others as his own conscience let him – it is notable how often Gandhi resorted to such selective or 'representative' satyagraha after the experience of mass violence in the big nationwide campaigns. But the question still remained, and often pressed itself on practical issues where there was great divergence of opinion, such as the partition of India on Independence.

Gandhi's view that everyone could see the Truth if they had the courage to face it was not enough by itself to deal with this situation, and he knew it. He was realistic enough to recognize that people could in all honesty and integrity differ in their perception. But this recognition led to a deeper understanding on his part, which I think we shall find particularly valuable in problems of religion. He observed that a person's understanding of an issue was determined in part by the situation in which he or she was placed, and by the specific needs of that person; also that a person can see only part of the Truth anyway, namely that part which his/her vantage point allows him/her to see. These limiting factors of perception led Gandhi to talk of the 'relative truth' which is available to us in distinction from the 'Absolute Truth' which eludes us.

This concession might be thought to be fatal to the whole exercise, for it seems to imply that everyone has, in fact and inevitably, a different view of things relative to his/her situation and that therefore no general agreement is possible. In this 'sea of relativity' what has happened, we might ask, to the one universal Truth?

We have a record of an interesting debate on this point in the Hunter Commission of 1919, when a member of the committee, Sir Chimanlal Setalwad, shrewdly pressed Gandhi on this apparent contradiction in his thinking:

SIR CHIMANLAL: However honestly a man may strive in his search for truth, his notions of truth may be different from the notions of others. Who then is to determine the truth?
GANDHI: The individual himself would determine that.
SIR C: Different individuals would have different views as to the truth. Would that not lead to confusion?
G: I do not think so.
SIR C: Honestly striving after truth is different in every case.
G: That is why the non-violence part was a necessary corollary. Without that there would be confusion and worse.
SIR C: Must not the person wanting to pursue truth be of a high moral and intellectual equipment?
G: No. It would be impossible to expect that from everyone. If A has evolved a truth by his own efforts which B, C and others are to accept, I should not require them to have the equipment of A.
SIR C: Then it comes to this – that a man comes to a decision, and others of lower intellectual and moral equipment would have to blindly follow him.
G: Not blindly.[26]

Gandhi could have responded by either making claims for his leadership or for public debate and democratic decision-making (in the English fashion, for example), but he chose to emphasize the importance of an individual's own perception, walking into deeper water still, it would seem.

That particular discussion was not resolved, obviously, but Gandhi certainly had other things to say at other times which help to clarify it and perhaps also to resolve it. Most importantly, I think, Gandhi talked about differences in the *perception* of Truth, rather than differences of opinion in the normal sense. Opinions can be false, but perceptions of Truth, by definition, cannot be false, only more or less adequate, or clear. The relativity that Gandhi talked about was, therefore, not to be confused with the Western doctrine of relativism which tends, of course, to lead to very skeptical conclusions about the possibilities of Truth: 'We will never all think alike and ... we shall always see Truth in fragment and from different angles of vision',[27] which, in Indian-English, makes the point precisely.

We must also note what Gandhi means by 'conscience' and the

phrase 'according to one's lights'. These were popular terms among the English people Gandhi had to deal with, but they express rather poorly the kind of personal insight Gandhi had in mind. He preferred to speak about 'the Truth in the heart', 'the light within', or 'the voice within'. He goes so far as to equate the Truth with what the voice says: 'What is Truth? A difficult question: but I have solved it for myself by saying that it is what the voice within tells you.'[28] We get some clue as to what this means in practice from his autobiography. It is related to introspection, silence, dreams, 'flashes' of insight, as well as near-audible voices. In 1918, 'one morning – it was at a mill-hands' meeting – while I was still groping and unable to see my way clearly, the light came to me. Unbidden and all by themselves the words came to my lips: "Unless the strikers rally", I declared to the meeting, "and continue the strike till a settlement is reached, or till they leave the mills altogether, I will not touch any food."'[29] One night the following year, after the alarming news that the Rowlatt Bill had been published as an Act, 'I fell asleep while thinking over the question. Towards the small hours of the morning I woke up somewhat earlier than usual. I was still in that twilight condition between sleep and consciousness when suddenly the idea broke upon me – it was as if in a dream. Early in the morning I related the whole story to Rajagopalachari. "The idea came to me last night in a dream that we should call upon the country to observe a general *hartal*."'[30] Looking back on such occasions as he is about to conclude his 'story' he says: 'My object in writing these chapters is simply to describe how certain things, as it were spontaneously, presented themselves to me in the course of my experiments with Truth.'[31]

Gandhi's habit of waiting for the voice may have infuriated his more secular-minded colleagues, such as Nehru, but it was clearly an integral part of Gandhi's own discipline. The voice was a privileged disclosure of Truth for which he longed, and often had to struggle to receive. It was an insight beyond the normal scope of reason, gained only by developing a mystical sensitivity to feelings and situations which are not otherwise observable, although Gandhi also insisted that no idea should be accepted which contravened reason. At any rate, his own example of listening to Truth is enough to assure us that his concept of inward Truth has nothing to do with personal opinion, still less with prejudice or ideology, which belong rather to the untruth of maya.

It is significant too that he made a point of undergoing 'well-tried disciplines' in the pursuit of Truth, by which he meant, among other things, the disciplines of yoga and meditation, of prayer, silence and restrictive diet. He developed his own disciplines as well of course, and in accordance with his view of the social dimension of maya he developed the communal discipline of the ashram, including vows of nonviolence, chastity and non-possession. 'It is because we have at the present moment everybody claiming the right of conscience without going through any discipline whatsoever that there is so much untruth being delivered to a bewildered world.'[32]

In addition to all this, there were in Gandhi some counterbalancing emphases on objectivity. To begin with, his experiments often entailed meticulous attention to the *facts* of the case. It is hard to see at first how this fits into the picture. Subjective perception is usually distinguished sharply from objective factuality. But we have seen that for Gandhi Truth has a social aspect and that falsehood and illusion often take the form of social prejudice or ideology. There must, therefore, be an objective and empirical component in Truth. It is noticeable in Gandhi's campaigns how carefully he assembled the relevant facts, especially direct testimonies from those involved, combining his legal training and a *bania* meticulousness with the inner spiritual quest. 'When (in 1893) I was making preparation for Dada Abdulla's case, I had not fully realized this paramount importance of facts. Facts mean truth, and once we adhere to truth, the law comes to our aid naturally.'[33] I do not fully understand, I must admit, how these two modes of search were brought together, nor am I aware of a particular discipline that was intended for this purpose, except that Gandhi spent a lot of time talking with people and listening to them. Perhaps there is more than a metaphor in his saying, 'the voice of the people is the voice of God', and perhaps, conversely, he was trying to sense the needs and aspirations of the people when he listened for the voice of God within.[34] However that may be, there can be no doubt that any insight gained had to be tested, and that the crucial test was always how it worked out in practice. This, essentially, is what he meant by *'experiments* with Truth', although these too combined two apparently incongruous features of openness to change and adherence to Truth as he knew it – what Erikson calls 'an altogether rare mixture of detachment and commitment, and . . . an almost mystical conflux of inner voice and historical actuality'.[35] But the connection is not so mysterious in this case because we know that when Gandhi talked of putting truth into practice he meant going some way towards realizing the 'Absolute Truth' of the oneness of things which meant, simply, loving them. Bringing wholeness to individuals or communities is to some extent realizing their truth, so that the appropriate test for any idea or hunch about their truth is whether it makes for wholeness in practice. 'The "Inner Voice" may mean a message from God or the Devil, for both are wrestling in the human breast. Acts determine the nature of the voice.'[36] 'By their fruits you shall know them', Jesus had said in a passage Gandhi had marked well, but more pertinent is a statement in the *Mahabharata* which Gandhi might have been actually alluding to: 'It is indeed noble to speak the Truth, but one is never sure what the Truth is. I tell you, that alone is Truth which is wholly beneficial to others' (12.276.19).

These amount to important qualifications of his doctrine of the relativity of truth. They suggest, for example, that differences of perception do not necessarily imply a conflict of views, nor, if there are such conflicts, that they are insoluble. On the contrary, this doctrine of relativity points the way to the resolution of conflicts. Another way of expressing this positive potentiality is to speak of the 'manysidedness' of Truth, as the Jains did, or as Gandhi quaintly phrased it, 'the manyness' of Truth: 'I very much like this doctrine of the manyness of reality. It is this doctrine which has taught me to judge a Musalman from his own standpoint and a Christian from his.'[37]

Now that is going beyond a mere acceptance of diversity towards a more dynamic conception in which a person can learn to see reality as others see it – thereby, of course, enriching his or her understanding of reality. If this really is possible as Gandhi claims, then the implications for religion are tremendous. It means that in situations of religious diversity or conflict it is possible not only to accept other religious viewpoints as valid in an attitude of tolerance, and not only to learn from others in dialogue in an attitude of openness, but also to see reality from others' points of view in an attitude of positive affirmation. John S. Dunne has described this process of temporarily identifying with the experience of others as 'passing over', and I agree with him in thinking this to be particularly important in the religious situation of our time. 'The holy man of our time', he suggests, 'is not a figure like Gotama or

Jesus or Mohammed, a man who could found a world religion, but a figure like Gandhi, a man who passes over by sympathetic understanding from his own religion to other religions and comes back again with new insights to his own. Passing over and coming back, it seems, is the spiritual adventure of our time.'[38]

There are at least these two positive implications of the doctrine then: the possibility of resolving differences of view by recognizing the situations out of which they arise; and the possibility of enriching our knowledge of Truth by 'passing over' from one view to another and one situation to another.

I cannot discuss the political implications here, but it is worth pointing out at least, as Joan Bondurant has done so clearly,[39] that the political techniques of satyagraha are made intelligible by Gandhi in terms of the inevitable relativity of our perception of Truth. Satyagraha is a form of action appropriate to the dual character of Truth as one in essence but diverse in practice.

There is, however, one feature of satyagraha which applies more widely to the pursuit of Truth and the recognition of divergence. It is that in order to win a greater understanding or realization of Truth, a person or group must recognize the partiality of their own perception even in the process of insisting on it. This means that no perception of truth must be fashioned or defended in a dogmatic manner. The opponent must be listened to and expected to yield his or her truth too. Such openness to others, especially in cases of conflict or oppression, requires quite extraordinary courage, humility and goodwill. That is why all confrontations in the name of Truth have to be nonviolent, for violence would immediately close the door to dialogue and mutual regard.

The principle turns out to be especially important in Gandhi's attitude to religion. Religion, to Gandhi, is simply the pursuit of Truth under a different name. But that Truth as discovered in religion 'passes through the human medium'[40] and 'the human mind' in its turn 'works through innumerable media',[41] so that in one way or another religion is bound to assume a variety of forms. This simple and inevitable fact, however, has led to one of the greatest problems in religion. It has led people to see the particular form in which they have gained a glimpse of Truth as the final embodiment of that Truth. They mistake Hinduism, for example, for the essence of religion, which is to say they identify the relative truth of their religion with the Absolute Truth their religion was meant to lead them to. The first problem here is that religions can in this way become an obstacle to their own real purposes. The solution to this must be for people to relativize their own traditions, to become conscious both of the partiality of their perception and the provisionality of the specific forms in which it is expressed, that is, to consider the tradition as 'pointing beyond itself' (to use a phrase of Paul Tillich's) to the ultimate reality beyond all possible expressions. 'Even as a tree has a single trunk, but many branches and leaves, so there is one true and perfect Religion, but it becomes many, as it passes through the human medium. The one Religion is beyond all speech.'[42] Therefore, to be true even to the religion people profess, they must in a sense pass beyond it or see through it to something really ultimate and universal. For this reason Gandhi himself professed 'the religion which transcends Hinduism, which changes one's nature, which binds one indissolubly to the Truth within and which ever purifies. It is the permanent element in human nature which counts no cost too great in order to find full expression and which leaves the soul utterly restless until it has found itself.'[43]

The second problem is that religions can divide people and oppress them by making one form final and definitive, providing a criterion by which other religions can be judged more or less adequate or true, and in this way, again, they deny the Truth they are meant to bear witness to – in this case, the ultimate unity of human life. The fact is that we are never in a position of absolute knowledge from which we could presume to deny that others have some truth, and on that basis suppress them and their views, let alone do violence to them as a dangerous source of error.[44] The solution to this problem may be first of all to recognize the sources of dogmatism so that we can then discover means for its preventive cure. Gandhi makes an interesting distinction in this respect which if it doesn't stand up linguistically yet makes a valid theological point: 'Idolatry is bad, not so idol-worship. An idolater makes a fetish of his idol. An idol-worshipper sees God even in a stone and therefore takes the help of an idol to establish his union with God.'[45] A fetish is something a person clings to, as if that in itself were the source of salvation. It is a finite symbol, as Tillich put it, made into something infinite and absolute.[46] But Gandhi elsewhere made the point in a slightly different way so as to suggest also another solution to the problem: 'So long as there are different religions, every one of them may need some distinctive symbol. But when the symbol is made into a fetish and an instrument of proving the superiority of one's religion over others, it is fit only to be discarded.'[47] It is how the symbol is instrumental that is important here, that is, its practical use in relation to other human beings. It suggests a criterion of religious truth and validity which takes us beyond the bare intellectualism of Tillich into the practical realm of human relationships. It is for this reason, and not for a theoretical reason, that Gandhi said 'I cannot ascribe *exclusive* divinity to Jesus'.[48]

Once again then we must be careful not to confuse Gandhi's tolerance in religion with a bland liberalism which can happily regard all religions as much the same. Gandhi preferred to say that religions were 'equally false' than to say they were 'equally true'! The point is that he saw all religions as human mediations of Truth and as such, inadequate expressions of it. Each religion must be open to critique and to greater exposure to the truth it professes, even if that were to come through an encounter with other religions. Truth itself is the only final criterion, and the most reliable way of applying that criterion is to see how religion affects human relationships in practice.

This last point about practice raises a third problem in religion, which has often been regarded as so serious as to become reason enough for rejecting religion altogether. This is the tendency of religious symbols – and here we must include all the rituals and doctrines that make religion distinctive – to become such foci of devotion and commitment that they obscure the needs of the world and divert energy from the practical task of meeting them. It is yet another aspect of the fetishizing of symbols, but in this case the practical attitude is not so much disdain for other religious people as indifference to peoples' suffering. This of course was the brunt of Marx's critique of all religion. Without being aware of that critique (as far as I know), Gandhi was aware of the problem and regarded such religion as a gross distortion. 'Those who say religion has nothing to do with politics do not know what religion means', he said bluntly. 'True religion and true morality are inseparably bound up with each other.'[49] His repeated emphasis on morality or service to human beings as the 'essence of religion' can almost sound reductionist, as if in the last analysis that were all there was to it.[50] However, he did not wish to exclude God from the proper concern for humanity, but rather to include the concern for humanity in the concern for God, as the essential expression of that concern. Another reason for emphasizing morality was that it was itself a means of realizing Truth and being liberated from self-concern; it was the 'selfless action' recommended in the *Gita*. And as a *means* to Truth it could in practice take precedence over Truth, though ontologically Truth remained prior. Ahimsa, or love, and Truth

> are so intertwined that it is practically impossible to disentangle and separate them. They are like two sides of a coin, or rather of a smooth unstamped metallic disc. Who can say, which is the obverse and which is the reverse? Nevertheless *ahimsa* is the means; Truth is the end. Means to be means must always be within our reach, and so *ahimsa* is our supreme duty.[51]

In this practical expression of religion, as we have seen in Gandhi's own case, the poor can themselves become a symbolic 'face of God'.

Finally, there is the problem that religion provokes, by its own distorted forms, the total rejection of religion. We have noted one example of this in Marxism. But it seems to apply also to the very widespread phenomenon of atheism and secularism, which in various ways see religion as a hindrance to truth or morality or both. Gandhi's response to this phenomenon is quite original, and perhaps one of his most creative contributions to the practice and understanding of religion. For he sees the problem not in the rejection of religion as such but in the kind of religion that provokes this rejection. In the famous lecture in 1931 to a group of atheists in Lausanne, he makes what appears to be a defensive claim, that 'not even atheists have denied the necessity or power of Truth',[52] as if to suggest they might be honorary theists after all. But then he adds: 'Not only so. In their passion for discovering the truth they have not hesitated even to deny the very existence of God – *from their own point of view rightly*. And it was *because of their reasoning* that I saw that I was not going to say "God is Truth" but "Truth is God".'[53] Gandhi does not merely concede their right to be atheists, but in John Dunne's sense, he 'passes over' into atheism and positively affirms it. That is why he can say of his atheist friend and humanitarian Charles Bradlaugh that, 'that which sustained Bradlaugh throughout all his trials was God. He (God) is the Denial of the atheist';[54] and again, 'He is even the atheism of the atheist'[55] as part of a *definition* of God. Since it was 'self-styled believers (who) are often not so in reality',[56] who pushed others into unbelief, their unbelief was wholly right. This is not to say that atheists will be impressed by this argument, although they should be careful not to read it as subtle apologetic for belief in God. The Indian atheist Gora was not too impressed when he talked to Gandhi, at some length, on this matter; but this was partly because, as Gora himself admitted, he did not have Gandhi's breadth of view. He was stunned, however, when Gandhi said to him, 'I can neither say my theism is right, nor your atheism wrong', and Gora recognized in him, if not a good philosopher, 'a prophet who perceived the direction'.[57] Gandhi had relativized his own theism, and affirmed as ultimately true only what he and Gora could both affirm in good conscience, the ultimacy of Truth itself.

> I do not share the belief that there can or will be on earth one religion. I am striving, therefore, to find a common factor.[58]

Notes

1. M. K. Gandhi, *The Story of My Experiments with Truth*, 2nd edn (Ahmedabad: Navajivan Press, 1940) p. ix.
2. Ibid., p. xi.
3. Ibid., p. x.
4. A letter to Mahadev Desai, September 15 1919.
5. E.g., *The Story of My Experiments with Truth*, p. 260.
6. *Selected Writings of Mahatma Gandhi*, ed. R. Duncan (London: Fontana, 1971) p. 124.
7. *The Story of My Experiments with Truth*, p. 289.
8. This is a translation made by Donald Groom on his visit to the Sevegram Ashram, and it was given to me by one of the ashramites, Balwant Singh, when I visited the ashram myself in 1976 and asked for a translation of Gandhi's favorite *bhajans*, or hymns. Balwant Singh had lived with Gandhi there from the time of his move in 1936.
9. Consider the following statement from an article published on April 24 1924 after his long imprisonment in Yeravda, during which time he had read deeply in classical Hindu literature, including, apparently, the whole *Mahabharata*: 'If I were asked to define the Hindu creed, I should simply say: search after Truth through nonviolent means. A man may not believe even in God and still call himself a Hindu. Hinduism is a relentless search after Truth.'
10. See the discussion of this in G. Ashe, *Gandhi: A Study in Revolution* (London: Heinemann, 1968) p. 50; and in Erik Erikson, *Gandhi's Truth* (London: Faber, 1970), where Erikson claims that at this point

Gandhi 'solved his identity crisis' (p. 47).
11. *The Story of My Experiments with Truth*, p. 82.
12. An article in *Young India* in 1922, cited in R. Duncan (ed.), *Selected Writings of Mahatma Gandhi*, p. 65.
13. *Young India*, December 1924.
14. *Harijan*, November 1938.
15. *The Story of My Experiments with Truth*, p. 383.
16. The title of the 1969 UNESCO symposium, 'Truth and nonviolence in Gandhi's humanism', was not inappropriate therefore, provided that humanism is not taken to be an alternative to a religious outlook.
17. *Young India*, July 1931.
18. *All Men Are Brothers*, UNESCO (New York: Columbia University Press, 1958) p. 72.
19. *Harijan*, May 1936.
20. *Harijan*, November 1938.
21. He also gives some metaphysical backing to the claim that God is accessible to everyone with the barest human capacities. Note the significant 'therefore' in the following statement: 'Truth is not a mere attribute of God, but He is That. He is nothing if He is not That. Truth in Sanskrit means *Sat*. *Sat* means Is ... God is, nothing else is. Therefore, the more truthful we are, the nearer we are to God. We *are* only to the extent that we are truthful' (*Harijan*, March 1949). Also in *In Search of the Supreme*, vol. 1 (Ahmedabad: Navajivan Press, 1961) p. 38; it was originally a letter to a Mr P. G. Mayhew in September 1932.
22. Leo Tolstoy, *The Kingdom of God and Peace Essays* (London: OUP, 1936) p. 442.
23. Raghavan Iyer, *The Moral and Political Thought of Mahatma Gandhi* (New York: OUP, 1973) p. 69.
24. *Vinoba on Gandhi*, ed. Kantilal Shah (Varanasi: Sarva Seva Sang Prakashan, 1973) p. 52.
25. I came to appreciate this point from hearing a lecture by Dr James Manor on Gandhi's politics, delivered at Birmingham University (England) in May 1983.
26. Quoted in G. Ashe, *Gandhi: A Study in Revolution*, pp. 196f.
27. *Young India*, September 1921, also in *In Search of the Supreme*, vol. 3, p. 39.
28. *All Men Are Brothers*, p. 71.
29. *The Story of My Experiments with Truth*, p. 325.
30. Ibid., p. 348.
31. Ibid., p. 377.
32. *All Men Are Brothers*, p. 71.
33. *The Story of My Experiments with Truth*, p. 99.
34. Ibid., p. 164.
35. Erik Erikson, *Gandhi's Truth*, p. 411.
36. *Young India*, February 1930, in *In Search of the Supreme*, vol. 1, p. 257. Cf. Joan Bondurant's remark in her *Conquest of Violence* (Los Angeles: University of California Press, rev. 1965) p. 25: 'If there is dogma in

the Gandhian philosophy, it centers here: that the only test of truth is action based on the refusal to do harm.'
37. *Young India*, January 1926, in *In Search of the Supreme*, vol. 1, p. 340.
38. John S. Dunne, *The Way of All the Earth* (London: Sheldon Press, 1972; published in the USA by Macmillan, 1972), p. vii. See Margaret Chatterjee's *Gandhi's Religious Thought* (London: Macmillan, 1983), where she talks of the possibility beyond 'dialogue' of a 'combined witness' (p. 181).
39. Joan V. Bondurant, *Conquest of Violence*, e.g. pp. 16f.
40. *Selections from Gandhi*, ed. N. K. Bose (Ahmedabad: Navajivan Press, 1948) p. 225.
41. *All Men Are Brothers*, p. 71.
42. *Selections from Gandhi*, ed. N. K. Bose, p. 225.
43. *Young India*, May 1920.
44. Note the parallel case of divisive dogma in politics, as in Raghavan Iyer's eloquent passage in *The Moral and Political Thought of Mahatma Gandhi*, p. 175.
45. *Harijan*, March 1940, in *In Search of the Supreme*, vol. 1, p. 230.
46. Note the useful comparison between Gandhi and Tillich in Glyn Richards, *The Philosophy of Gandhi* (London: Curzon Press, 1982), Chapters 1 and 2 on 'the concept of truth' and 'truth and religion' respectively.
47. *Selections from Gandhi*, ed. N. K. Bose, p. 225; also in *All Men Are Brothers*, pp. 59f.
48. *In Search of the Supreme*, vol. 3, p. 17. Margaret Chatterjee's comment on this is also apt: 'Mere dialogue cannot bring peace. What is needed is the labour of reconciliation', in *Gandhi's Religious Thought*, p. 179.
49. *All Men Are Brothers*, p. 75.
50. I think Joan Bundurant makes this mistake when she compares his view with Feuerbach's, that talk about God is reducible to talk about humanity, and that the solution to the problem of disagreements about Truth 'is in terms of "man, the measure"' (*The Conquest of Violence*, p. 21); and to claim that he rejected Absolute Truth in preference for relative truth (ibid., p. 193) in the practice of satyagraha is surely to misunderstand him.
51. *From Yeravda Mandir* (Ahmedabad: Navajivan Press, 1957) pp. 8f.
52. *M. K. Gandhi: Select Speeches*, ed. B. K. Ahluwalia (New Delhi: Sagar Publications, 1969) p. 272.
53. Ibid., emphasis mine.
54. *Young India*, April 1925, in *In Search of the Supreme*, vol. 1, p. 9.
55. Ibid., p. 15.
56. *Harijan*, September 1940, in *In Search of the Supreme*, vol. 1, p. 26.
57. Gora, *An Atheist with Gandhi* (Ahmedabad: Navajivan Press, 1951) p. 56.
58. *All Men Are Brothers*, p. 78.

7
Gandhi's Moral Philosophy
Steven A. Smith

Among public figures in this century who significantly altered the course of history, none displayed such exacting moral discipline as Mahatma Gandhi. Gandhi's revolution was above all a moral revolution, which advanced social justice on a larger scale at less moral cost than any other in recent memory. It is often supposed that public figures can achieve their ends only by means that are to some degree unscrupulous: that public hands must be dirty. Gandhi's hands were extraordinarily clean. Furthermore, his moral rigor was not incidental to his success as a reformer, but integral to it. The life of Gandhi is thus of special interest for the moral philosopher, as an object lesson in the union of ethics and politics, of right and power.

I am concerned here not with the specific content of Gandhi's moral philosophy – his views on diet and celibacy, property and poverty, and so on – but rather with its broad features and their significance, for moral philosophers and for all of us as reflective moral agents. Placing the development of Gandhi's thought within the context of moral philosophy suggests a variety of lessons regarding the proper relation of thought to action, of religion to politics, of means to ends. I am concerned also with Gandhi's central moral doctrine, the principle of *satyagraha*, and with the strengths and dangers of moral suasion as a device for achieving social ends. Whether there was a certain inconsistency in Gandhi's own practice of nonviolence – a coercive element in purportedly non-coercive means – has been much discussed by scholars; I suggest a way of looking at this question by means of a distinction between moral attachment and moral non-attachment. Finally, I note that current trends in contemporary moral philosophy make this an especially propitious time for Gandhi studies.

What is the pattern by which a moral theory arises, and how does Gandhi's development as a moral thinker exemplify this pattern? Those who construct a normative moral philosophy typically seek to explain to themselves their own deeply felt moral sentiments: entrenched convictions about what is wrong and what is right, what should be prohibited and what required. Moral theories thus commonly rationalize pre-existing and firmly held moral intuitions – in somewhat the same way that an aesthetic theory may explain to us why we find certain things to be beautiful or fitting, and other things less so. In constructing moral theories, philosophers have frequently sought to base them upon an *a priori* foundation – such as God's will, or pure reason itself – so that moral applications may be derived in a quasi-deductive way as theorems within the system. But the 'theorems' typically play a more controlling role than this model suggests. And this is as it should be. If a moral philosophy with apparently impeccable *a priori* origins should imply, for example, that acts of gratuitous cruelty were obligatory, we should reject the theory on the basis of its consequences, much as we would reject an aesthetic theory which told us that all that we experience as beautiful is in fact ugly, and *vice versa*.

Moral intuitions are not sacrosanct, to be sure. The process of reconciling theory with application may prompt us to prune or revise our intuitions, bringing moral sentiments into harmony with principles of compelling pedigree. The best moral philosophy arises through a dialectic of theory and application by which, in John Rawls' felicitous phrase, we arrive at a *reflective equilibrium* between entrenched moral intuitions and credible moral principles.[1] If there is an Archimedian point in moral philosophy – a point from which we can move the world – we can approximate this point only by untidy trial and error; and while engaged in this process, we will do well to take as our motto Aristotle's remark in the *Nicomachean Ethics* that it is the mark of a reasonable person not to demand more exactness than is permitted by the subject matter.

In the life of Gandhi we see a graphic example of this dialectical evolution of moral thought. The profound insights of satyagraha were the product of decades of experimentation and revision, of gradual purification of views that in the beginning were unsystematic and immature. In the tempering fire of South Africa, Gandhi steadily refined his moral thought, at times striking forward with brilliant thrusts of insight, at other times falling back in confusion, always searching and questioning himself. Above all, Gandhi developed his moral views in response to practical problems that pressed in upon him or that he, in his moral fervor, sought out to confront. Increasingly, his judgment served not only as a guide to his own actions, but also as a norm for thousands, even millions of others who depended upon his moral wisdom for the guidance of their own lives. His moral outlook thus evolved under conditions very different from those of the academic philosopher, for whom theory may be comfortably insulated from active moral choice, and only the residue of that choice, our reflective intuition, remains as raw material for theorizing. Some have, on these grounds, denied any theoretical depth to Gandhi's thought, seeing him as primarily an inspired politician with a spiritual bent who used religious and moral language to promote his political goals. Such a description is false, however. Gandhi saw himself as first of all a seeker after religious Truth, for whom the realm of social involvement was a means to further his own spiritual liberation. He writes:

> I count no sacrifice too great for the sake of seeing God face to face. The whole of my activity, whether it may be called social, political, humanitarian or ethical, is directed to that end ... I am impatient to realize myself, to attain *Moksha* in this very existence. My national service is part of my training for freeing the soul from the bondage of flesh. Thus considered, my service may be regarded as purely selfish.[2]

A person who knew nothing of Mahatma Gandhi and who, wandering through a library, happened upon a shelf of Gandhi's collected works, might naturally conclude that one who wrote so extensively and penetratingly upon so many topics must be first a thinker, a man of libraries and studies, of discourse directed towards the task of writing. Yet, despite his voluminous literary output, Gandhi was primarily a moral activist, a reformer. In fact, the dichotomy of theory and practice is hardly useful in talking about Gandhi, for whom thought and action fused in a seamless fabric of moral commitment.

It might well be argued that moral philosophy ought to be developed only in this manner; that the divorce between contemplation and choice creates a false environment for moral reflection; that the ethics of the Oxford drawingroom or the professional philosophers' conference perforce cannot be the ethics of the engaged life. Perhaps, despite our best efforts to bring into academic discussion the urgency and concreteness facing an involved moral agent, something is lost, something whose absence leaves our ethical discourse anemic and distorted. Ideas forged in practice have an authenticity which no abstract principle can attain, despite all the niceties of careful academic balancing. Perhaps, in fact, such considerations call into question this very thing I now do: I, an academic moral philosopher, a man of the classroom rather than the streets or the corridors of power, ruminating ironically upon the necessity for moral philosophy to evolve in action. Still, here I am, and I must make the best of it. In my own defense, it is well to remember that even Gandhi himself did much of his moral reflection and writing at times of removal from action: in a jail in South Africa; during a fast in Yeravda Prison; in the quiet of his *ashram* in Ahmedabad before the day's activities. That moral reflection and writing were, nevertheless, developed in response to matters that arose in his life of action. There is a lesson here for academic moral philosophers: just as philosophy of science ought not to be conducted at too far a remove from the activities of the practicing scientist in laboratory and field, and the theory of musicology should retain close ties to the realities of actual musical performance, so the development of moral philosophy should arise from the realities of real-life moral choice.

Not all moral action takes place in a context of revolution, to be sure. Gandhi was a pivotal figure in a period of national upheaval, and the leadership role that he assumed – or that was thrust upon him – gave his moral actions a broad urgency and salience that distinguished them from the moral choices of most of us. If there is an ethics of revolution and reform, there is also an ethics of everyday life, to guide those not placed at the cutting edge of a mass political movement, but simply seeking to conduct their mundane affairs rightly. Yet even here, Gandhi does not permit us an easy distinction; for Gandhi's moral genius lay partly in his fusion of the personal and the political, the ordinary and the extraordinary, the banal and the exalted. No detail of life was too minor for his moral scrutiny, no matter of personal choice so trivial as to be divorced from political action. For Gandhi, the very act of salting one's food was politically significant. Like all great religious leaders, he insisted that political efficacy must not be separated from personal conduct and spiritual practice. In one of his most often-quoted affirmations, he declared that 'I can say without the slightest hesitation, and yet in all humility, that those who say that religion has nothing to do with politics do not know what religion means.'[3]

Nearly every political leader pretends to moral rightness and clothes his or her political objectives in the language of moral justification. Gandhi's uniqueness lies not in his claim of a moral rationale for his actions, but in the persuasiveness of that claim as evidenced in his life – so that even his political opponents were frequently compelled to acknowledge his moral stature.[4] Indeed, Gandhi often defined satyagraha as a means of achieving a moral victory by winning over the heart of the opponent.

Wherein lies the secret of success of such an approach? It is not enough simply to profess high ideals, nor even enough consistently to live by those ideals in one's own life. One must be prepared to suffer on their behalf, without turning one's suffering into hatred for those who cause it. Without these elements – strict self-discipline, and the willingness to suffer without retaliation in thought or deed – the profession of high moral ideals is mere sanctimony, commanding little respect and less cooperation. In contrast, Gandhi put himself on the line – again and again. Though he often held up his own moral choices as a standard for others, the charge that he assumed a posture of 'holier-than-thou' is blunted by his willingness to accept upon himself the ill effects of others' misbehavior for the sake of a higher moral end. 'The end does not justify the means', we say; yet repeatedly we justify coercive and destructive means for the sake of ends that we regard as of overriding importance. Gandhi insisted that means must be wholly consistent with ends, or the ends are not worthy of our pursuit. Because the ends that Gandhi sought went well beyond the achievement of specific political goals (such as home rule for India) to a way of life manifesting the highest ideals of human harmony and spirituality, the means used must, in Gandhi's view, be subject to thorough scrutiny to ensure that they were consistent with such ideals. Repeatedly throughout his life, Gandhi withdrew himself and his followers from confrontation with his adversaries when it became apparent to him that success could not be achieved without resorting to violent or coercive means. At such times, his strategy was to purify himself and to strengthen the moral basis of his movement. Justice was to be achieved not through power over others, but through power over oneself.

But if there are dangers in the use of amoral means to achieve moral ends, there are also dangers in the assumption of moral purity to gain leverage over others. Moral posturing may be employed in a subtly coercive manner, to shame the opponent into compliance. It may be used disingenuously, to arouse partisan public indignation and favorable publicity. And it may promote self-deception; for the mantle of moral righteousness is a gratifying guise, which may hide not only from others, but also from oneself one's own motives of resentment and need to control. Erik Erikson argues in his searching and generally favorable study, that Gandhi's exacting moral demands upon himself and upon those around him at times constituted a kind of 'displaced violence where nonviolence was the professed issue'.[5]

Thus any attempt to assess Gandhi's moral views must come to grips with the status of his moral practice. Was satyagraha merely a morally presumptuous means to achieve various political, social and personal ends, as capable of misuse as any other? Was it an inspired expression of God-consciousness, whose integrity surpassed that of any other mass movement in history? Or did it lie somewhere between these extremes? This is well-trampled ground in Gandhi scholarship. I propose to approach it by delineating a spectrum or continuum of moral involvement, and then by exploring where Gandhi's moral practice may be placed on this continuum. The continuum I have in mind is defined by the means favored by moral agents to promote their preferred moral values. At one end of the continuum is what may be called *moral attachment*: the commitment to certain moral values together with an attachment to their enforcement, and hence a willingness to ensure compliance by various informal and/or formal means, such as legal sanctions, social ostracism, or direct physical coercion. Several Western moral philosophers, including John Stuart Mill and Kurt Baier, have declared that by definition all moral commitment is attached in this sense; to affirm that an act is morally wrong, for instance, is to imply that people should be prevented from doing it, and that those who do it may legitimately be punished. Mill writes that 'It is part of the notion of duty in every one of its forms that a person may rightfully be compelled to fulfil it...'[6] And Baier asserts that to regard a matter as morally significant is to 'license interference' in the affairs of others.[7] From this standpoint, morality is necessarily attached, entailing an element of coercion, a commitment to control the behavior of humans, if necessary against their will.

But Mill and Baier are mistaken in declaring coercion to be a logically necessary feature of morality. Whether one favors sanctions to support compliance with one's moral values varies from person to person and from situation to situation. I may be fully committed to certain moral values, yet not favor coercive measures to promote them. I may, for instance, hold that the actions of another are wrong, but believe that no one should interfere – perhaps because I adhere to supervening values such as respect for privacy and self-determination which prohibit interference in cases of this kind. Or – more to the point here – I may trust that without intervention the wrong will in the end be righted, and that my interference will make things worse rather than better. Thus I may adopt an attitude of *benign forbearance*, akin to the Taoist notion of *wu-wei* or non-action, allowing events to go forward in the conviction that they will work themselves out eventually.

An example from the role of parenting may be useful here. A father watches his son playing in the park. The boy is teased by another child and an altercation ensues. At first, tempted to intervene, the father chooses instead to let the children deal with it themselves. Believing that no serious harm is likely to occur, and convinced that his son must learn how to manage such experiences, the father refrains from imposing his own solution to the problem. He is watchful and aware, willing to be present for the children if they need him; and he feels compassion for their pain. But he does not attempt to control the situation. His attitude of benign forbearance is rooted in a decision to trust the course of events.

As this example makes clear, benign forbearance is decidedly not callous indifference. In the case as described above, the father's attitude is not 'I don't care' but 'It's better that I not interfere'. His inaction is concerned and compassionate. Nor is benign forbearance identical with a lazy passivity. As any parent knows who has lived through such a moment, 'doing nothing' may require distinct effort and discipline.

Benign forbearance – the willingness to allow events to unfold according to their own imperative, in the belief that the process may be trusted – may be termed *moral non-attachment*, to distinguish it from a normative moral stance that seeks to force compliance through the use of various sanctions. It is often found in a developed form in religious settings, where belief in a spiritual or divine order provides a rationale for the conviction that in a deeper sense, all is well. As exemplifed in the lives of many saints, *bodhissatvas* and others, moral non-attachment does not entail literally doing nothing to right wrong; such spiritual leaders typically spend much of their energy in efforts to relieve suffering. But they are unlikely to attempt to coerce others by moral sanctions; more typically, they seek to purify themselves and thus to manifest moral and spiritual leadership in their own person. Such self-discipline typically includes the willingness to accept suffering rather than to cause it for others, even – or especially – in a morally upright cause.

I have emphasized the role of trust in moral non-attachment. The coercive sanctions of moral attachment seek to control the behavior of others, manifesting a fear that things will go awry if left to themselves. When this fear is replaced by an open trust, the desire to control fades and is replaced by an attitude of acceptance, of willing acquiescence. In its more heightened forms, moral non-attachment merges into a loving acceptance of all that exists, the mystic's blissful embrace with the universe.

Yet despite the pejorative connotations of words like 'fear' and 'desire to control', and the positive associations with a trusting, open attitude, it is not my purpose here to advocate one form of moral involvement over another. Trust seems often misplaced, and inaction may be, if not uncaring, simply foolish or naive. Furthermore, what may be appropriate for a moral saint may be less appropriate for others. In the moral repertoires of most of us, moral non-attachment is one available response, to be adopted in some circumstances and not in others; and our decisions about whether to allow things to go forward or to interfere, to trust that things will work out or to act on our fear that they may not, are among the most difficult moral choices we make. Probably in no case is our moral judgment wholly attached or wholly unattached; between complete attachment and complete non-attachment is an infinite gradation of degrees, and where we place ourselves on that continuum in a given situation reflects our judgment on a variety of questions: How likely is it that things will work out on their own? How serious will be the consequences if they do not? How intrusive would interference be? How certain can we be of our own convictions about how things should go? How willing are we to risk? How willing to suffer? How willing to see others suffer? And so on.

On this continuum from moral attachment to moral non-attachment, where does the moral practice of Gandhi fall? I have defined moral non-attachment as a moral commitment which, because it rests on an attitude of trust or love, finds coercive sanctions unacceptable or unnecessary. Gandhi's doctrine of satyagraha exemplifies such an attitude. Gandhi accepted Patanjali's dictum that 'violence ceases in the presence of nonviolence'.[8] A genuinely pure nonviolence would, he believed, be invincible: its very presence would pacify the violent person, and would achieve moral ends without coercion of any kind. 'Nonviolence carries within it its own sanction ... A fully non-violent person is by nature incapable of using violence or rather has no use for it. His nonviolence is all-sufficing under all circumstances.'[9]

Such nonviolence is, however, not merely a way of acting, but more importantly a way of being: an attitude, a frame of mind that must be won through unremitting discipline: 'It is not a mechanical thing. You do not become non-violent merely by saying "I shall not use force." It must be felt in the heart.'[10] Gandhi repeatedly confessed that he himself had not wholly mastered nonviolence; even less were his followers uniformly nonviolent in their actions and attitudes. Further, Gandhi held that for those who have not achieved a nonviolent spirit, the effort to promote moral ends will in some instances require coercive means. For example, Gandhi declared that 'He who cannot protect himself or his nearest and dearest or their honor by non-violently facing death, may and ought to do so by violently dealing with the oppressor. He who can do neither of the two is a burden. He has no business to be the head of a family. He must either hide himself, or must rest content to live for ever in helplessness and be prepared to crawl like a worm at the bidding of a bully.'[11]

Gandhi thus recognized a need for coercive means to achieve moral ends – though he regarded this need as 'a fall from the pure doctrine'.[12] If we are literally unable to prevent evil by 'nonviolently facing death', we must employ coercive means, but we should at all times cultivate our own moral and spiritual discipline so as to render violence unnecessary. Gandhi's concession to an imperfect world does not provide a rationale for the conventional use of force, for in such cases, nonviolent means have not been employed to their limits.

Gandhi's doctrine of nonviolence thus exhibits a high degree of moral non-attachment. But his determined commitment to moral reform caused him to affirm a qualified need for coercive means to achieve moral ends. His life was, for example, utterly different from that of the Taoist sage as described by Chuang Tzu, 'wandering free and easy'[13] opposing nothing, 'chiming in'[14] with whatever social practices prevail. Gandhi's moral activism committed him to a degree of moral attachment, and to a program of distinct moral sanctions to bring about his intended goals. He was from the beginning and remained until his death a moral reformer rather than a pure witness to moral truth.

Perhaps Gandhi was right that a soul governed wholly by the principle of nonviolence would be morally invincible, perfectly uniting spiritual purity with moral power. Such is the description commonly given of Guatama Buddha and Jesus Christ. But for all those (including Gandhi himself) in whom these dual aspects are imperfectly joined, there exists a continuing tension between the goal of spiritual harmony and programs for transforming the world. Many seek to escape this tension by repudiating the spiritual path altogether, and establishing ethics on a purely secular basis. Others avert their eyes from the pressing moral tasks before them and, turning inward, seek a spiritual solace that is otherworldly. Committed as he was to the unity of politics and religion, Gandhi would take neither approach. By his own admission, however, pursuit of the spiritual path was Gandhi's predominate motivation; morality, politics, reform were his appropriate means to *moksha*. And this emphasis left him vulnerable to certain dangers. Whereas those who place reform first may pay mere lip service to religion or reject it altogether, those who devote themselves above all to spiritual liberation run another risk: that of using a spiritual language and rationale to disguise their own private projects for controlling their world. In his formative book, *Satyagraha in South Africa*, Gandhi wrote that 'Satyagraha may be offered to one's nearest and dearest...' and, a few lines later, 'Satyagraha postulates the conquest of the adversary by suffering in one's own person.'[15] The juxtaposition of these two statements is striking. Gandhi presumably did not consciously intend to describe his 'nearest and dearest' as 'adversaries' to be 'conquered'. Yet throughout his life he often relied upon the techniques of satyagraha to exact changes in the behavior of his wife, his children and other intimates, in a manner which at times resembled nothing so much as a moral wrestling match. One example may serve to illustrate the point here.

Gandhi recounts in his *Autobiography* an exchange between

himself and his wife. Kasturba had been ill, and Gandhi was convinced that she would recover if she eliminated salt and pulses from her diet. Kasturba was unwilling to comply, however, and in an ill-advised moment, blurted out that Gandhi himself would not be able to give up salt and pulses (which he loved) if he were advised to do so. Gandhi writes that in response to this retort, he 'was pained and equally delighted – delighted in that I got an opportunity to shower my love on her.'[16] Taking up Kasturba's unthinking challenge, Gandhi on the spot declared, 'But there! Without any medical advice, I give up salt and pulses for one year, whether you do so or not.' A shocked and sorrowing Kasturba immediately pledged to forgo salt and pulses, and begged Gandhi to relent of his own vow; but he was adamant, citing his religious duty and the need to support Kasturba in her pledge. Finally, Kasturba gave up. 'You are too obstinate. You will listen to none', she said, and dissolved into tears. Gandhi's next words are 'I would like to count this incident as an instance of Satyagraha and as one of the sweetest recollections of my life.' In his own moral defense, Gandhi adds that 'all self-denial is good for the soul'.[17]

The words 'conquest of the adversary' are not too strong here. A battle of wills is joined, and Gandhi wins the battle by means of his insistent self-righteousness. His evident delight in the moral triumph over his wife's resistance bespeaks a degree of moral attachment, the need to control others by the pressure of moral sanctions. Satyagraha is here a means for psychological manipulation; what purports to be an attitude of moral non-attachment is in fact attached, insistent upon compliance.

Numerous other such incidents may be found in Gandhi's life, some of them highlighted in Erikson's study.[18] Yet if they suggest a degree of inconsistency in Gandhi's moral practice, they pose no serious blemish to the larger picture of his life. Gandhi's personal secretary, Nirmal Kumar Bose, perhaps sets the right tone: Gandhi's writings 'do not exactly give a correct representation of what he actually *is*, but what he has always tried to be . . .'.[19] Gandhi's moral misdemeanors may be grist for the debate about whether he can be counted a saint or an avatar (descriptions that Gandhi himself repudiated), but when measured against a human standard, Gandhi's life serves rather to exalt our image of how good a person can become. Of his own achievements, he declared simply: 'I have not the shadow of a doubt that any man or woman can achieve what I have, if he or she would make the same effort and cultivate the same hope and faith.'[20]

Renewed interest in the life of Gandhi comes at a propitious time for the contemporary development of moral philosophy. After decades of arid discussion of highly technical issues in meta-ethics, Anglo-American moral philosophy is gradually returning to a serious investigation of major problems of conduct and policy. At first inclined to treat such large normative topics in a piecemeal fashion, moral philosophers show increasing willingness to address issues more broadly: some, instead of confining themselves to a series of specific and apparently unrelated questions, are enlarging the scope of moral investigation, seeing morality as a comprehensive characteristic of life well lived. The recent success of Alasdair MacIntyre's provocative book, *After Virtue*, is one indication of this trend.[21] Such a concern with the broad features of the moral life joins naturally with *moral biography*: attention to actual individuals whose lives may serve as exemplars or models of moral excellence. In the contemporary world, no individual provides a richer source for such study than Mahatma Gandhi, whose life, as John Hick observes, may be the most minutely scrutinized and recorded in human history.[22] Uniting theory and practice, religion and politics, the personal and the social into one extraordinary whole, Gandhi's life is a superb subject for the moral philosopher who cares about a morally engaged life.

Notes

1. See *A Theory of Justice* (Cambridge, Mass.: Harvard University Press, 1971) pp. 20f., 48–51.
2. *My Philosophy of Life*, ed. and published by Anand T. Hingorani (Bombay, India: Pearl Publications Private Limited, 1961) pp. 4f.
3. Ibid., p. 12.
4. Upon Gandhi's final departure from South Africa in 1914, General Smuts exclaimed, 'The saint has left our shores, I sincerely hope for ever.' Quoted in Robert A. Huttenback, *Gandhi in South Africa* (Ithaca and London: Cornell University Press, 1971) p. 330.
5. *Gandhi's Truth: On the Origins of Militant Nonviolence* (New York: W. W. Norton & Co., Inc., 1969) p. 231.
6. *Utilitarianism*, ed. by Oskar Piest (Indianapolis, Indiana: The Library of Liberal Arts, 1957) p. 60.
7. 'II. Moral Obligation', *American Philosophical Quarterly*, 3, 3 (July 1966) p. 224.
8. 'Discussion with Pacifists', February 1940, in *The Collected Works of*

Mahatma Gandhi, vol. LXXI (Ahmedabad, India: Navajivan Press, 1978) p. 225.
9. Ibid., p. 225.
10. Ibid., p. 225.
11. From *Young India*, 1928, reprinted in *For Pacifists*, ed. by Bharatan Kumarappa (Ahmedabad, India: Navajivan Publishing House, 1949) p. 13.
12. From *Young India*, 1925, reprinted in *For Pacifists*, p. 27.
13. *Chuang Tzu: Basic Writings*, transl. by Burton Watson (New York and London: Columbia University Press, 1964) p. 21.
14. Ibid., p. 68.
15. *Satyagraha in South Africa*, translated from the Gujarati by Valji Govinji Desai (Ahmedabad, India: Navajivan Publishing House, 1928) p. 114.
16. *An Autobiography: The Story of My Experiments With Truth* (Boston: Beacon Press, 1957) p. 326.
17. Ibid., p. 327.
18. *Gandhi's Truth*. See especially 'A Personal Word', pp. 229–54 *passim*.
19. *Selections from Gandhi* (Ahmedabad, India: Navajivan Publishing House, 1948) p. v.
20. *My Philosophy of Life*, p. 6.
21. *After Virtue: A Study in Moral Theory* (Notre Dame, Ind.: University of Notre Dame Press, 1981).
22. Foreword to *Gandhi's Religious Thought* by Margaret Chatterjee (Notre Dame, Ind.: University of Notre Dame Press, 1983) p. ix.

8
Gandhi on Civilization and Religion
Raghavan Iyer

Within the tangled worlds of both politics and religion Mahatma Gandhi moved freely; challenging sacrosanct dogmas about the limits of the possible, he explored daringly simple alternatives. Owing to his early experience of the meretricious glamor of modern civilization, he could at once declare that its influence was insidious, and deny that it was inescapable. Rather than retreat into stoical aloofness, he lived insistently in the world to show that even an imperfect individual could strive to purify politics and exemplify true religion – thereby restoring the lost meaning of humanity. By holding out at all times for the highest potential in every person, he raised the tone and refined the quality of human interaction.

As a thinker, Gandhi was more resilient than rigorous. Having laid down the foundations of his thought during the pioneering days of his campaigns in South Africa, he elaborated upon its diverse applications as problems arose in his eventful life. With his superb sense of occasion and his assured faith that God provides what is needed by the aspiring soul, he used the inquiries of correspondents, speaking engagements and the demands of day-to-day business to set the pace and scope of his pronouncements. Convinced that he should never take the next step until he was ready, Gandhi preferred to lead when persuaded, without claiming any messianic mantle. He would not be prompted or pushed; instead he waited for his inner voice to show the way, and often halted large-scale movements because that voice was silent. On one such occasion, when many were clamoring for his counsel, Gandhi simply explained his reticence by saying: 'I am trying to see light out of darkness.'[1] He was unerring in perceiving opportunities without becoming an opportunist, serving as an effective leader without recourse to expediency.

In the Preface to his autobiography, Gandhi declared that his devotion to Truth had drawn him into politics, that his power in the political field was derived from his spiritual experiments with himself, and that those who say religion has nothing to do with politics do not know what religion means. He was concerned with the purification of political life through the introduction of the *ashrama* or monastic ideal into politics. Politics was to him not a profession but a vocation, and he was a politician only in the sense that he was conscious of a mission to serve the masses in the political and social sphere and to inspire them with a love of the common ideal. In the last analysis, Gandhi's political ethic rests upon his metaphysical presuppositions, which introduce a strong subjectivist element into his basic concepts, as well as a sustaining conviction that the morally right must necessarily be the most effective course of conduct in the long run.

Gandhi's moral and political insights grew out of a coherent set of concepts, the nuances of which he explored over six decades. Even the claim that he was a man of action rather than introspection could be misleading. Gandhi worked from within outwardly. Through praying each day, repeatedly consulting his 'inner voice', probing his own motives, he would reach general conclusions. Then, after carefully considering the views of others, he would decide upon a course of action. This elusive and indefinable process, which he called 'heart churning', arose out of his unwavering conviction that constructive thought and timely action are inseparable. If skill in action can clarify and correct thought, soul-searching deliberation can purify action. Gandhi stressed fidelity to the greater good even when it remained hidden from view, together with the perseverance that springs from trust. Maintaining such faith was for Gandhi true *bhakti*. He also demonstrated that this practice need involve neither indecisiveness nor ineptitude in worldly matters. A keen alertness to detail can, he showed, be accompanied by a cultivated lack of interest in immediate results. Upon a basis of unalterable conviction, one can confidently refine thoughts and redirect action. For Gandhi, this bedrock was spiritual Truth gained through intense search and deep meditation; a developed art of fundamental commitment to *satya* and *ahimsa*, a moral dedication to self-chosen vows and sacrificial action.

Gandhi did not think that all human beings are alike, but he did fervently believe that all humanity originates in the same transcendental godhead. Recognizing that he could not define that sacred source, he found in satya or Truth its best expression. God is Truth, and Truth is God. Since every human being can know and exemplify some Truth – and indeed cannot live otherwise – every human being participates in the Divine. From this conviction, one is compelled to affirm universal brotherhood while attempting to enact it through authentic tolerance, mutual respect and ceaseless civility. If Truth is God, man, who cannot exist without some inward Truth, must at some level be sincere. Each individual enjoys both the ability and sacred obligation to grow in Truth whilst acknowledging disagreements.

Gandhi could say without exaggeration that his all-absorbing goal in life was to seek and to serve God as Truth. Longing to obtain *moksha*, spiritual freedom, he maintained that it could not be won through great learning or preaching, but only through renunciation and self-control (*tapascharya*). Moksha for Gandhi signified the vision of Absolute Truth, to be attained by means of *tapas* or 'self-suffering', and the relation between moksha and tapas was mirrored in the relation between satya and ahimsa. The test of love is *tapasya* and tapasya means self-suffering. Self-realization is impossible without service of, and identification with, the poorest. The quest for Truth involves tapas – self-suffering, sometimes even unto death. Satya then requires the tapas of ahimsa and this means self-suffering and self-sacrificing in the midst of society. Gandhi's interpretation of moksha as the full realization of Truth and his justification of ahimsa as an exercise in tapas, the self-suffering and service needed for the attainment of satya, gave traditional values a new meaning and a fresh relevance to politics and to society. In deriving satya and ahimsa from what were essentially religious notions he not only gave spiritual values a social significance but also infused into his political vocabulary an otherworldly flavor, whilst divesting religion of exclusive claims to moral authority.

Self-control was to be won through action, and the course of action to which Gandhi gave his life was the service of the downtrodden. Service of humanity alone could generate the disinterested self-control essential to spiritual emancipation. Through the selfless embodiment of satya and ahimsa, Gandhi believed theophilanthropists could ameliorate human misery whilst freeing themselves from worldly hopes and fears. Freedom, he felt, lies in *anasakti*, selfless service. He was certain that he could never be a votary of principles which depended for their existence upon mundane politics or external support. While even social work is impossible without politics, political work must ever be judged in terms of social and moral progress, which are in turn inseparable from spiritual regeneration.

Gandhi viewed civilization as that which assists moral excellence, moving individuals and society to Truth and nonviolence. True civilization aids self-realization and nurtures universal brotherhood. In his definition, civilization is that mode of conduct which points to the path of duty. The Gujarati equivalent for civilization means 'good conduct'. For Gandhi the *polis* is nothing more or less than the domain in which all men and women are free to gain skill in the art of action and learn how to exemplify satya and ahimsa; the arena in which both the individual quest can be furthered and social virtues displayed among the masses of citizens in a climate of tolerance and civility; a morally progressive society in which neither the State nor any social organization is allowed to flout with impunity the sacred principle that every man is entitled to his relative truth and no one can claim the right to coerce another, to treat him as a means to his own end.

Gandhi decried modern civilization because he felt that it was less an instrument for soul-growth than a supposed end in itself. Its vaunted intellectual and technological achievements deflect it from any authentic concern with moral welfare. Its 'isms' and social structures, sciences and machines, are not evil in themselves – though in a true civilization many of them would not exist – but they actively participate in the contagion of corruption that pervades it. Modern civilization is diseased in the Socratic sense because it blinds the soul and eclipses Truth. It is, as Tolstoy also thought, bondage masquerading as freedom. Gandhi derived his outlook from the traditional Indian doctrine of maya, or illusion, and he also stressed the notion of *moha*, delusion or glamor. The evident evil in this world and in modern civilization is enormous and deep-rooted, while what seems to be good is merely delusive and ephemeral. The apparent good is almost worse than the admitted evil because it has a hypnotic and narcotic effect on the moral perception and will of man. If this spell could be lifted for the individual, he could then proceed to purify human society of its dross, and restore the natural strength and activity of the spiritual and moral faculties. Modern civilization was for Gandhi a positive menace to the moral growth of man rather than simply a magnifying mirror of his moral deficiency. Even *Hind Swaraj* conceded that 'civilization is not an incurable disease, that people are not bad at heart and their mode of thought is not inherently immoral'. Civilization stands self-condemned, but it is possible for courageous and compassionate individuals to adopt a massive program of action rather than resign themselves, like Spinoza's wisely silent philosophers, to a stoical philosophy of apparent submission. Nor is it necessary to turn society violently upside down or vainly attempt to reduce it to a primordial *tabula rasa*.

Gandhi contended that the earth has enough resources to provide for human need, but not human greed. He held, therefore, that every man, woman and child would eat adequately, clothe and shelter themselves comfortably, if there were a greater sharing of wealth in all parts of the world. Spurning equally the insatiable acquisitiveness of capitalism and the mechanistic materialism of communism, Gandhi condemned the very basis of modern civilization. In his conception of authentic civility, a sense of spiritual and social obligation is fused with a spontaneous sense of natural reciprocity. He further upheld the belief, steadily undermined since the eighteenth century, that social institutions and political actions are by no means exempt from ethics. For social institutions are, he felt, the visible expression of moral values that mold the minds of individuals. It is, therefore, impossible to alter institutions without first affecting those values. Like Dr Stockmann in Ibsen's play, he felt that all our spiritual sources of life are poisoned, our whole bourgeois society rests on a soil teeming with a pestilence of lies. The function of cant in society is to allow an individual or a people to do anything whatsoever, provided they preserve appearances and obstinately maintain that everything is going on for the best of everybody. Since modern civilization is one complete tissue of intertwined evils, no plan of partial and gradual reform from within the system can produce a lasting remedy. Gandhi sought to destroy systems, not persons; but he argued that the 'soulless system' had to be destroyed without its reformers themselves becoming soulless.

Holding that one should repudiate wrongs without reviling wrong-doers, Gandhi could not bring himself to condemn the British for their mistakes and even misdeeds in India. They too, he felt, were the hapless victims of a commercial civilization. The theme of *Hind Swaraj* was not just the moral inadequacy and extravagant pretensions of modern civilization, but its treacherously deceptive self-destructiveness. 'This civilization is irreligion', he concluded, 'and it has taken such a hold on the people of Europe that those who are in it appear to be half mad.'[2] Yet, he added, 'it is not the British who are responsible for the misfortunes of India but we who have succumbed to modern civilization'.[3] For Gandhi, the villain is hypocritical materialism, the judge is he who frees himself from the collective hallucination, and the executioner is the Moral Law (*karma*) that inexorably re-adjusts equilibrium throughout the cosmos.[4]

Gandhi did not preserve his feeling for common humanity by remaining conveniently apart from it. He knew poverty and squalor at first hand; he knew, too, the desperate violence found in those who have lived on the edge of starvation. Yet he could still extol the Indian peasant with ringing authority:

> The moment you talk to them and they begin to speak, you will find wisdom drops from their lips. Behind the crude exterior you will find a deep reservoir of spirituality ... In the case of the Indian villager, an age-old culture is hidden under an encrustment of crudeness. Take away the encrustation, remove his chronic poverty and his illiteracy and you have the finest specimen of what a cultured, cultivated, and free citizen should be.[5]

Gandhi's longing to transform contemporary civilization was mirrored in his political thought and action. No more than civilization is politics an end in itself. Gandhi invoked Indian tradition in rejecting the modern dichotomy between religion and politics, but he went much further than most classical Indian thinkers in dispensing entirely with notions of *raison d'état* and in hoping to counter the propensity of politics to become corrupt. Even if all wished to shed their pretensions and nurture the 'enlightened anarchy' of an ideal world community, politics would be necessary since human beings differ in their perspectives, needs, and desires. Accepting, then, that politics cannot simply be abolished, Gandhi sought to purify politics by showing that its sovereign principle is neither coercive nor manipulative power, but moral and social progress.

As with Gandhi's view of civilization, so with his views of politics. He rejected the view that politics is inherently sinful and irremediably so, whether for reasons of theological or secular pessimism. He also rejected the view that politics is intrinsically moral *in its own way* and that this political morality could be perfected, whether through religious or worldly institutions or leaders. He further rejected the view that politics is characteristically pragmatic and that some form of prudential or utilitarian justification, whether put in religious or sociological terms, is adequate in the long run. Gandhi's own view is that politics is inherently impure and involves pollution and can never be ideal in any sense, but that it can and must be purified, and this requires, as a first step, the repudiation of any distinction between public and private, political and personal, morality. Politics is dangerous but it is not sinful or beyond redemption. It could become a means to spiritual perfection as legitimate and sacred as any other spiritual path because it should, in principle and in practice, be possible to enter it without losing one's soul. Politics, as usually understood, cannot be morally justified or spiritually utilized, but it has a potential legitimacy of the highest order if its corrupting nature is understood and continually countered through a process of spiritual self-purification.

Gandhi rejected collectivist theories of both state and society. He argued that only the individual could exercise conscience, and, therefore, morally legitimate power. Refusing to hold political office himself or to endorse those compatriots who did, he saw power as a by-product of social activity at the family and community level. Through *satyagraha* he sought to introduce religious values into politics by extending the rule of domestic life into the political arena. Ascribing the underlying continuity of mankind to the sacrificial exercise of soul-force within families, he was convinced that the same energies could be brought to bear self-consciously in the larger sphere of life. For the *satyagrahi*, the individual committed to Truth, the only power that can be legitimately exercised is the capacity to suffer for the errors of others and on behalf of the welfare of all – whether it be the family, the nation, or the world.

Self-direction, for Gandhi, involves passing moral judgment on one's own behavior, justifying or condemning it. But man mistakenly believes he has set right what was wrong; he tries, fails and does not always recognize that he has failed. Yet, he progresses at least insofar as he recognizes as wrong what he once regarded as right, and he tries to avoid it, even if he cannot always assess correctly his level of effort and the extent of his failure. Gandhi explicitly declared that the right to err and the freedom to experiment constitute the universal and indispensable condition to all progress. Evolution is always experimental, and all progress is possible only through mistakes. This, he felt, is the law of individual moral growth as well as of social and political evolution.

Gandhi did more than base his view of ends and means on a metaphysical faith in the Moral Law or his account of the necessary as well as contingent connection between satya and ahimsa, Truth and nonviolence, tolerance and civility. He also rejected the moral model underlying the sharp dichotomy between ends and means. Moral life was not for Gandhi mainly a matter of achieving specific objectives, nor was politics like a field game in which a concrete objective is given in advance and known to all. No doubt, he regarded satya as the supreme common end for all men and women, but its content cannot be known in advance. For Gandhi, as for the ancient Greeks, satya refers to the highest human activity rather than an imposed and predetermined target. He evolved his political and social ethic in terms of a theory of action under which all our thinking and activity can be corrected and justified only by reference to satya or ahimsa, which are good in themselves and not merely the means to a higher good. It is only for the sake of these goods – in order that as much of them as possible may at some time exist – that anyone can be justified in undertaking any social or political activity. They are the *raison d'être* of virtue and excellence, the ultimate test of human endeavor, the sole criterion of social progress.

The individual is, therefore, always to be treated as an end in himself, while social institutions are always to be treated as corrigible means to some greater end. The satyagrahi should be active in politics if he can stand firmly for social justice and initiate constructive change. Where he cannot, he must practice non-cooperation. One can at least refuse to participate in evils that one cannot directly alter, even if the satyagrahi soon finds that he can alter more than he previously supposed. Far from denying the existence of conflicts of interest, Gandhi evolved ahimsa so as to resolve such conflicts by limiting, if not wholly removing, their *himsa* (violence). Gandhi further advocated voluntary poverty as an essential prerequisite for any social or political worker who wished to remain untainted by the wasteful greed of power politics. He even maintained that possessions are anti-social: it is not enough to continue possessing goods in practice under the sincere illusion that one has given them up in spirit. Possessions, he believed, should be held in trust at the disposal of those who need them. Furthermore, those who trusted the community to provide for essential needs could come to experience true freedom.

The religious component in satyagraha may be seen not merely in the ideal constructions that Gandhi offered but also in his attempt, following the *Gita*, to regard the earthly battlefield (*Kurukshetra*) as a righteous struggle (*Dharmakshetra*) between truth and falsehood, love and hate, justice and injustice, greed and altruism. The concept of tapas, upon which the doctrine of satyagraha is based, is religious rather than political, and those who object to satyagraha as unworthy of consideration are often merely expressing their distaste for introducing religious notions into politics. For Gandhi this was a religious as well as a political necessity. He believed that the best and most lasting self-defense is self-purification. In its appeal to public opinion, to the prevailing or potential respect in society for satya and ahimsa, and to the moral sensitivity of those whose acts are being challenged, satyagraha differs from the methods of rational persuasion and violent action chiefly in its unique reliance upon tapas or self-suffering.

Firmly believing in the fundamental unity of life, he rejected any distinction between public and private, between secular and sacred, and ultimately, between politics and religion. In order to understand Gandhi's position, we must, first of all, see that he both narrowed and broadened the connotation of 'politics', and secondly, that he used the word 'religion' in a special sense quite different from its common sectarian implications. When he spoke disparagingly of politics, he referred to the politics of power and regarded it as an overestimated segment of politics as a whole. In his attempt to make politics religious and religion practical, he based his beliefs upon a neglected strand of Indian tradition – the path of karma yoga, or spiritual realization through social action, that is associated with classical heroes like Rama and Janaka. Neither *artha* (politics) nor *moksha* (salvation) could be separated from *dharma* (social and personal morality). Gandhi was, in fact, following in the footsteps of the Buddha in showing the connection between the service of suffering humanity and the process of self-purification. He rejected the distinction between the mundane and the ultramundane, the natural and supernatural.

Religion, for Gandhi, signifies a spiritual commitment which is total but intensely personal, and which pervades every aspect of life. Gandhi was always concerned more with religious values than with beliefs; more with the fundamental ethics that he saw as common to all religions than formal allegiance to received dogmas which hinder rather than aid religious experience. He staunchly refused to associate religion with sectarianism of any kind. Truth for Gandhi was a matter of experienced knowledge, not of borrowed belief, and hence his distrust of ideologies and isms. We are dogmatic to the extent of the inadequacy of our experience, and we become more truly tolerant as we have made more experiments and acquired greater experience of 'truth in action'. A political judgment is made true only when it works satisfactorily in experience. Values without action are barren and action without values is blind. 'Isms', he thought, appeal only to the immature; through religion he sought nothing less than Truth itself. In his vision, each soul resembles a drop of water from the ocean of divinity, fallen into a muddy pool. To experience consanguinity with God it must cleanse itself of the mud. Whatever its tenets, assumptions or practices, every true religion holds out this hope of self-regeneration. All true religions are, therefore, equal in Gandhi's estimation. He regularly advised inquirers to discover the true meanings of the faiths they were born into under karma. The seeker pledged to Truth must, however, abstain from proselytizing others. He should rather encourage, or inspire, others to elevate the inner and outer practice of their own faiths. Different religions and sects emerge only because no tradition and no individual can be the exclusive receptacle for boundless Truth.

Gandhi found no difficulty in accepting his own religion, while also acknowledging that he was at heart a Christian, a Jain, a Muslim and a Buddhist. He thought that accepting the *Bible* did not require rejecting the *Qur'an*, just because one scripture speaks more directly to an individual than another. The *Bhagavad Gita* was the most accessible text in the Indian tradition. As it affirmed that God represents perfect Truth, and that imperfect man, whatever his path, can follow its precepts and come closer to God, the *Gita* has universal application. Gandhi felt that enduring help could come only from within, from what one learns through tapascharya.

For Gandhi, religions and religious concepts grow through human experience just as individuals mature morally, socially and spiritually. No religion can claim to be complete in time. No formulation is final. He could thus say, without condescension, that Hinduism included Jainism and Buddhism, while freely criticizing Hindu sectarian disagreements and dogmatism; he praised Islamic brotherhood, while decrying the intransigence of some Muslim zealots; he upheld Christianity as a 'blazing path of *bhakti yoga*' and the Sermon on the Mount as a model, while dismissing most theology because it invidiously tends to explain away what should be taken to heart and applied. Gandhi's radical reinterpretation of Hindu values in the light of the message of the Buddha was a constructive, though belated, response to the ethical impact of the early Buddhist Reformation on decadent India.

The pursuit of Truth was clearly a social activity for Gandhi; it could only emerge out of our daily struggle with the concrete problems of living. A man's devotion to Truth, his veracity and integrity, are most sharply tested in his relations with opponents and opposing views. The problem for the seeker is to put himself in advance in the very position in which alone he can properly receive the fruit of his search, and which is the position he aspires to attain. The practical implication of the paradox is that our concern must continually be with the next step rather than the summit, and the exhilaration of climbing becomes an end in itself, rendering irrelevant the attainment of the peak. Gandhi's favorite Christian hymn was that of Newman and he often repeated the phrase 'one step enough for me'. The searcher for Truth advances step by step; he aims at increasing his understanding and cannot, of course, forsee what he will know when he has increased it. In practice, Gandhi urged the importance of 'infinite patience and inward longing'. If we would serve God or become one with the universal life-principle, our activity must be as unwearied as that of Krishna.

Given such beliefs, religion is ultimately priestless, because the capacity for prayer lies latent within human nature. Prayer and all devotion (*bhakti*) are, for Gandhi, a kind of petition. The noblest and purest petition is that one should become outwardly what one is inwardly – that one's thoughts, words and deeds should ever more fully express the soul's core of Truth and nonviolence. Prayer is to God as thought is to Truth, but since God and Truth are beyond all limiting conceptions, they cannot accommodate egotistic petitions. Prayer is truly an intense supplication towards one's inmost ineffable nature, the source of one's being and strength, the touchstone of one's active life. Just as politics and religion should endeavor to reduce the gap between theory and practice, so too prayer must narrow the gulf between one's real being and one's manifest appearance.

Gandhi's heartfelt reverence for all religions and for their spiritual founders and exemplars, together with his restraint in attributing to any of them uttermost divine perfection, arose from his concept of Deity. Although at times Gandhi spoke of God as a person and the ideal man as a servant (*dasa*) of God, he really regarded God, as the Stoics did, as an indefinable and universal Power that cannot be conceived apart from humanity or from the whole of Nature. Each man is a ray or a part (*amsha*) of that divine Power that underlies all change, that is changeless, that holds all together, that creates, dissolves, and re-creates all forms of life. Gandhi declared explicitly that he was a believer in *Advaita*, the Indian doctrine of monism, the essential unity of God and man and of all that lives. This is similar to the Stoic idea of the universe as a divine whole and of mankind as an essential unity in which the individual can realize himself. Man alone is made in the image of God.

The doctrine of man's oneness with God and humanity has several implications. First of all, this doctrine is incompatible with the belief that an individual may gain spiritually and those that surround him suffer. Gandhi believed that if one man gains spiritually, the whole world gains with him and if one man falls, the whole world falls to that extent. Secondly, the monistic doctrine implies that all human beings are working consciously or unconsciously toward the realization of that identity. Thirdly, what one man is capable of achieving is possible for all to attain. Fourthly, it is quite proper to resist and attack a system, but to attack and resist the author is tantamount to resisting and attacking oneself. Fifthly, man's ultimate aim is the realization of God, and all his activities, social, political, religious, have to be guided by the ultimate aim of the vision of God. The immediate service of all human beings becomes a necessary part of the endeavor, simply because the only way to find God is to see God in creation and be one with it. This can be done only by service of all.

To Gandhi the moral solidarity of mankind was an ever-present fact rather than merely a contrived political ideal that remains to be realized. God is alien to no human being, not even the atheist who risks sundering himself from his source. 'To deny God', Gandhi believed, 'is like committing suicide.'[7] Since the divine is reflected within every individual as his or her inalienable core of Truth, God will appear in as many forms and formulations as there are possibilities of human thought. There are, at least, as many definitions of God as there are individuals, and God transcends them all. Beyond the boundaries of reason and imagination, God is ineffable, indescribable, without form or characteristic. Fundamentally, Gandhi believed in what he called the absolute oneness of God and, therefore, also of humanity. To believe in Absolute Truth, which is God, implies that every man embodies a portion of that Truth, i.e. is a soul possessing 'soul-force'. As Truth is the substance of morality, man is a moral agent only to the extent that he embodies and seeks Truth.

Gandhi thought that the concepts and images used to express the Divine, including his own formulations, were at best derived from glimpses of immense but partial truths. As aids, these images may assist human growth; but as dogmas, they tend to breed sectarianism and violence. As aids, they may foster the universal religion of duty and detachment (*dharma* and *vairagya*); but as dogmas, they tend to reinforce a harsh insistence upon rights and privileges. For Gandhi, all conceptions of God are merely means to be used in the service of Truth. The religion of our conception, unlike ideal religion, and similarly the political truth of our conception, unlike ideal Truth, are always subject to a process of evolution and reinterpretation. There must be no barbarity, no impatience, no insolence, no undue pressure in politics or in religion. Intolerance betrays want of faith in one's cause. We shall retard our cause if we suppress opinion by intolerance. The indispensable condition of success in the common pursuit of Truth is that we encourage the greatest freedom of opinion. Tolerance is not indifference and it is real only if it brings true understanding and purer love. Bitterness means bias, and intolerance based in insecurity breeds violence.

Gandhi knew that his ideas and ideals were difficult to instantiate precisely because of their inherent simplicity. He recognized, therefore, that he could only clarify and illustrate them to all who sought his counsel. Those others would, through tapas, have to assimilate and apply them for themselves. But the hero and villain jostle in every soul. The morally sensitive individual must learn to detect self-deception with firmness and forbearance, mellowness and maturity. He must come to know the obscuration of light within before he can ferret out evil at its roots. Eventually, 'a man with intense spirituality may without speech or a gesture touch the hearts of millions who have never seen him and whom he has never seen'.[8] Through meditation, the individual can attain that elevated plane on which thought becomes the primary and most potent mode of action. Gandhi unwaveringly affirmed that living this conviction would bring sacrifical suffering, as well as an inner joy that cannot be conveyed in words.

On his 78th birthday in 1947, when well-wishers showered him with lavish and affectionate greetings, Gandhi thought only of the violence and suffering of his recently independent and hastily partitioned homeland:

I am not vain enough to think that the divine purpose can only be fulfilled through me. It is as likely as not that a fitter instrument will be used to carry it out and that I was good enough to represent a weak nation, not a strong one. May it not be that a man purer, more courageous, more far-seeing, is wanted for the final purpose? Mine must be a state of complete resignation to the Divine Will ... If I had the impertinence openly to declare my wish to live 125 years, I must have the humility, under changed circumstances, openly to shed that wish ... In that state, I invoke the aid of the all-embracing Power to take me away from this 'vale of tears' rather than make me a helpless witness of the butchery by man become savage, whether he dares to call himself a Mussalman or Hindu or what not. Yet I cry, 'Not my will but Thine alone shall prevail.'[9]

By upholding vows, any person, Gandhi held, can align his conduct to the motionless center of the wheel of life. But the individual must first adopt stern measures to control the mind in its everyday vagaries, monitoring or even selecting his every thought. Only in this way can one become single-minded and so incarnate one's beliefs in one's sphere of dharma. Gandhi felt that conscience is kept alive not by a preoccupation with intention, but by concern for rectitude of action. He deliberately shifted emphasis from the spiritual emancipation of the individual to the collective benefit of all.

Gandhi's fundamental convictions constitute a world-view of far-reaching dimensions. They cannot be proved for 'Truth is its own proof, and non-violence is its supreme fruit'.[10] But Gandhi never doubted that if these ideals were practiced with sincerity and humility, aimed not at applause of the world but the support of the soul, they would gradually prove to be self-validating, helping the individual, painfully but assuredly, to mature into a joyous state of spiritual freedom and self-mastery. Gandhi did not wish to be considered an inspired prophet. His metaphysical presuppositions only deepened his disarming faith in a human solidarity that admits of no degree. He persisted in seeing himself as a somewhat unworthy exemplar of his exacting ideals. And yet, by his lifelong fidelity to his vows, Mahatma Gandhi demonstrated the liberating and transforming power of any attempt to fuse metaphysics and conduct, theory and practice, through an enormous effort of the will.

Notes

1. *Amrita Bazar Patrika*, November 7 1924.
2. *Hind Swaraj*, Ch. IV (Navajivan, 1938).
3. Preface to second Gujarati edition of *Hind Swaraj*, (May 1914).
4. For a fuller treatment, see the author's *The Moral and Political Thought of Mahatma Gandhi*, Chs. 2 and 3 (Oxford University Press, 1973; 2nd edn, Concord Grove Press, 1983).
5. *Harijan*, January 28 1939.
6. Preface to *Gitapadarthakosha, Harijanbandhu*, October 25 1936.
7. *Mahadevbhaini Diary*, vol. 1, p. 82 (Navajivan, 1953).
8. *Young India*, March 22 1928.
9. D. G. Tendhulkar, *Mahatma*, vol. 8, pp. 144–5 (V. K. Jhaveri & D. G. Tendulkar, 1951–54).
10. *Navajivan*, October 11 1925.

9
Gandhi's Interpretation of the *Bhagavad Gita*

Kees W. Bolle

Gandhi's life-long concern for the Harijans is well-known. The name 'Harijan' that he favored is the most eloquent expression of his concern. The Untouchables, the lowest people of the social scale, for him were to be called children of God, Hari, Vishnu.

It has been said that the only book in Gandhi's possession at his death was the *Bhagavad Gita*. The question that cannot fail to come up is: how does Gandhi's political activity, his social action, indeed, how does action in general find its impetus for Gandhi in the text? The answer we must give, I believe, is: 'not very well'. I am painfully aware that asking such a question in the case of a man known for his sainthood can become an exercise in pedantry. And how could the answer by a mere scholar rise above that level of academic futility?

The question of how Gandhi felt stimulated in his activities by the text of the *Gita* does not go away even if it is not expressed at all, or relegated to a late, hesitant footnote. My footnote intends to show that if the exercise does not take us closer to sainthood, it may help us discover one perspective improving our admittedly merely academic, historical understanding. There are clear vantage points for such understanding of one unclear facet of Gandhi's life and work and its significance for twentieth-century India. My thesis is that Gandhi becomes more understandable through his interpretation of the *Gita*, if we see him in that act of interpreting as one (very great) exponent of a nineteenth- and twentieth-century international cultural community of a special type: he is a towering figure within a 'neo-romanticism' that had passed beyond the borders of the Western nations that saw its beginnings in the 'real' Romantic movement.

★ ★ ★

Gandhi was not a scholar, certainly not a Sanskrit scholar, and did not pretend to be one, but his views on the *Gita* greatly influenced others. One of those others was a scholar, Mahadev Desai, friend of Gandhi, devoted to him, and occasionally used almost as an errand boy – or so it seems from Gandhi's autobiography.[1]

Mahadev Desai wrote his translation with commentary and entitled his work *The Gospel of Selfless Action, or the Gita According to Gandhi*.[2] Gandhi himself wrote the Preface. The year of publication was 1946.

It so happens that in that same year another translation came out, also aiming to present a very particular leader's view. It is the translation by Anilbaran Roy: *The Gita, with Text, Translation and Notes, Compiled from Sri Aurobindo's Essays on the Gita*.[3]

Any comparison of people has weaknesses, and we may well ask whether it is fair to compare Gandhi and Aurobindo, or their personal influences. If it is unfair, the consolation is that it is equally unfair in both directions. Aurobindo will not be remembered as father of the country, while Gandhi's name will be forever glorified in that manner, even by detractors. On the large canvas of history, he is the paramount figure. But on the other hand, Gandhi's influence on the interpretation of the *Gita* cannot be assessed without realizing that Gandhi did not spend a great deal of time philosophizing, no matter how much he meditated. Sri Aurobindo, by contrast, did nothing but philosophize, perhaps even while meditating. No wonder that his influence on minds and souls of text interpreters is clearer to us, intellectually traceable in detail. The conclusion that in this area he outshines Gandhi is predictable. The endeavor to set the two men and their influences on others side by side may be of value just the same. This value, I admit it once more, is limited, but it is heuristic, as scholars in their limited area have to call it. It is not meant to belittle or idolize, but to understand.

When we think of Gandhi's limitations in interpreting the *Gita*, one issue comes up at once: he preached nonviolent resistance, while in the text of the *Gita* Krishna repeatedly calls Arjuna to action – and that action is war. But this peculiar fact by itself, no matter how important, may not be crucial in distinguishing Gandhi's and Aurobindo's impact on their followers; it certainly does not make Gandhi unique. Aurobindo was also an advocate of nonviolent resistance, and was the first to formulate the doctrine.[4]

The harshest statement to be made about Gandhi himself in

discovering the *Gita* is that his account betrays a certain shallowness, something uncritical, on the verge of the sophomoric.

Gandhi's autobiography first describes his study of law in England as a rather uninspiring affair. The young Gandhi studied some books, thereby doing more, as he does not fail to tell us, than most of his fellow students; he learned things by heart and passed his bar exams. At a certain moment, he began to read some things that older and presumably wiser counselors told him to read. Thus also the *Gita* in English translation, to begin with, the beautiful rendering by Edwin Arnold, *The Song Celestial* (New York: Heritage Press, 1965), comes in. In the entire account he displays a naiveté that is quite disarming, charming even. (If the movie on Gandhi is completely true in one respect, it is in the display of his naiveté, from the moment he arrives in South Africa, being completely surprised by racial antagonism – a subject he apparently never observed in England in any manner, and something he had never guessed from his limited readings.) He began reading the *Gita* text for the first time in his life on the advice of two Theosophist friends, and tells us he was ashamed to have to admit to them that he had never become acquainted with it in Sanskrit or his native Gujarati.[5]

Shallowness more than charm shows when he begins to speak about his *serious* struggles with the text. This occurs much later in his life. By then (around 1903), he is in South Africa. The *Gita*, he writes, became 'an infallible guide of conduct' to him.[6] He leaves no doubt concerning the seriousness of his intent:

> Just as I turned to the English dictionary for the meanings of English words that I did not understand, I turned to this dictionary of conduct for a ready solution of all my troubles and trials. Words like *aparigraha* (non-possession) and *samabhava* (equability) gripped me. How to cultivate and preserve that equability was the question. How was one to treat alike insulting, insolent and corrupt officials, co-workers of yesterday raising meaningless opposition, and men who had always been good to one? How was one to divest oneself of all possessions? Was not the body itself possession enough? Were not wife and children possessions? Was I to destroy all the cupboards of books I had? Was I to give up all I had and follow Him? Straight came the answer: I could not follow Him unless I gave up all I had. My study of English Law came to my help. Snell's discus-

sion of the *Maxims of Equity* came to my memory. I understood more clearly in the light of the Gita teaching the implication of the word 'trustee'. My regard for jurisprudence increased, I discovered it in religion. I understood the Gita teaching of non-possession to mean that those who desired salvation should act like the trustee who, though having control over great possessions, regards not an iota of them as his own.[7]

Of course, I do not want to raise any doubt about Gandhi's serious intentions and his interest in religious matters. Many of his pages speak of them explicitly. The fact that neither of the two terms he mentions (*aparigraha* and *samabhava*) occur in the text of the *Gita* is a trivial irrelevancy. Gandhi was not a philologist and should not be judged as if he were one. He uses the word 'dictionary' almost poetically. He picked up religious terms from various sources. In this stage of his life he turned to several Indian texts. For instance, he had turned also to Patanjali's *Yoga Sutras*. He tells his readers that he was stimulated by Western friends who trusted his instinctive association with Indian spirituality, his insights that had to derive from many cycles of rebirth. His growing acquaintance with the *Gita* provided a special focus for him. It helped him turn his mind to ideas that were new to him; a new habit of perceiving changed his world.

But before we are ready to see a profound experience of conversion behind the trivial inaccuracies, it is necessary to look also at the concluding lines, because they may mean trouble for our desire to detect evidence of profundity. The *Gita*'s teaching of non-attachment to the fruits of our work is well-known. The idea of non-possessiveness, of non-egocenteredness permeates the text. What is the precise imagery that opens Gandhi's eyes? It is the concept of trusteeship as defined in one of his law textbooks. A trustee *has control* over possessions, but does not regard them as his own. What is one to make of this entry into the *Gita*'s meaning? The growth of international corporations had not reached its climax during Gandhi's life, but it was certainly not an unknown fact of economics. The stock-market had increased enormously in size and importance. The power in the hands of managers ('trustees' if you prefer) not owning the managed capital, one would imagine, could not be an unknown fact to a lawyer. Then, can 'control' be so easily separated from ownership? The legal separation is clear, but the illumination it provides for aparigraha (or for the thoughts and ideas of the *Gita*) casts a strange shadow.

Immediately upon his discovery of the *Gita*'s lesson, Gandhi discontinues his life insurance, or more precisely, he issues the order to a peon to allow 'the insurance to lapse'.[8] From now on, Gandhi is merely a trustee of sorts, but he does seem to manage all right. He concisely states the reason for his decision: '... I had become convinced that God, who created my wife and children as well as myself, would take care of them'.[9]

Countless readers must have concluded that Gandhi was strangely out of touch with the world he was in, and many have observed his inability to govern once a conflict was resolved and the time for managing began in earnest.

We have to return to the question: how did he inspire others to read the *Gita* in his way? But even from the few lines drawn we can see details that I would not like to ignore.

Gandhi's style of writing is charming, but has become also charmingly old-fashioned. One does not have to be a militant feminist to realize that we could not write anymore like that about our wives and children as possessions. There is above all a touch of late romanticism that probably only the middle-aged and older people among us can remember as part of the world of our parents. It is a touch of the same feeling that made some Westerners ascribe to the young Gandhi profound insights not because they knew he was going to be a saint, but because he was an Indian. It takes us back to a world that adored Albert Schweitzer, the genius giving up his own fame to live as a medical recluse doing good to the natives of darkest Africa. It takes us back to a world that give the Nobel prize for literature to Rabindranath Tagore (1913), Knut Hamsun (1920), and Hermann Hesse (1946). That world produced a Gandhi consciously giving up the craving for life and security, a self-made ascetic severing his ties with insurance companies, those live symbols of this-worldliness. This is also the world of Sri Aurobindo. The similarities between him and Gandhi are striking because of the sameness of their world, yet also dissimilarities may seem clearer to us now that our own distance from that world has become measurable in light-years.

Like Gandhi, Aurobindo enjoyed and suffered from an education in England. Like Gandhi, he became acquainted with the *Gita* in English. As in the case of Gandhi, English remained the major vehicle of communication for him all his life. Both had their share in friendships with Westerners, both more than an average share in contacts with Theosophists and sundry romantically inclined and optimistic world-improvers, and both had their many discussions about religion in those circles. Both shared in the very serious world of Western philosophy struggling for sense in a chaos of investigations, scholarly methods, new academic disciplines, mutually contradictory scientific hypotheses. It is the age marked by such men as Henri Bergson, Edmund Husserl, and A. N. Whitehead. Did those truly serious thinkers 'influence' Gandhi and Aurobindo? The question cannot be fully answered. Gandhi does mention his Western heroes occasionally (Tolstoy being the most prominent), but Aurobindo in his voluminous writings does not make it a habit to quote his inspirations. However, Gandhi and Aurobindo both quite obviously were involved in a period in which the greatest minds were searching for a rupture, a breaking away from outdated, fossilized certitudes.

Aurobindo's thought developed a 'process philosophy' on a large scale, and without having to name any direct influences, it is natural for us to think of Bergson and Whitehead when we think of that recent period in the past. A vision of the future is a most arresting concern in Aurobindo's writing, just as the idea of a unity of thought in spite of all apparent conflicts fascinates readers of Husserl.

Even if we did not want to see differences, here they begin to appear. Gandhi's early training in law and his life-long concern with politics seem to hamper his understanding of an authoritative Hindu text. In his endeavors at interpretation he remained caught in intellectual fashions that he was not prepared to resist. Aurobindo, on the other hand, did develop the patience to scrutinize the consequences of ideas governing the task of interpretation. Examples are not hard to find; I choose some passages that have a bearing on the issue of involvement in action and the structure of society.

The starkest example of a difference in interpretation concerns the four *varnas*. The lines on that subject in the text send Mahadev Desai into ecstasy in his eulogy of a supposed Vedic past:

> Quite an amount of ignorant criticism is levelled against the doctrine of the performance of *svadharma* (one's duty or funtion) taught in the Gita and the reason for it is the much-abused varna-system. This is no place for making out a case for or against the so-called 'caste-system' ... Much of the criticism is

directed against a thing which is just a shadow of *what existed ages ago. There was a system which existed in ages gone by,* which served the *then existing* social organism magnificently, which was elastic and hence made it possible for a number of different groups of the same race and several races to live together in amity and peace. *What we see today is its travesty,* a fossil formed out of the incrustations of customs and practices of several centuries ... The system of *varnas* we find described (in the Gita) is certainly no rigid one. The division is no division into water-tight compartments. Let us note then the main features of that elastic system: (i) The division was entirely vocational, in order that each might serve the best interests of the organism. *If men devoted themselves to tasks for which their character and aptitude best fitted them, they would be able to give their best to the community.* The criterion was not what one needed but what one could give to the community; (ii) The division had regard to the requirements of the *then* existing society and these were broadly divided into (a) intellectual and spiritual, (b) defense, (c) production of wealth by (1) intelligent economy and by (2) labor.[10]

This sort of presentation sounded eminently reasonable to many people for decades, provided they shared a similar inspiration for romanticizing the past. Let us note the peculiarities and shortcomings which today are not difficult to detect. The past (the Vedic times, conveniently including the time of the *Bhagavad Gita*) is indeed beautified and set up in opposition to the present. What was perfect then has become a travesty. Further, the author is careful to point out that the documents of that perfect past still have relevance today, and thus he translates the meaning of the varnas into the vocabulary of modern social science: the division was entirely *vocational*, and before our mind's eye arises a neat structure of professional organizations, trade unions of sorts. No, it was even better, for *then* every person could follow his own aptitude and character, thereby serving the whole society most eminently. In giving us this picture, the author does not have another way than that of a bit of historical pretentiousness and distortion: he has to suggest a society in which only three (or four) vocations needed to exist: it is a picture of arcadian simplicity and nobility. That was all *then* (as he keeps repeating) – but how relevant for today! He hammers the point home. The ability of every member makes the whole perfect; it is in fact the great ideal of utopian socialism. At the same time, it becomes the great ideal of the modern India of Gandhi and Nehru by just a slight extension; at that time everything could function so well because of two additional achievements: an intelligent economy, and labor.

We are not quite at the climax of this neo-romanticism that 'went international', with its permutation of fiction and history. In his eagerness to document the reality of the perfect past, after having telescoped Vedic and Epic times into each other (a forgivable act of enthusiasm), the author proceeds to bring the Medieval Bhakti movement into the same line of vision. This really becomes too much:

> ... salvation was more difficult for those who had greater tasks to perform and easier for those entrusted with humbler functions. For these were not cumbered with much knowledge. Whilst it was easy, for instance, for a butcher or for a scavenger to carry on his forefather's profession with equanimity and detachment and as a sacrifice offered to God, it was quite likely for a learned Brahmana to darken counsel with much learning and even 'with devotion's visage and pious action sugar o'er the devil himself.' Among the Indian saints we have fewer from among the Brahmanas than from the non-Brahmanas. Among the saints of revered memory, Sena was a barber, Sajana was a butcher, Gora a potter, Raidas a cobbler, Chokhamela an untouchable, Tukarama a kunbi, and so on.[11]

In conclusion, *dharma* turns out to be for the author merely this: to do what you should in the particular time and place you are in. It seems a bit meager as a conclusion, but a final cement in the entire conglomeration, supporting the author's attempt to define *svadharma* ('one's own duty'), comes from a Western textbook on ethics, Mackenzie's *Manual on Ethics*, reprinted and revised over and over since its first publication in 1883: 'Thou shalt labour within thy particular province, with all thy heart and with all thy might and will all thy strength and with all thy mind.'[12] This piece of unimpeachable and generally accepted scholarship is followed up by an absolutely final piece of scholarship Mahadev Desai adds on his own, a bit incongruously, but obviously with the assumption that all these pieces of science together will clinch the case. He states that history changes, that different times demand different action, and if killing a foe may have been right at one time, laying down one's life 'in defending a sacred principle or individual or national honor' may be the thing to do at another time.

One cannot speak of clarity and consistency in the business of interpreting the *Bhagavad Gita* in these comments. The romanticizing tendencies are plain, the disregard for history is obvious, a certain arbitrariness is given full rein, and the only thing constant (but hardly flattering) is the willingness to lean on modern and scientific doctrines to fill the gaps in the exposition.

★   ★   ★

The interpretations given in Aurobindo's 'school', even if developed in the same very general climate of thought and feeling (the 'internationalized neo-romanticism'), are distinct, and certainly much more consistent and clear, much less vulnerable to critical questions. At the first instance where the varnas demand our attention, Anilbaran Roy paraphrases Aurobindo as follows:

> Varna is usually translated as caste, but the existing caste system in India is a very different thing from the ancient social idea of Chaturvarna, the four clear-cut orders of the Aryan community, and in no way corresponds with the description of the Gita.[13]

It is important to notice that here the difference between Vedic and Epic is not obliterated. Further, it is of great significance that the varnas and the castes are not spoken of *as if* they were matters of the same material, empirical reality, one a product of the other. The four varnas are called 'orders'. They are less a matter of visible reality, and more a matter of principles governing human social life. Concrete, empirical, far from abstract problems concern Arjuna most in his complaint in *Bhagavad Gita* I. Anilbaran Roy translates verse 42:

> By these misdeeds of the ruiners of the family leading to the confusion of the orders, the eternal laws of the race and moral law of the family are destroyed.

What is here rendered as 'laws of the race' is *jatidharmah*; *jati* is the common Sanskrit term we should understand as related to the actuality of existences, births, 'castes' (or 'race').

That varna in Aurobindo's thought should indeed be understood in a distinct, special sense ('order') is perfectly clear from his writings. (Mahadev Desai, unlike A. Roy, left *varna* untranslated, thereby befuddling the issue even more than through his comments.) Aurobindo makes no attempt to prove the pure, pristine existence of the varnas in some ideal past, but he makes them into principles with a universal validity. One may quarrel with that procedure, but it does avoid useless argumentation about history.

> There is always in human nature something of all these four personalities developed or undeveloped, wide or narrow, suppressed or rising to the surface, but in most men one or the other tends to predominate and seems to take up sometimes the whole space of action in the nature. And in any society we should have all four types, – even, for an example, if we could create a purely productive and commercial society such as modern times have attempted, or for that matter a Sudra society of labor, of the proletariat such as attracts the most modern mind and is now being attempted in one part of Europe and advocated in others. There would still be the thinkers moved to find the law and truth and guiding rule of the whole matter, the captains and leaders of industry who would make all this productive activity an excuse for the satisfaction of their need for adventure and battle and leadership and dominance, the many typical purely productive and wealth-gathering men, the average workers satisfied with a modicum of labor and the reward of their labor.[14]

Thus Aurobindo universalizes the varnas both psychologically and sociologically. He even goes one more psychological step. The inner, spiritual meaning of the four orders is given with the inner realization of man. Every individual in the world is given the potential and opportunity to develop through the four orders as *stages* in his own growth. That, Aurobindo says, is the reason why the *Gita* asserts 'that even the Sudra or Chandala can by turning his life Godwards climb straight to spiritual liberty and perfection'.

The entire reasoning resembles the reasoning of Gandhi and his follower Mahadev Desai to some extent. There is a common flavor, which we can detect in certain intellectual circles of the period. At the same time, it would be absurd to suggest that all those intellectuals of 'internationalized romanticism' were the same. The differences in detail between Gandhi's and Aurobindo's style are hard to miss. Although Aurobindo had drunk from the same fashionable intellectual sources as Gandhi, his words never reach the sort of sentimentality of the Gandhian interpretations. There is no need for conjuring up butchers and potters and washermen who could reach God so much more easily than could the learned. The similarity between the two men, or rather their schools in reading the *Gita* text, remains the most important thing to notice in the present historical footnote. The details, no matter how striking, are variations on the same theme; they are matters of degree of scholarship, intelligence, philosophical ability to anticipate critical questions, and of the communities in which their most developed thoughts 'made school'. Gandhi remained a political leader throughout all his spiritual exertions, Aurobindo a thinker, in spite of his political involvements. For both, a certain evolution mattered more than anything else; it was an evolution for all mankind and meant to reach the supreme. 'Internationalized romanticism' triggered that principal concern in both men and their movement.

One might daydream and imagine that Gandhi's movement, his inspiration for India and the Indians might have profited, gained in strength, lasted as a spiritual force, if it had recognized and accepted the integral Yoga of Aurobindo. But this wishfulness goes beyond the realm of the mere historian.

The only note to be added without such indulgings in *post factum* prophecies and plain nostalgia is that Aurobindo's militant philosophical interpretations have received a modicum of support from industrious scholarship. Georges Dumezil has demonstrated in a large number of his comparative historical studies that the division in varnas must be seen in a manner that is surprisingly analogous to Aurobindo's views. For Dumezil, however, this is not a philosophical decision, but the result of a careful analysis of the ancient texts (see, for example, *Mythe et Epopée* (Indic Mythology) Paris: Gallimard, 1968). The varnas are governing, ideological principles, rather than a way of describing an empirically given, existing society. One might also think of the important recent work by the sociologist Louis Dumont, the writer of *Homo Hierarchicus* (Chicago: University of Chicago Press, 1970), who has helped us see that indeed caste is a very different thing from varna, and that it is only through a habitual self-delusion that we have ignored for so long the natural quality of hierarchies in human life. But all these scholarly matters are secondary to our present subject. And most certainly, Gandhi will continue to be remembered and praised, but as for the details of this *Gita* interpretation and the summarizing efforts of Mahadev Desai (and they are of course only a detail of Gandhi's work) – they are not likely to last.

* * *

I still consider the preceding pages a footnote, yet I do not want to pretend that there are no further ramifications and implications. It is true that my pages are no more than a footnote in the sense that they have tried to show a neglected feature in our historical understanding of Gandhi. No one can be surprised to discover that Gandhi was a man of international format, and hence no one will be astonished to hear that he partook of Western ideas that had become international. He was not the only one to do so, and his countryman Aurobindo has provided us with a special instance. The primary purpose of my historical footnote is to suggest that the international climate must not be ignored. Our understanding would be quite incomplete, on the basis of *Gita* interpretations alone, if we saw either Gandhi or Aurobindo merely as examples of renascent Hinduism. Such a designation would be far too narrow, and deprive both of their real significance.

The best term I can find to pinpoint Gandhi's significance beyond the confines of Indian and Hindu history is 'internationalized (neo-)romanticism'. My friend Arvind Sharma has offered me another term: 'nostalgia for the future'. I like that term as a description. Just like the much less aesthetic term I proposed, it is applicable to Gandhi as well as Aurobindo (and to a great many others in the climate of the period: Jean Jaurès, Leon Blum, Troelstra, Henriette Roland Holst, and many others, especially writers with socialist sympathies). Both Gandhi and Aurobindo were emphatic in their concerns for the future, both lived and worked with hope for mankind. There is, however, a good historical reason for not being quite satisfied with a term that merely describes a psychological or mental predisposition of individuals. The historian insists on indicating the conjuction with Romanticism. The most crucial component of the new vision of the future, in spite of individual differences and articulations, comes from the West.

It is in order to indicate briefly that not only the study of history in general, but the history of religions in particular must pay particular attention to this special 'nostalgia for the future'. A variety of social, religious, political, generally anthropological and literary and artistic moods and ideas coalesced. I have argued that the 'influence' of this Western climate on Gandhi and Aurobindo is difficult to document for specific reasons. Without a doubt, these influences went without saying at the time; more often than not, they were prevalent assumptions in the circles in which these men moved. The impulses they received do not make them less, but more important, from the point of view of the historian of religions.

We may be inclined to see Gandhi, and also Aurobindo, triggered rather than inspired by prevalent Western ideas. However, even such triggering should not be seen as a negligible quantity. The Romantic movement has engendered a variety of fashions and ideas, including the unwholesome entitity of modern nationalism. In our century this monstrous birth, exported from the West, has sickened the entire planet. One certainly would hate to speak of 'inspiration' in this case. But one has to take notice of it.

When the historian of religions turns to the nineteenth and twentieth centuries, he has no option but to conceive of crucial chapters on international ties. These ties are only to a small extent the seemingly so obvious subject of Christian missions, and the missionary efforts by Hindu, Buddhist, and Muslim organizations. Here the institutions are known and well delineated, and the literature is explicit. The major attention of the historian of religions will have to go out toward more concealed, but ultimately much more important relations. The history of the nineteenth and twentieth centuries has brought about a growth of international intellectual relations of an intensity for which the only parallels could be found in late Antiquity, or in the Hinduization process of South and Southeast Asia. Then, gods of different traditions and nations and with different names were identified, or conceived as fundamentally the same. In recent history, the general idea of evolution, almost invariably in an identifiably romantic vein, has brought about some measure of intellectual coherence; it developed and freely crossed the borders of nations. Those who developed their hope for the future of man, even if merely 'triggered' by typically Western notions, found – or rather rediscovered – sources in their own religious heritage. Bergson spoke of the role of prophecy in his own peculiar manner as a central factor in his philosophy of creative evolution. Aurobindo developed his integral Yoga, leaning on ancient Samkhya and Yoga ideas of development, as well as Advaita. Most of the Mahatma's life was dedicated to the justice and equality that were to be reality in the end.

The future of mankind is an unavoidable subject of concern, if not anxiety, for statesmen today. It would be a great error to see the reasons for concern only in the terror of new weaponry. The future of mankind can never and nowhere be fathomed unless we are willing to see the impulses of a religious kind below the surfaces of military, as well as political, social, and economic history.

The term 'internationalized neo-romanticism' is still the most adequate, if we want to gain a clearer understanding of the widely shared concern for the future. It is especially helpful if we want to preserve our sense of critique in an investigation of the religious roots of our own time. It is true, of course, that idealizing the past (especially the distant past), of which we have seen some examples, is a very obvious predisposition of the great Romantics in the early part of the nineteenth century. It is equally true, however, that the wide circle of later romantics, in the late nineteenth and early twentieth centuries, are characterized quite often by their hope for the future. In the history of anthropology as an academic discipline, we can see the contrast between the two tendencies. Some see the beginning of culture in very crude forms: the descent from earlier primates, the indulgence in magic, etc.; only a long evolution will lead to refinement and elevation. The opposite tendency turns toward the beginnings as most meaningful; it is as if the beginning were the nucleus that contained everything that developed in human culture, but the nucleus, exactly because it was the first principle, remains somehow the most meaningful; moreover, development brings about misunderstanding of all that was first understood. The two tendencies, however, are by no means mutually exclusive, even in anthropology. In the general climate of thought of neo-romanticism, we frequently find the two side by side; in this respect, the comments quoted from Mahadev Desai in this essay are a clear illustration.

Notes

1. Mohandas K. Gandhi, *An Autobiography. The Story of My Experiments With Truth*, trans. from Gujarati by Mahadev Desai (Boston: Beacon Hill, 1957) pp. 463, 499.
2. Mahadev Desai, *The Gospel of Selfless Action or The Gita According to Gandhi* (Ahmedabad: Navajivan Publishing House, 1946)
3. Anilbaran Roy, *The Gita, with Text, Translation and Notes Compiled from*

Sri Aurobindo's Essays on the Gita (Pondicherry: Sri Aurobindo Ashram, 1946).
4. Aurobindo Ghose, *The Doctrine of Passive Resistance* (Calcutta: Arya Publishing House, 1948). First published in 1907.
5. Gandhi, *An Autobiography*, p. 67.
6. Ibid., p. 265.
7. Ibid., p. 265.
8. Ibid., p. 265.
9. Ibid., pp. 265–6.
10. Mahadev Desai, pp. 98–9. Italics are mine.
11. Ibid., pp. 100–1.
12. Mahadev Desai refers to p. 101 of John F. Mackenzie, *A Manual of Ethics*. In my edition the quoted words occur on p. 309 (London: University Tutorial Press, 6th edition).
13. Anilbaran Roy, *The Gita*.
14. Ibid.

10
Gandhi and Christianity
Margaret Chatterjee

Gandhi's attitude toward Christianity and his relationships with Christians can perhaps be treated in combination with his approach to religious pluralism, and yet in some ways, it needs to be addressed as a matter distinct in itself. This distinctness stems from at least four considerations. First, Christianity was the religion of the imperial power, something which inevitably colored the relations of British and Indians during Gandhi's leadership of the nationalist movement. Secondly, while Jainism and Buddhism, which are both woven into Gandhi's religious thought, belong to the family of religions of Indian origin, Christianity does not. Thirdly, Gandhi's attitude to Christianity illustrates in an interesting way what I have elsewhere discussed under the rubric of understanding, and sharing religious insights.[1] What emerges is that understanding and sharing, however sincerely embarked on, and however deep, have limits. Fourthly, Christians see their religion specifically in terms of the challenge of the *person* of Christ in a way which is probably not claimed by Jains in connection with Mahavira, or by Buddhists for Buddha, and certainly not by Muslims for Mohammed. The Christian asks the question 'What think ye of Christ?' Gandhi's implicit response to this question brings out both the extent of sharing and its boundaries.

It is pertinent in this context to raise the question whether, for example, Gandhi misunderstood Christianity in any way, thanks to the particular theological garb in which he encountered it. Would a more modern theology have eased his difficulties over such doctrines as the atonement and the uniqueness of Christ, or was he up against an irreducible core that the most advanced theologizing would not have been able to soften for him? To speak of misunderstanding Christianity, however, raises a hornet's nest if we take our hermeneutics seriously. Does not each generation, or even each individual, redefine the core for itself? Moreover, it would be a mistake to give greater weight to such a question than to one which might be rarely asked but which in all fairness should at least be framed, i.e. 'What prevents the Christian from becoming a Hindu?' The latter formulation in many ways sets the record straight, for one should not assume that, for example, 'if it were not for doctrines X, Y, and Z, Gandhi could very well have become a Christian', any more than it would make sense to say that 'only A, B, and C features prevent a Christian from becoming a Hindu'. Neither situation can be conceived in the abstract. Only for any particular *individual* can the question of taking a stand *vis-à-vis* another faith arise. Even to say this immediately brings into prominence another difference between Christianity and Hinduism. Within Christianity the issue of taking a stand is *built into* the tradition. This is seen most sharply in the life and writings of Kierkegaard. The Hindu does not face the issue of commitment in quite this way.[2] Given his own Hindu heritage, it is remarkable that Gandhi should have seen 'taking a stand' as incumbent on the *Hindu* of his own generation in such innovative ways, for example, the Hindu should take a stand *against* untouchability, take a stand *for* fostering Hindu/Muslim relations, take a stand by undertaking bread-labor as something which *inter alia* would break down caste barriers.

POSITIVE IMPACT

It was not until Gandhi started studying the New Testament in his student days in London that the leaven of Christ's personality began to work within him. Perhaps this is to put the matter too strongly. At the very same time Gandhi was studying the life of Buddha through Sir Edwin Arnold's *The Light of Asia* (Boston: Roberts Brothers, 1879). He seems to have been struck by the similarity between the two central figures of each religion, Christianity and Buddhism, finding therein the same compassion and complete renunciation. Gandhi never thought of Buddhism as in any great way different from the Hindu tradition within which it had its birth. But Christianity grew out of a very different cultural milieu. Gandhi seems to have been torn between his response to an infinitely appealing figure with a world-shaking message and disillusionment with the civilization which paid but lip-service to Him and which was torn by warfare and bore the sour fruits of colonialism. The anomaly which lay at the heart of Western civilization never ceased to strike him. C. F. Andrews to some extent shared this particular disquiet.

Would it be close to the truth to say that what made an impact on Gandhi was not a package called 'Christianity' so much as the person of Christ and his teaching as seen in the Gospels? We seem to come near Kierkegaard once more in putting it this way. If Kierkegaard was disillusioned with the fossilized conventional religion of his day, that is, with the Christians he saw around him, Gandhi had every reason to be unhappy about aggressive evangelizing and the trade/flag/Bible syndrome in general. A word on the evangelical question may be in order here. There is no doubt that it was evangelical Christianity that Gandhi encountered in Porbandar (from a street corner perspective and, in South Africa, among people who personally showed him much kindness and for whom he had great affection). Now Hinduism is par excellence a non-proselytizing religion. Those Westerners who claim these days to be Hindu, especially in the particular state I happen to be in now, that is, California, are scarcely regarded as such by the inhabitants of Hindustan. It is not so much the consideration that Hindu society is an in-group to which outsiders cannot gain entry (although there may be a grain of truth in saying this) but that the idea of *Swadharma* limits the exercise of attempting to acquire the *dharma* of someone else. It is far more individualistic a matter than Hinduism is usually given credit for by those who latch on to Advaitic monism or, another common view, always see dharma in caste terms rather than in terms of individual destiny.

Conversion is a non-issue for the Hindu – one might put it like that. Gandhi's advice to Mirabehn is relevant here.[3] At one time she felt that maybe conversion to Hinduism should be a natural accompaniment of all the many ways in which she identified herself with Gandhiji and the causes dear to him. But Gandhi was firm on the point that she should not abandon her own religion even though she had certainly abandoned the ways of life to which she was originally accustomed. She should remain a Christian and assimilate the spirituality of Hinduism within its framework. Behind this we uncover Gandhi's attitude to other faiths and to Christianity in particular. All religions are 'almost as dear' to him as his own 'in as much as all human beings should be as dear to one as one's own close relatives'.[4] This suggests love for the *person* professing a certain faith along with respect for the religion adhered to by him or her. However, what he says immediately after this is as follows: 'My own veneration for other faiths is *the same* as that for my own faith; therefore no thought of conversion is possible' (my emphasis).

We need to try to understand all this in the light of Gandhi's experiences in the company of Christians both in South Africa and elsewhere. No doubt many of those who took him along to their services and prayer meetings during the South African days were hopeful that their new friend would 'see the light', 'be saved' and 'become a Christian'. The same language, it must be remembered, would still be used by contemporary evangelicals in comparing conventional Christians with the 'born again' Christian. The transition from Hinduism to Christianity would be comparable to the conversion of the latter type. It was to a gathering of Christians that Gandhi gave the famous advice that they should 'help a Hindu to become a better Hindu, a Mussalman to become a better Mussalman, and a Christian a better Christian'. It is to be noted that this was not a mere injunction that each should be a better embodiment of his own tradition but that a *Christian* should be able to help a Hindu to become a better Hindu, etc. That this can come about through prayer is clarified when he said that our prayer for the other must be *not* 'God, give him the light that Thou hast given me', *but* 'give him all the light and truth he needs for his highest development', and that we should pray merely that our friends may become better men, whatever their form of religion. This reveals the extent to which Hinduism makes room for diversity of religious needs – a diversity of greater extent than say Baron von Huegel's recognition of the difference in temperament between those who tend to a Christ-centered religious experience and those whose experience is God-centered. The *istadevata* idea gives radical sanction for a plurality of paths and, as such, goes in a contrary direction to the 'there is none other Name' approach. But let us pursue the trend of thinking given in Gandhi's position. A Christian *helps* the Hindu to become a better Hindu (and the Muslim etc.) by praying for him in a particular way, i.e. that he should receive what he needs at his particular stage of development so that he can proceed to a higher stage of development along his own particular *marga*. What the relation between being a better Hindu/Christian/Muslim and being a better man is seems to amount to an identity. For he told a different Christian audience, 'Make us better Hindus, i.e. better men and women'.

Conversion would only make sense if one faith were inferior to another. Unfortunately, evangelical Christianity in the India of Gandhi's day did regard other religions as inferior. The attitude expressed in Bishop Heber's famous hymn typified what many missionaries thought.[5] They had come to bring enlightenment to a benighted land. There was, therefore, every reason why there should have been a gulf between this school of thought and Gandhi's loving approach to all, regardless of caste and creed. Another way of focusing this is to bring in the consideration of truth claims. If truth is internalized in the way that Gandhi sees it, how is the *mahavakya* of the New Testament 'I am the Way, the Truth, and the Life' to be understood? One of Gandhi's answers is this: 'I concern myself not with belief but with asking to do the right thing.' This takes the aspirant not to Christ, but to dharma. In the performance of dharma imitation of an exemplar is not prescribed, but rather the correct discernment of duty and the carrying out of it, strengthened by divine grace.

We cannot at this juncture, it seems to me, ask a straightforward question as to whether Gandhi had misunderstood Christianity or not, and for the following reasons. First, Gandhi had correctly gauged missionary desires to 'convert' others to what they believed to be the true path and to lead them from darkness to light. But the sages of ancient India had also prayed for guidance on the path from darkness to light, and by this something very different had been meant. Grace was invoked in the *metabasis* from the *tamasik* to the *sattvik*, from the bondage of ignorance to the clear light of *moksha*. The prayer had never led an aspirant out of his *swadharma* to embrace an alien dharma.

The second consideration brings in what could be called the cultural packaging of Christianity. Gandhi once asked: 'Why should a man, even if he becomes a Christian, be torn from his surroundings?' It is a historical fact that converts in Gandhi's day changed their names, dress, and food and often appeared to be aping their rulers. After Independence things often went in reverse, with Christians acquiring Indian names, especially in North India, although usually retaining their first names ('Christian names'). Gandhi in his early youth associated Christianity with beef-eating and other customs alien to Hindus. An inculturated type of Christianity came along after Gandhi's day, and, oddly enough, even up to present times is found least of all in nonconformist circles. Christian theology historically incorporated Judaic and

Greek concepts. Contemporary Indian Christian theology, or at least some of it, seeks to incorporate elements from Advaita Vendanta / Sri Aurobindo etc. There are Indian Christian theologians who were influenced by Gandhi and some of these will be mentioned later.

GANDHI AND CHRISTIANS FROM OVERSEAS

Of Christians from overseas who were close to Gandhi, the names of C. F. Andrews and E. Stanley Jones come immediately to mind. His friendship with C. F. Andrews was, no doubt, of a special order. If Andrews saw in Gandhi something which reminded him of St Francis of Assisi, Gandhi saw in Andrews someone who practiced the message of love rather than preached it and who in later life was humble enough to make an act of contrition by touching the feet of a Punjabi who was full of resentment against the imperial power. The friendship between the two great souls was at the level of *common action* and it was this that brought Gandhi closest to his fellow human beings, no matter what their religious label might be. Gandhi and Andrews both shared a common streak of asceticism and, at the same time, a deep capacity for and need for emotional warmth. It was even, after a time, a hardship for each to be away from the other. Through his friend Charlie, I venture to say that Gandhi's understanding of the Sermon on the Mount was deepened, seeing in this central message of the New Testament, a love *at work*, a love that ever serves, and that is faithful even to the point of death. To name Andrews 'Deenbandhu', friend of the poor, was to invoke powerful associations ranging from the Magnificat and the Beatitudes to St Francis. For all his rooting in the Anglican form of Christian belief, Andrews was able to embody for Gandhi, I believe, a discipleship of Christ that transcended denominational boundaries. It was a happy thing that Gandhi should have found a close friend in one who may have begun his career in India as a missionary but who, along with Gandhi, was subsequently able to engage in something more, a *mission* which would not only bring his own people closer to India but make Hindus and Christians more intelligible to each other. It was a labor of love, a work of reconciliation that took them across continents.

Gandhi always found the religious component of life most

vividly present in the world of action. This perhaps gives us a key as to how he saw the man Jesus. To say he was the Son of God did not have for Gandhi the compelling force it has for the Christian. If all are the sons of God wherein lies the uniqueness of Christ? To stress the historical Christ, moreover, does not impress the Hindu. It is the teaching, rather than the man, that matters. I have suggested elsewhere[6] that it was the Son of Man rather than the Son of God that made a deep impact on Gandhi. There is no doubt that, among Christians, Gandhi had no closer friend than C. F. Andrews and that in turn Andrews was his most eloquent ambassador in the cause of peace and justice, whether it was in South Africa, India or Fiji.

E. Stanley Jones, an American Methodist missionary, spent some time with Gandhi at the Sabarmati ashram in the early 1920s. Along with M. M. Thomas he found that Gandhi 'had only touched the Person at second-hand through the principles'.[7] There is no such expression of regret, as far as I know, in Andrews' writings. Jones, sensitive as he was to the concept of a Christ of the Indian Road, was more of a 'missionary' in the old sense of that term than Andrews was. This shows in all his writings about Gandhi, even though he must certainly be numbered among Gandhi's genuine admirers. A brief mention of Albert Schweitzer here may not be out of place. Among overseas Christians, Schweitzer was on the wrong track in thinking that Gandhi was wedded to the 'traditional Hindu philosophy of self-negation ... the inactive ethic of perfecting the self alone'. Certainly the British would have been the last to see any such signs of an inactive ethic in such an active nonviolent adversary!

GANDHI AND CHRISTIANS IN INDIA

It is in fact not easy to try and assess Christian reactions to Gandhi in India. Gandhi's theological discussions with Kali Charan Bannerjee during his visit to Calcutta in 1901 are well known to researchers on this subject. The main theological stumbling blocks for Gandhi were the doctrine of the atonement, once-and-for-all salvation, and the divine sonship of Christ. He had not moved in sufficiently sophisticated theological circles (mercifully perhaps!) to be worried about the Trinity, although one can discern in Gandhi's own religious thought something very like a Trinitarian structure of God *beyond* (God as Lord), God *among* (the Jesus who collected dust on his feet and who suffered as men suffered) and God *within* (the inner voice). Significantly, though Gandhi could greet in the person of Kali Charan Bannerjee a friend and fellow devotee, their intimacy was, as far as one can pronounce about such matters, far less than that between him and his Christian friends in South Africa.

Bengal had numbered W. C. Bannerjee, the Calcutta barrister, among distinguished Congressmen. However, dates and circumstances must not go unforgotten. At the all-India meeting in Bombay in December 28 1885 over which Bannerjee presided, he spoke of 'the merciful dispensation of Providence' which had brought India under the dominion of the great British power! Much the same had been said by Rammohun Roy many decades earlier in the century. There were precedents in Bengal for involvement of upper-class Christian intellectuals in the cause of social justice. It was Michael Madhusudan Dutta who, most probably, was the anonymous English translator of Dinabandhu Mitra's *Neel Darpan*. It was published by Rev. James Long and the latter suffered imprisonment for it – surely a very interesting example of activism and a fearless combination of forces between an Indian Christian and an English missionary! Once the Brahmo Samaj movement was under way, the Christians could no longer claim to be the only monotheists in India (apart from Muslims of course). Many of the causes which Gandhi espoused had already been championed, as far as Bengal was concerned, by Vidyasager and by Tagore – I refer here to things like the cause of womankind, and opposition to caste restrictions and untouchability. The imagination of Bengal had been captured by the revolutionary movement, the movement of which Tagore was frankly critical in his novel *Ghore-baire*. Christians, as far as I know, and I am really guessing here, were not associated with the secret societies. While the latter could not draw them in, Gandhi to some extent did so. It was Jawaharlal Nehru who wrote that the nationalist movement in Bengal from 1906 onwards had for the first time shaken up the upper classes, and 'infused a new life into the Bengali lower middle class and to a small extent even the masses'.[8] Tagore's disapproval of Gandhi's burning of foreign cloth must not blind us to the large areas of common agreement between the two men, especially their dislike of humbug, their concern for the rural sector, and their ability to combine nationalist sentiments with a love for all men across frontiers.

Christians were swept up in Gandhi's nationalist movement no less than others were. To explore this further one would need, for example, data about the class and caste composition of converts in, say, Madras, Punjab and Bengal, and also some idea of the difference in 'style' of the various missionary societies such as the LMS, BMS and CMS. There was no question of people becoming nationalists or following Gandhi *on account* of a Christian affiliation. Hindus have indeed sometimes thought that those they described as 'dal/bhat' Christians (referring to missionary activity among the lower castes and the poor) kept conveniently close to the Raj. As far as Bengal is concerned, what Gora realizes at the end of Tagore's novel of this name, is most significant. He confesses his need for a mantram: 'the mantram of that deity who belongs to all, Hindu, Mussalman, Christian and Brahmo alike – the doors to whose temple are never closed to any one person of any caste whatever – He who is not merely the God of the Hindu but who is the God of India herself.' In such a statement we hear an echo of Brahmo assimilation of unitarian belief, and perhaps even an intimation of a Christ figure who is somehow identified, by Christians certainly and even by Brahmo Hindus, with suffering India, or even suffering man. Gandhi's appeal to overcome evil with good was already familiar to an English-educated upper class whose school curriculum was likely to have included the study of the Bible. It was, needless to say, immediately intelligible to Christians and found an echo in their own commitment to the Gospel. But the more orthodox, that is those who, through conversion, distanced themselves from their original community or were distanced by the latter, probably had difficulty over the teaching that 'he who is not for us is against us'. The situation was clearer after Independence once the association of Christianity with the imperial connection disappeared. Governor Haren Coomar Mookerji, Bengal's first Indian Governor and a Christian, was a gentle unassuming man who had been associated with Gandhi's rural programs. His unostentatious mode of dress and manner endeared him to the people of Bengal. In post-Independence India, the phrase 'Indian Christian' would gradually lose its tinge of odium among caste Hindus. Interestingly enough, in his *Autobiography* Gandhi used not this expression, but 'Christian Indian'. Christian hymns continue to be sung at the memorial functions held on Gandhi's birth and death anniversaries. If in Bengal there were Christian enthusiasts for Gandhi's constructive program, the same was the case in Madras.

In the Kumarappa brothers, especially Bharatan Kumarappa, he has very eloquent advocates of villagism. For J. C. Kumarappa, the precepts of Jesus (a phrase that immediately recalls the Brahmo Samajists of Bengal) have precedence over high Christology. Those who 'follow precepts such as the ones Jesus taught can be deemed Followers of Jesus, be they Hindus, Muslims, Buddhists or perchance, even Christians, irrespective of their own religious affiliations'.[9]

S. K. George is another Christian from South India, who was deeply influenced by Gandhi. S. K. George writes:[10]

> The organized church in India was at no time entirely sympathetic towards the national struggle. There were, of course, individual Christians who took an active and creative part in the nation's fight for freedom, but their participation was as private individuals; it was primarily personal commitment, not involvement as a community, that drove them into the ranks of freedom fighters. This assessment is probably correct.

In 1938, S. K. George wrote a book called *Gandhi's Challenge to Christianity* during a year spent at Manchester College, Oxford. He had stayed in Gandhi's ashram in Sabarmati at a time when Gandhi was in jail. The two corresponded and George found in Gandhi, he wrote, 'The essence of Christianity lived out in the Indian Setting'.[11] In *satyagraha* he found the Cross in action; moreover a sense of conversion therein, deeper than the change of label to which missionary efforts were directed. The *satyagrahi*, by taking suffering upon himself, aims at converting the heart of the adversary. For George, the Cross overshadows the Christ. In this respect George singles out the symbolic power of sacrificial suffering rather than the crucifixion of the historic Jesus. The Hindu, however, does not believe in vicarious suffering. The single one cannot bear on his shoulders the sins of many. It is those who suffer a particular injustice that can offer satyagraha in order to remove it. The satyagrahi does not atone for others' sins. George, it seems, had learned from Gandhi the latter's own understanding of the Cross, i.e. the power of suffering love.

George noted the strange reaction of some Christians (especially in missionary circles) to efforts to uplift the Harijans within the Hindu fold, and of course the subsequent safeguards provided for them in free India, detecting a strange disappointment, 'for the obvious reason that it would stop the flow of converts to the Christian churches'.[12]

George's analyses in his various writings correlate initial inertia *vis-à-vis* the nationalist movement among Christians in India with the consideration that a large proportion of the converts came from the lower castes. But the prominent nationalist names that come to mind from the Christian community during the struggle for Independence are of people from the upper castes. George writes of free India that 'the Harijan need no longer look for social uplift in folds other than Hinduism'.[13] Whatever suspicion of Gandhi might remain in the minds of some Christian Indians might contain two elements, firstly, the realization that the Christians were no longer in the vanguard of meliorist elements in society since this meliorism was now built into state policy, and the older and much more long-standing apprehension that Hinduism can well assimilate Christianity as it has assimilated so many other elements in the past, and that this attitude is typified by Gandhi's own assimilation of such a large amount of Christian teaching, symbolism and language. George's writings were not liked much by Christians such as M. M. Thomas. The latter refers to him as a Christian of the Inner Gandhi Circle. But what he objects to is probably reflected in his own characterization of what he conceives George to have looked forward to (he died in 1960): 'Christianity finding its rightful place in the catholicity of Hinduism'.[14]

Thomas' own position needs consideration at this point for he is still an eloquent advocate of indigenized Christianity. Author of *The Acknowledged Christ of the Indian Renaissance*, he writes of Gandhi: 'Because of his life and death, the meaning of suffering love has been deepened and its larger application to the struggle for political and social justice opened up for the whole world'.[15] But Thomas identifies suffering love with vicarious suffering in a way which I think is unwarranted in Gandhi's case, as indicated earlier in discussing S. K. George. Thomas, moreover, seems to find in Gandhi's quest for self-purification 'the spiritual sin of pride', an accusation which is not justified in the light of Gandhi's reiterated mention of his attempts to reduce the self to zero. Thomas also fails to note that the Vaishnava tradition, which is woven into the warp and woof of Gandhi's religious thought, does indeed lay a great stress on Divine grace. But, to be sure, the Hindu will not look upon Christ as a mediator. For Gandhi, the example of Jesus' suffering was a factor in the composition of his undying faith in nonviolence which ruled all his activities, worldly and temporal.[16] When Thomas speaks of the 'tragedy inherent in man's pursuit of a righteousness of the law',[17] (in the course of his critique), he is taking a backward look of the kind that Christians tend to direct toward Rabbinical Judaism, and the comment misfires as far as Hindu *sanatan dharma* or Gandhi's principle of *ahisma* is concerned, for neither of these are on a law-like wavelength.

Gandhi believed that 'the highest Truth needs no communicating for it is by its nature self-propelling. It radiates its influence silently as the rose its fragrance without the intervention of a medium.'[18] On another occasion he remarked that there is no truer evangelism than life. The image is that of drawing others to you rather than going out to preach to them. The principle of *swadeshi* encourages being rooted where one is, and this, *inter alia*, goes against the veering of Harijans towards Christianity or, as advocated by Ambedkar, their moving into Buddhism, or for that matter, their conversion to Islam.

The earlier writings of M. M. Thomas and other leaders of indigenized Christianity recognized that depressed and backward classes were on the move but associated Hindu desire to do justice to them with 'nationalistic and humanitarian' rather than religious considerations. In turn, the reaction to this desire shows ambivalence, on the one hand a welcoming of the Hindu spirit of reform and on the other hand the sense that fewer Harijans will need to join the Church in order to get a place in the sun. The context of the discussion takes us back almost fifty years ago. Gandhi's rejoinder to the manifesto called 'Our Duty to the Depressed and Backward Classes', which was drawn up by a group of Christian leaders who had in any case been influenced by Gandhi, appeared in *Harijan*, on April 3 1937. Gandhi cannily pinpoints the way the document (which he dubs 'unfortunate') switches from the idea of duty not only to the downtrodden but to all sections of people to a *right* to 'awaken hunger in all' (the language of the manifesto). Gandhi suggests to the signatories that 'in the spiritual sphere, there is no such thing as a right'. Looking upon Christ's own nonviolence as the most appealing thing in Christianity, Gandhi believed that the very same message was there in Hinduism, Jainism and Buddhism, so there was no basic spiritual hunger which went unsatisfied in the adherents of these three religions. Some of this has the ring of battles fought long ago. Christians and members of other communities make their contribution to national life as citizens rather than as adherents of this or that particular faith. If one were to ask to what extent Christians today were influenced by Gandhi, in all fairness the same question should be asked of Indians from other communities as well. In pre-Independence days I think it correct to say that Gandhi made Christians in India aware of their Indianness. After Independence the community learned to stand on its own feet, set free from association with the former rulers.

As far as Gandhi's own assimilation of Christian elements in his thinking is concerned, the matter may be put something like this. He found in Christ's message of love something deeply consonant with his own belief in nonviolence. But creeds and castes were something which the man of goodwill should be able to surmount. What Gandhi had imperceptibly assimilated in dozens of evangelical meetings in South Africa flowered in a concept which was uniquely his own, that of soul-force. This was something which *all* could experience – Hindu, Muslim and Christian alike. This is why those, like Charlie Andrews, who understood him best, never tried to convert him. Words must become flesh and dwell among us as deeds bearing good fruit. The resonances of more than one culture can be heard in these phrases. The idiom, however, was Gandhi's own. His religious life had already gone beyond labels. He went deep enough to tap the living waters which feed all faiths.

Notes

1. See *Religious Studies*, March 1984.
2. See my forthcoming *The Religious Spectrum* (Delhi: Allied Publishers).
3. *Christian Missions* (Ahmedabad, 1940) p. 196.
4. *Sabarmati*, 1928, 17–19.
5. From Greenland's icy mountains,
   From India's coral strand,
   Where Afric's sunny fountains
   Roll down their golden sand;
   From many an ancient river,
   From many a palmy plain,
   They call us to deliver
   Their land from error's chain!
   From Reginald Heber, *Hymns* (New York and London: Garland Publishing, 1978) p. 139.
6. See my *Gandhi's Religious Thought* (London: Macmillan, 1983) Ch. 3.

7. *Mahatma Gandhi: an Interpretation* (Lucknow: Lucknow Publishing House, 1948) p. 76.
8. *An Autobiography*, p. 29.
9. *Practice and Precepts of Jesus* (Ahmedabad: Navajivan Publishing House, 1946) p. ix.
10. *The Witness of S. K. George* (Bangalore: The Christian Institute for the Study of Religion and Society, 1970) p. 4.
11. Ibid., p. 13.
12. Ibid., p. 58.
13. Ibid., p. 82.
14. *The Acknowledged Christ of Hinduism* (Bangalore: CISRS, 1970) p. 224.
15. Ibid., p. 234.
16. Paraphrased from *The Message of Jesus Christ* (Ahmedabad, 1940). p. 79.
17. *The Acknowledged Christ of Hinduism* (Bangalore: CISRS, 1970) p. 236.
18. *The Message of Jesus Christ* (Bombay, 1940) p. 32.

11

Gandhi's Religious Universalism

Elton Hall

It is a very strange thing that almost all the professors of great religions of the world claim me as their own. The Jains mistake me for a Jain. Scores of Buddhist friends have taken me for a Buddhist. Hundreds of Christian friends still consider that I am a Christian and ... Many of my Mussalman friends consider that, although I do not call myself a Mussalman, to all intents and purposes, I am one of them ... still something within me tells me that, for all that deep veneration I show to these several religions, I am all the more a Hindu, none the less for it.

– Mahatma Gandhi[1]

If Gandhi's life and thought are an enigma to the casually interested, they are a deepening mystery to the serious student and devotee. His remarks were public and widely shared, his correspondence voluminous, his articles and speeches translated into half a dozen tongues, and his style open and plain. He was never secretive and seldom cryptic. More than any thinker in the twentieth century, he was concerned to explain his views to anyone who asked about them, whatever the mood of the inquirer or level of the question. Writer, editor, public speaker, social reformer, preacher, leader of prayers, diplomat, politician, lawyer, experimenter in diet, health and social structures, his recorded words fill more than ninety volumes. Despite being perhaps the most visible public figure in three generations, the more one examines the great treasury of his thought, the more elusive his views become. Some writers will fare better perceived from a sympathetic distance, where their work can be appreciated as a coherent whole, rather than looked at closely, where flaws in the edifice are revealed. Mahatma Gandhi's unsystematic and diverse writings, however, have misled superficial readers into detecting

Religious Universalism

alleged discrepancies and inconsistencies throughout, but the closer one draws to them – letter by letter, speech by speech – the more solid his foundation is seen to be.

If Gandhi can be said to exhibit any reticence, it is in specifically spiritual matters. Here the depth and the mystery of his thought emerge in a striking way: the more we discover the meaning of Gandhi's religious universalism, the more we are compelled to ask difficult questions of ourselves. Indeed, we might say that it is only to the extent that we ask ourselves difficult questions that we can begin to understand Gandhi's religious universalism. In an age when ecumenical thinking is respectable, if somewhat muted, and many individuals profess a universalist belief, if vaguely defined, Gandhi's religious universalism seems unexceptional. And the growing interest in 'interreligious dialogue' may dim awareness of his boldness in presiding over sacred occasions in several religions.[2] What will not disappear even as understanding amongst the religious increases is that Gandhi was accepted as a brother, companion and co-religionist by many adherents of different religions. It is not his acceptance of non-Hindu religions that demands our thoughtful attention, but that he was welcomed by them. Why did he do this? How did he do it? What are its implications for mankind today?

Gandhi claimed that he knew little of Hinduism until he was a young man, save for his mother's devotions and a few ritual occasions. While a student of law in England, he met several influential Theosophists and read *The Key to Theosophy*. Sir Edwin Arnold's *The Light of Asia*, a life of the Buddha in verse form, and his *The Song Celestial*, a rendering of the *Bhagavad Gita*, deeply impressed Gandhi. The *Ghita* became his daily reference book, and he spoke of *The Light of Asia* throughout his life. When he went to South Africa to practice law, he was a Hindu employed by a Muslim firm and a member of the executive board of the Christian Esoteric Union. From youth Gandhi had the sublime good fortune to appreciate spiritual ideals and religious ideas without having to be concerned about the labels attached to them. Nonetheless, as he found himself impelled into the arena of social reform in Africa, his religious universalism found living roots in his metaphysical presuppositions. It would be as fruitless as it is impossible to determine whether his ideals grew out of the same fertile soil that nurtured his religious universalism or whether his broad spiritual views fostered his metaphysical conception.

Reduced to its simplest expression, Gandhi's religious universalism followed from his concept of God, for the other two pillars of his faith – Truth and nonviolence – are aspects of God. 'God is certainly One. He has no second. He is unfathomable, unknowable and unknown to the vast majority of mankind . . . He is the most elusive.'[3] Again, 'The real God is beyond conception. He neither serves nor receives service.'[4] This conception of Deity has led some philosophers to reject all religious activity as superfluous or superstitious. Others have seen in it the exaltation of reason and, in more recent centuries, science. But for Gandhi, it was the starting-point for three critical and interrelated distinctions that gave particular emphasis and limitation to both religious practice and reason.

Like Plato, Gandhi rejected Meno's paradox and held that intellectual and spiritual growth are possible. First of all, he accepted the classical distinction between Absolute Truth and relative truth, *paramarthasatya* and *samvrttisatya*. By definition, Absolute Truth cannot be wholly captured by any formulation or instantiation, just as relative truth can never be justifiably absolutized. In this sense, Absolute Truth is real precisely because it cannot be stated. In Johannine Christian terms, it is prior to the Word. If one accepts this much, one would be bound at the minimum to reject dogmatism, a standpoint which would be inadequate by itself to meet Gandhi's standards. In addition, Gandhi felt that relative truths were not fragments of Absolute Truth, but rather approximations to it in an almost mathematical sense of the term. In one sense, a statement might be true from one point of view, but not true from another.[5] In another sense, a statement might be less an approximation of truth than a distortion or misconception which contains a kernel of truth. Relative truth reflects Absolute Truth to some more or less obscure degree. Because the degree of reflection can vary, relative truths are not all equal, but because they are reflections, they all deserve a minimal respect. To use a Buddhist metaphor, the reflection of the moon on a lake varies with the disturbance of placidity of the surface of the water, yet the shimmering light is a reflection nonetheless. If rejection of dogmatism is a negative virtue required by Gandhi's stance, respect for truth however it appears is a positive step beyond.

Secondly, Gandhi recognized what might be called two gods. 'Since we do not understand the ways of God', he wrote 'we have necessarily to think of a power beyond our conception. And the moment we think of it, the God of our imagining is born.'[6] If God transcends all possible categories, characteristics and conceptions, then even the concept of God as transcendent falls short. One ends up with two gods, the real God and the God of one's imagination. This distinction, summarized in Paul Tillich's famous phrase, 'the God behind God', is parallel to that of the 'two truths'. From the beginning, Gandhi saw a connection between them, which he indicated in the affirmation: 'God is Truth.' In 1929 Gandhi's maturing insight led him to reverse the equation and say, 'Truth is God.' For Gandhi, this solved a philosophical problem which exercised a number of his correspondents. While he frequently admitted that the existence of God cannot be proved, he insisted that the existence of Truth is shown even in the act of questioning it. Never mind that the existence of truths does not prove the existence of Absolute Truth. Specific instances can never prove a general principle, but they do lend weight to it. Since many people cannot honestly claim to see God about them, yet can recognize truth everywhere, reversing the equation instantly lends the credibility of the possibility of Absolute Truth to the possibility of God. More important, however, linking the idea of 'two gods' to that of 'two truths' suggests that relative conceptions of God mirror something of Deity Itself. 'God is not a person.'[7] 'Man is a person, God is not in the same sense ... Our difficulty arises through our effort to measure God by our little selves. And he eludes all measure.'[8] Even so, Gandhi felt a deep joy in singing the praises of Krishna and Rama, and honored Allah and Ormazd alike. The god of one's understanding, like relative truth, has something of Deity in it. 'He is a personal God to those who need His personal presence. He is embodied to those who need his touch. He is the purest essence. He simply Is to those who have faith. He is all things to all men.'[9] In the language of the Gospel, 'The Word was with God and the Word was God'.

Thirdly, Gandhi clearly distinguished between reason and experience, the head and the heart. Again like Plato, he was convinced that reason is essential to human evolution, but that it is a tool and not the agent. Without experience imbued with fundamental ethics, reason is cold and can become twisted. But without reason, experience, even ethically suffused experience, is blind and without purpose. For Gandhi, ultimate values are not matters of reason, although ways of embodying them in particular circumstances must involve reasoning. 'You may have faith in the principles which I lay down', he advised, 'but conclusions which I draw from certain facts cannot be a matter of faith.'[10] Just as he warned young people not to confuse feelings with conscience, since conscience was the result of tremendous self-examination and *tapas* (self-suffering), so one could not claim to have real experience if one's powers of thought were not awakened. Reason judges the application of principle; it can also lay the groundwork for faith, which can lead to spiritual experience:

> Reason may be a useful instrument of knowledge at one stage. But anybody who stops there will never enjoy the benefits of true spiritual knowledge ... God or the *atman* is not an object of knowledge. He Himself is the Knower. That is why we say that He is above reason. There are two stages of knowledge of God. The first is faith, and the second and the last is first-hand experience to which faith leads.[11]

One cannot prove the existence of the Divine nor describe it, but one can experience it.

These three convictions are utterly fundamental to Gandhi's life and thought. He takes them together in his letters and discourses, sometimes treating them as if they were interchangeable. The first two regarding Truth and God lay the groundwork and give direction to his thought and aspirations, and the third concerning reason, faith and experience provides the prerequisites for knowledge and effective action. Only faith which leads to spiritual experience yields that penetrating insight which Gandhi called knowledge of God. Faith, which can never be proved through reason, is nonetheless supported by it. Like conscience, faith cannot be claimed lightly and without strenuous efforts to cultivate it. One's faith, however conceived, is invariably faith in Truth. Just as we cannot pretend to ourselves that what our profoundest experience shows us to be truth is false, so we cannot expect others who see truth differently from ourselves to do so. The irreversibility of true faith and the recognition of it in others entails that 'We should not harm others for what we regard as Truth or right. We should be prepared to die for Truth and when the call comes give our life for it and sanctify it with our blood. This in my view is the essence of all religions.'[12] Unshakeable faith requires reason for its support, never for its justification. Reason under the illumination of faith, the head guided by the heart, allows a discerning interpretation of one's experience.

Intuitions, visions and inner certitude, like dreams, require cool assessment. An insight can be authentic and spiritual, but if it is forced into a prisonhouse of preconception, it will be enervated if not twisted into a grotesque parody of itself. Thus dogmatists, conventionalists and those bound by custom undermine and erode their faith by subjecting it to limiting interpretations and narrow categories. But one who clings to some belief out of fear – fear of death, change, loss of identity, role or whatever – corrupts the fruition of faith. A dream may be intense with meaning, yet if it is subjected to a mechanical Freudian interpretation or is forced into Jungian archetypes, subtle and open-textured significance may be lost and the whole distorted. Modes of interpretation should be rooted in faith and applied by reason. Skeptics who apply interpretive principles without faith contribute little to religious understanding.

The cultivation of the faith which may lead to spiritual insight necessitates preparation. To this end, Gandhi established a variety of observances in his ashrams. Designed to deepen faith and quicken application of principle, they also prepared one to understand insights and to become truly religious. Late in life, Gandhi set out eleven vows: nonviolence (*ahimsa*), which applied to thought and feeling as well as word and deed; truth (*satya*); nonstealing (*asteya*), which included misappropriation, negligence and unnecessary use of objects and resources; *brahmacharya*, celibacy in the broadest sense of self-restraint and purity in all things; non-possession (*aparigraha*), which included persons and relationships; body-labor; control of the palate; fearlessness on all occasions; equal respect for all religions (once called 'tolerance'); *swadeshi* or self-reliance in the fullest sense of the word; and *sparshabhavana* or the refusal to recognize untouchability in theory or practice.[13] The ashram was, for Gandhi, an arena for self-testing, but the observance of vows was not limited to ashram life; they would have to be taken up by anyone earnestly seeking wisdom. Much earlier, Gandhi enumerated five conditions necessary 'to approach a study of religion', which are the first five *yamas* of the eleven vows just given.[14] In this list, Gandhi placed brahmacharya first and translated ahimsa as 'absolute innocence'. If these are taken as the conditions for assimilation of one's own religion, it is clear that the ground rules laid down by scholars and historians of religion for interreligious dialogue not only fall short of what is needed but are almost irrelevant. They may provide for tolerance amongst religions, but that passive condition is insufficient for equal respect between them.

The preparation Gandhi insisted upon as a devotee of Truth was endorsed by experiments in his own life. The findings he commended to his audience, however, were not to be accepted simply because he had arrived at them, nor even because he had aspired ardently and labored sincerely to do so. His sympathetic listeners had to test them for themselves, and they could not do so without the determination and perseverance enjoined by the yamas. He held that his own experience had been repeatedly tested and verified by others who gave their lives for Truth. In the scriptures and *shastras* they left, they said:

> 'We cannot deliver the truth to you.' It is incapable of being delivered through writings, it is incapable of being delivered with the lips, it is capable of being delivered only through life. It transcends reason. But it is not past experience. So they said: 'We tell you that such and such is the fact, but you will have to test it for yourselves. You will apply your reason, we do not want you to deaden your reason, but you yourselves, even as we, will come to the conclusion that reason which God has given is after all a limited thing, and that which is a limited thing will not be able to reach the limitless. Therefore, go through these preliminary conditions ... Observe them and then you will find that what we tell you with our own experience will also be yours.'[15]

Self-validating inner experience is possible because every creature mirrors something of Truth which is God in the very fact of its existence, and man, being self-conscious, is capable of recognizing that Truth, reflecting upon it, nurturing it and making it grow. The 'two truths' doctrine gives everything purpose, a divine but non-utilitarian function which for man becomes the *dharma* or duty to realize God in his thought and life. All knowledge is referred to self-knowledge, which, in its pure form unstained by truncated concepts and involuted ideas of identity, is ultimately equivalent to knowledge of God. Preconceptions, fears, and identification with limited notions of oneself as a separate being block such knowledge, and this is why Gandhi insisted that an individual who would gain knowledge must reduce himself to a cipher. This radical reduction is not easy and cannot be accomplished suddenly, but vows and observance, when kept, will eventually lead to it. In the words of Professor Raghavan Iyer:

> The advantage of vows lies . . . in the fact that acts which are not possible by ordinary self-denial become possible with the aid of vows which require extraordinary self-denial. Vows are both a recognition of the fickleness of human nature and an additional aid to even the strongest of minds . . . Vows are thus a sign of the fullness, intensity and authenticity of personal commitment to chosen ideals and social ends.[16]

Gandhi's view of life, human nature and the possibility of progress affected and was conditioned by his religious universalism. He rejected weak doctrines of universalism which claim that all religions are one at the cost of betraying their significance. He was convinced that religious unity within and amongst faiths could be achieved only be intensifying one's religious sense.

> We must believe in God if we believe in ourselves . . . The denial of God is injurious in the same way as denial of ourselves. That is to say, to deny God is like committing suicide . . . I can live only by having faith in God. My definition of God must always be kept in mind. For me there is no other God than Truth; Truth is God.[17]

Statements in this vein imply that belief in God is not a matter of conviction arrived at through the exercise of reason; rather it is bound up with a precise conception of what it is to be a human being, and this conception is not simply logical but the result of seeking the kind of experience he advocated. Gandhi did not think that identification with a religious tradition prevented one from appreciating other religions, but *how* one identifies with a religion is critical. It places on one the willingly accepted obligation to engage in that self-examination and encounter with the Divine that enhances one's appreciation of all religions. 'My religion is Hinduism', he often said, 'which, for me, is the religion of humanity and includes the best of all the religions known to me.'[18] Gandhi fearlessly penetrated to the heart of his religion and was delighted to find in it the heart of every other religion as well.

Gandhi could make this discovery without engaging in reductionism because he did not equate religion with externals of any kind – traditions, customs, rituals, scriptures, organizations or structures. The distinction between Absolute Truth and relative truth finds its parallel in religion. Religion can be thought of in ideal terms, in which its revelatory force is embodied in spiritual teachers of supreme purity; the message, sent into a world unscarred by history, would awaken men and women to selfless service and harmonize them in a realized universal brotherhood. Religion must also be considered in a historical context, a radiation of spiritual truth imperfectly interpreted by well-meaning yet imperfect men, handed down by teachers who could not claim spotless purity and followed by individuals who are not free from the flaws of custom, prejudice and conditioned reaction. The great religions of the world should not be rejected in favor of irreligion, which confuses basic awareness of right and wrong and offers neither values nor purpose, but they should be ceaselessly re-examined and purifed, just as relative truths must be critically searched for the fuller Truth they veil.

For Gandhi, the gap between the ideal nature and actual condition of religion compels anyone committed to religious unity to investigate critically all aspects of one's religion in exactly the spirit which would make examination of other religions valuable, and to conduct such examination within oneself, not against others. Purification of religion cannot occur independently of purification of individuals, and that has to be done each for himself. While Gandhi never claimed adeptness in self-examination or scholarship in the investigation of religions, the sincerity, consistency and constancy of his concerns gave him the moral authority to uphold his idea of the equality of religions and to encourage others to be more serious about their own religions. Declaring that 'The time has now passed when the followers of one religion can stand and say, ours is the only true religion and all others are false',[19] he added, 'We must not, like the frog in the well who imagines that the universe ends with the wall surrounding his well, think that our religion alone represents the whole Truth and all the others are false. A recent study of the other religions of the world would show that they are equally true as our own, though all are necessarily imperfect.'[20]

Interreligious understanding requires a tolerance grounded in one's own being and tradition. 'I do not think', Gandhi wrote to a friend, 'that it is necessary to forget one's own faith in order to be tolerant towards the rest. In fact, tolerance loses its value when one's own faith is forgotten.'[21] When speaking with members of the Council of International Federation, Gandhi provided a criterion of true tolerance: 'If we do not feel for other religions as we feel for our own, we had better disband ourselves, for we do not want a wishy-washy toleration.'[22] Although Gandhi disclaimed knowledge of all major religions and declined to speak for minor sects, he refused to escape religious exclusiveness by the expedient of widening the circle of self-arrogated superiority. 'I have no feeling that from a spiritual standpoint I am necessarily superior to the so-called savage. And spiritual superiority is a dangerous thing to feel.'[23]

> I have come to the conclusion, in my own experience, that those who, no matter to what faith they belong, reverently study the teaching of other faiths broaden their own, instead of slackening their hearts.[24]

Gandhi eventually made this conclusion a principle in his conception of religious education.[25]

Growth in authentic interreligious understanding requires recognition of the logical corollaries which follow from respect for all religions. First of all, just as one cannot respectfully approach another religion from the standpoint of superiority, so one cannot harbor the intent to convert others under the guise of dialogue amongst equals. 'I disbelieve in the conversion of one person by another. My effort should never be to undermine another's faith but to make him a better follower of his own faith.'[26] Although honest conversions are possible, they come, like all spiritual insight, from within, and Gandhi refused even to pray in secret for the conversion of another.[27] Secondly, respect for all religions shows that

> ... it is impossible to estimate the merits of the various religions of the world, and moreover I believe that it is unnecessary and harmful even to attempt it. But each one of them, in my judgment, embodies a common motivating force: the desire to uplift man's life and give it purpose.[28]

Appreciation does not entail judgmentalism, and because of their common motivating force it is possible, thirdly, to adopt whatever satisfies one from all the religions.[29] When satya or Truth is taken as a pure ideal, its expression is ahimsa, nonviolence, although the two can be seen as one from a different perspective. 'To me religion means truth and *ahimsa*', Gandhi wrote, 'or rather truth alone, because truth includes *ahimsa, ahimsa* being the necessary and indispensable means for its discovery.'[30]

By factoring religious beliefs into a few fundamental principles of faith and emphasizing the need for self-purification, tapas and perseverance, Gandhi made ethics central to religion. He no more reduced religion to ethics than he reduced Truth to nonviolence, but as in the relationship between ahimsa and satya, ethics becomes the means for discovering, expressing and living religion, which is Truth. Beliefs and practices vary tremendously within major religious traditions, and they may be alien to the point of incomprehensibility between them. Nonetheless, Gandhi discerned in all the religions he encountered that ethics – moral commitment to a moral life – remained remarkably constant within and across religions. For him, this showed more certainly than any argument or analysis that all religions are at root one. And so he found nothing difficult in saying, 'I think I am as much a Christian, a Sikh and a Jain as I am a Hindu.'[31] Ethical commonality provides a foundation for a fraternal communion that can lead to spiritual union.

Gandhi freely criticized the tyranny of custom and the confusion of religion with convention. His sustained attack on untouchability is famous. But he was equally open in his criticisms of the shortcomings found in the interpretation and practice of other religions. He told Christian missionaries that 'there should be less of theology and more of truth in all that you say and do'.[32] 'You all read the Koran', he told Muslims, 'but how few put into practice what you read?'[33] He praised the spiritual and moral tone of Sikh scriptures and stated his belief that Sikhism is a reformation of Hinduism and not distinct from it.[34] He made statements in this vein about Zoroastrianism and Buddhism, Judaism and Jainism. His prerogative to do so was not based upon claims of scholarship, subscription to particular beliefs or practice of specific rituals. Rather, he spoke with authority about religions because he approached them with reverence and a willingness to learn from them, he honored the words of their founders in his life; and he strove for the practical realization of universal brotherhood.

Perhaps historians, philosophers and sociologists encountered problems in attempting to understand Gandhi's standpoint; the great stream of humanity, the 'masses', did not. They did not consult him on details of religious belief or practice – they asked him *how* to live the religious life. Regardless of their religions, Gandhi answered all of them in the same way. Just as the rose imparts its fragrance to those who can smell, so the religious life imparts its transforming force to those with spiritual sight.[35] One demonstrates the sublimity of a religion by living it. Adherents of the different religions accepted him as their own because they sensed and understood that he had assimilated the quintessence of their traditions and that they could learn from him without being urged to become something else. In undertaking whole-heartedly the disciplines necessary to be worthy of a great religious heritage, he lived the spiritual life, and in living it he lived their religion, whatever its name. His own experiments with Truth confirmed their innermost longings for self-transcendence.

The secret of Gandhi's religious universalism lies in its simplicity. His eye for essentials and his purity of thought uncovered principles which were simple because fundamental. In matters of religion, he was more of an alchemist than a chemist. The chemist is concerned with the composition and structural interconnections of elemental substances; the alchemist seeks the *prima materia*, the root from which all elements arise. Just as the alchemist uses the chemist's equipment, so Gandhi imbued the chemistry of politics with the alchemy of religion. For most individuals, the eye is conditioned to complexity and thought is bound by preconceptions, and therefore simplicity is hard to discern and to separate from simple-mindedness. Gandhi's secret lay in the fact that he was simpler than most people, but his simplicity was not that of the untested child or the simplistic adult: it was the product of a conscious endeavor to become and remain simple at heart and in habit. The chemistry of the head and alchemy of the heart must become one science. The aim of life is to simplify, and simplicity is the beginning of wisdom.

One might think that Gandhi had little to say to the historian of religion, the scholar or philosopher, or the anthropologist or sociologist. He could appreciate their work and even be grateful to them for a few insights, but he found much intellectual effort irrelevant when placed against his universal measure – is the work for *lokasangraha*, the uplift of the whole? Yet when he urged students to study all religions, he gave an invaluable suggestion to all those who are concerned with interfaith understanding and interreligious dialogue:

> There is one rule ... which should always be kept in mind while studying all great religions and that is that one should study them only through the writings of known votaries of the respective religions. For instance, if one wants to study the *Bhagavata* one should do so not through a translation of it made by a hostile critic but through one prepared by a lover of the *Bhagavata*. Similarly to study the Bible one should study it through the commentaries of devoted Christians. This study of other religions besides one's own will give one a grasp of the rock-bottom unity of all religions and afford a glimpse also of that universal and absolute truth which lies beyond the 'dust of creeds and faith'.[36]

Men and women today, and especially those who believe that religion is essential in human life, can draw a lesson from this. In respect of our own religion as well as the religions of others, have we undertaken the preparation necessary to genuine inquiry? Have we consistently sought to live our religion? Put another way, do we have the moral and spiritual integrity which are prerequisites to claiming to have a view in these matters? Are we more devoted to mastering scholarly and intellectual paraphernalia than to performing Gandhian experiments with Truth? To what are we devoted? Are we seekers of Truth or skeptics prowling for meaning in a devalued world? Do we examine ourselves for prejudices, preconceptions and stifling categories, or do we work to reinforce them? In sum: can we emulate Gandhi in unconditional commitment to an ideal, knowing in advance that every expression of it will be imperfect?

These questions push the intrepid inquirer back toward fundamentals. Whether or not the discoveries made at the heart of religion and of humanity will be put in Gandhian terms did not concern him. His lifelong aspiration was not that humanity should accept his formulations but that it should reach Truth. To the degree that human beings strive to do that, religious conflict, mutual suspicion and manipulation, misunderstanding and irreligion masquerading as religion will diminish in scope and seductive power.

Gandhi was less interested in a wistfully held universalism that envisaged a vague synthetic religion for all human beings than in a fearless universalism built on an honest recognition of the sanctity of every human effort to come to terms with ultimate reality (*sat*).

The need of the moment is not one religion, but mutual respect and tolerance of the devotees of the different religions. We want to reach not the dead level, but unity of diversity ... Wise men will ignore the outward crust and see the same soul living under a variety of crusts ... Truth is the exclusive property of no single scripture.[37]

When fundamental affirmations like these irreversibly affect our thinking, we will be prepared for the disciplined experiments Gandhi taught as essential to faith and spiritual knowledge. We will no longer dither over our beliefs, worry about conversion or wonder whether Jesus or Krishna or Allah has a place in our hearts.

If you will do the proper scavenger's work, clean and purify your hearts and get them ready, you will find that all these mighty teachers will take their places without invitation from us.[38]

Notes

1. 'Speech at Buddha Birth Anniversary', delivered at the Buddha Vihara, sponsored by the Mahabodhi Society), *Amrita Bazar Patrika*, May 9 1925; *CWMG*, vol. xxvii, no. 23, pp. 61–2.
2. Ecumenism suffers chronically from a tendency to high-flown affirmations coupled with paralysis in practice. Interreligious dialogue – known by many names – has advanced warily in contrast to Gandhi's robust universalism. Raimundo Panikkar and Ninian Smart have outlined ambitious modes for interreligious understanding, though from quite different perspectives. Richard Henry Drummond attempted a sympathetic Christian understanding of Buddhism in *Gautama the Buddha* (Grand Rapids: Eerdmans, 1974), but his effort is subtly undermined by scholarly assumptions endemic to the history of religions. It is not clear whether a treatment of Jesus by him would encounter the same difficulties. Recently, Leonard Swidler has attempted to articulate the basis of authentic interreligious dialogue in 'The Dialogue Decalogue: Ground Rules for Interreligious Dialogue', *Journal of Dharma*, vol. viii, no. 3 1983, pp. 311–15. Swidler's 'Tenth Commandment' is 'Each participant must attempt to experience the partner's religion "From within".' Gandhi would no doubt point out that everything hangs on the last two

words. What does 'from within' mean? The level of understanding of another's religion which one can achieve depends upon the level one has achieved in one's own religion. An excellent discussion of the problem and prospects for genuine dialogue between Christians and Marxists (and applicable in broader contexts) can be found in Raghavan Iyer's '*Civitas Dei* and the Classless Society', in *Parapolitics – Toward the City of Man*, (New York: Oxford University Press, 1979).

3. 'God is One', *Young India*, September 25 1924; *CWMG*, vol. xxv, no. 130, p. 178.
4. 'Letter to Bhuskute', *Mahadevbhaini Diary*, vol. 1, p. 364; *CWMG*, vol. L, no. 387, p. 376.
5. This sense of truth is often sought after in contemporary parlance in queries such as 'Where are you coming from?', which ask for one's perspective or frame of reference as well as the historical and psychological experience associated with it. Such questions suggest that a perspective is a stage in a journey, unique for each individual – a subtlety Gandhi would have appreciated.
6. 'Letter to Bhuskute', p. 377.
7. 'Note to Gope Gurbuxani', March 9 1945; *CWMG*, vol. LXXIX, no. 381, p. 228.
8. 'Letter to P. G. Mathew', September 26 1930; *CWMG*, vol. XLIV, no. 242, p. 169.
9. 'God and Congress', *Young India*, March 5 1925; *CWMG*, vol. XXVI, no. 132, p. 224.
10. 'Letter to Mathuradas', *CWMG*, vol. XXXVIII, pp. 216–17.
11. 'Letter to Ibrahimji Rajkotwala', *Mahadevbhaini Diary*, vol. I, pp. 136–7; *CWMG*, vol. XLIX, no. 491, p. 399.
12. 'A Christmas Message', *CWMG*, vol. LXXVIII, no. 556, p. 389.
13. See, for example, 'Letter to Mahadevshastri Divekar', November 1 1945; *CWMG*, vol. LXXXII, no 7, p. 4. Here Gandhi lists the eleven vows which were recited in the daily prayers.
14. 'Speech at Young Men's Buddhist Association, Colombo', *Young India*, December 8 1927; *CWMG*, vol. XXXV, no. 210, p. 311.
15. Ibid., p. 312.
16. Raghavan Iyer, *The Moral and Political Thought of Mahatma Gandhi*, 2nd edn (Santa Barbara: Concord Grove Press, 1983) pp. 74–5. This fundamental and revolutionary work has been indispensable in exploring the depths and ramifications of Gandhian thought.
17. 'Letter to Hanumanprassad Poddar', *Mahadevbhaini Diary*, vol. 1, p. 82; *CWMG*, vol. XLIX, no. 345, pp. 284–5.
18. 'Questions and Answers', in Sir S. Radhakrishan, *Contemporary Indian Philosophy* (London: G. Allen & Unwin, 1952) p. 21; *CWMG*, vol. LX, no. 123, p. 106.
19. 'The World's Religion', *Indian Opinion*, August 26 1905; *CWMG*, vol. V, no. 69, p. 49.
20. 'Foreword to *The Persian Mystics*'; *CWMG*, vol. LXVII, no. 35, p. 24.
21. 'Letter to S. V. Venkatanarasayyam', April 1 1926; *CWMG*, vol. XXX, no. 243, p. 216.

22. 'Discussion on Fellowship', *Young India*, January 19 1928; *CWMG*, vol. xxxv, no. 351, p. 461.
23. 'Difference Stated', *Young India*, March 22 1928; *CWMG*, vol. xxxvi, no. 157, p. 137.
24. 'Speech at Central College, Jaffna', *The Hindu*, December 2 1927; *CWMG*, vol. xxxv, no. 229, p. 343.
25. See 'Religious Education', *Young India*, December 6 1928; *CWMG*, vol xxxvii, no. 296, pp. 254–5.
26. 'Interview to Dr. John Mott', *Young India*, March 21 1929; *CWMG*, vol. xl, no. 61, p. 60.
27. 'Discussion on Fellowship', p. 462.
28. 'What Jesus Means to Me', *Modern Review*, October 1941; *CWMG*, vol. lxxv, no. 97, p. 70.
29. 'Letter to Kasamali', June 13 1926; *CWMG*, vol. xxx, no. 690.
30. 'Religious Education', p. 254.
31. 'Speech at Prayer Meeting', *Hindustan*, September 8 1946; *CWMG*, vol. lxxxv, no. 332, p. 328.
32. 'Discussion with Christian Missionaries', March 12 1940; *CWMG*, vol. lxxi, no. 326, p. 328.
33. 'Speech at Meeting to Commemorate the Prophet's Death', *The Hindu*, June 29 1934; *CWMG*, vol. lviii, no. 116, p. 99.
34. 'Sikhism', *Young India*, October 1 1925; *CWMG*, vol. xxviii, no. 153, p. 263.
35. See 'Discussion on Fellowship', p. 463, and 'Difference Stated', p. 136.
36. 'Religious Education', p. 255. Elsewhere, Gandhi translated this conviction into concrete terms.

> Churches, mosques and temples, which cover so much hypocrisy and humbug and shut the poorest out of them, seem but a mockery of God and His worship, when one sees the eternally renewed temple of worship under the vast blue canopy inviting every one of us to real worship, instead of abusing His name by quarrelling in the name of religion.'

('God's Temple', *Young India*, December 8 1927; *CWMG*, vol. xxv, no. 249, p. 368.)
37. 'God Is One', pp. 179–80.
38. 'Speech at Central College, Jaffna', p. 343.

Part III
Gandhi on Politics and Economics

Introduction to Part III
Lamont C. Hempel

We live in a time of wrenching economic dislocations, widespread political upheaval and, paradoxically, unprecedented human potential for improvement. The tides of technological progress seem to sweep us simultaneously toward higher hopes and deeper fears, while the moral progress that Gandhi championed seems to recede into the shadows of his fame. Although today's world is perhaps no more violent than it was in Gandhi's time, the nature of that violence, amplified through technology, is far more sinister. A dozen or more nations will soon have the capacity to engage in pushbutton slaughter on a massive scale. Even India and Pakistan appear bent on joining the nuclear arms race. As a consequence, the international peace that Gandhi dreamed of seems less attainable now than in the cautiously optimistic, hope-filled days following World War II and Indian Independence.

Shortly before the development of the atomic bomb, Gandhi wrote:

> One thing is certain. If the mad race for armaments continues, it is bound to result in a slaughter such as has never occurred in history. If there is a victor left the very victory will be a living death for the nation that emerges victorious. There is no escape from the impending doom save through a bold and unconditional acceptance of the non-violent method ...

Putting an end to the arms race, Gandhi noted, meant putting an end to the spirit of exploitation gripping material civilization. The very essence of his political and economic thought seems to be embedded in the courageous expression of nonviolent noncooperation with all forms of authority engaged in exploitation of the weak and afflicted. Ending this exploitation involves not only a renunciation of greed and coercion, but also the creation of an economy that ceases, in Gandhi's words, 'to multiply wants'. The socially engineered creation of needs and desires for material things was perhaps the most insidious form of exploitation in Gandhi's eyes. He believed that the world's supply of resources was sufficient to meet all basic human needs, provided that the ideal of nonpossession was widely embraced and that a system of trusteeship was established to help with redistribution. In the absence of these conditions, economic development became just another form of exploitation or violence.

Gandhi sought to destroy systems of exploitation, not persons. His politics and economics were thus oriented to the problems of structural violence and industrial development in the modern nation state. Achieving development without destruction – progress without poverty – required the building of a new social order. In Gandhi's view, such an order had to begin in the heart of the individual where the goals of personal and political self-rule became one. It could then develop socially in what he called a 'constructive program' – a massive, grassroots movement of voluntary service to improve human relations and the quality of life. Combined with political action, in the form of nonviolent resistance directed against the established order, the constructive program was to provide the social 'glue' needed for peaceful revolution.

The Gandhian political and economic system, though experimental and focused on India, was designed to facilitate this process universally. No doubt the influence of Tolstoy, Thoreau and John Ruskin helped to shape Gandhi's thinking in these matters, but his synthesis of their ideas and his personification of their meaning would have been reason enough to grant him a prominent place in history. Gandhi's unique contribution is that he went beyond the ideas, and even their application, to inspire a shared vision of a nonviolent, socially just and democratic world order – one that anticipated in both spirit and scope the World Council of Churches' recently proclaimed goal of a 'just, sustainable, and participatory society'.

Gandhi's antipathy toward industrial society was manifested by what many would call his romantic notion of a village culture based on 'bread labor' and an agrarian or craft economy. The squalid character of rural life in India did not dissuade him from pursuing such a notion. As the late Sugata Dasgupta suggests in his essay, 'The Core of Gandhi's Social and Economic Thought', poverty was Gandhi's only wealth. India's two million villages and encampments provided laboratories where Gandhi could carry out his experiments with Truth on a human scale; places where the goals of self-sufficiency and *sarvodaya* – the uplift (welfare) of all – could be impressed upon those in greatest need. Industrial society, in contrast, offered only pampered affluence and what Gandhi described in terms of seven deadly sins: 'politics without principles, wealth without work, pleasure without conscience, knowledge without character, commerce without morality, worship without sacrifice, and science and technology without humanity'.

For a Westerner, there is something quaint, perhaps anachronistic, about all of this, especially in an age of space shuttles and instant global communication. To the beneficiaries of industrial growth, Gandhi's views must seem utterly out of step with reality. But as Dasgupta points out in his essay, the industrialized world's understanding of Gandhi is severely hampered by an inability – both moral and cultural – to identify with the human tragedies and privations in which Gandhi immersed himself. The heroic image that we extract is that of the moral cowboy or David confronting Goliath, not the frail, half-naked little man who placed his hands on the wounds of a leper.

Regardless of which image of Gandhi we choose to emphasize, the man and his message cannot be separated from the impoverished masses and victims of discrimination with whom he identified. Though his politics and economics were far from complete and never systematically developed, Gandhi's ongoing contribution to human liberation, particularly among the weak and disadvantaged, exceeds almost anything that development economists and modern political leaders have conceived. As Thomas Kilgore, Jr. shows in his essay, 'The Influence of Gandhi on Martin Luther King', the civil rights movement in America owes a deep debt of gratitude to Gandhi. Sushila Gidwani makes a similar point about the movement for women's liberation in her essay on 'Gandhian Feminism'.

From all of this it would appear that Gandhi's contribution to humanity is still unfolding through the various movements and ideas that his example has helped to spawn or at least influence. Evidence that Gandhi's message is continuing to evolve and to find new forms of expression is presented by each of the contributors to Part III. Geoffrey Ostergaard, for example, in an analysis of developments in Gandhi's constructive program and Sarvodaya campaign ('The Gandhian Movement in India Since The Death of

Gandhi'), shows how India's Sarva Seva Sangh and other Gandhian organizations have, despite factional differences and political setbacks, carried on Gandhi's quest for the emancipation of peasants from the despotic conditions of village life.

Ashis Nandy, the final contributor to this volume, calls for yet another form of Gandhian liberation – the liberation from Western-style secularism. His essay, 'An Anti-Secularist Manifesto', examines the post-Gandhian politics of religious and ethnic tolerance. Nandy shows how official secularism in India has robbed religion, culture and ethnicity of their vital roles. In the process, he provides yet another glimpse of the unbreakable link between Gandhi's religion (Part II) and his politics (Part III).

If all of these authors are correct, Gandhi's presence is still with us; a latent imprint, perhaps, but nevertheless forceful. The legacy we take from him is a developing one, not some time-bound bequest left over from the first half of the twentieth century. It is elusive, in part, because it is dynamic. The essence of Gandhi's message is not easily captured by those of us who have only his disjointed and sometimes inconsistent writings to rely on for insights. Nor can we be certain that changing times have not eroded the efficacy of his methods. To the extent that our memory of Gandhi seems dimmed by the specters of nuclear war, terrorism or starving children, there is reason to question the power of his legacy. But if the world has not turned out to be a safer place because of Gandhi, it has at least been treated to a higher standard of human decency and a stirring demonstration of nonviolent revolution. That so many have chosen to ignore these developments is not, in itself, reason to discount the legacy. The popularity of Gandhi's message, or lack thereof, is not a fitting indicator of its merit. What really matters is that his message provides a strong moral basis for nonviolent politics and non-exploitative economics. From today forward, as John Hutchison noted in his remarks to The Claremont Graduate School's 1984 Colloquium on Gandhi, 'We do our ethical thinking with Gandhi looking over our shoulders.'

12

The Core of Gandhi's Social and Economic Thought

Sugata Dasgupta

There is enough in this world for everybody's need: there isn't enough in this world for anybody's greed.

M. K. Gandhi

There has, of late, been a plethora of writings on Gandhi by social scientists, historians, political commentators, and journalists. Even the media-men have now turned the searchlight on Gandhi. It is indeed amazing to find today how little writing there was on Gandhi up to only a few years ago.[1] The priorities of social commentators were then fixed elsewhere. They were on anomie, social pathology, prostitution, crime, alcoholism, the expanse of industrial culture, the emergence of the urban megalopolis and on reaching the moon. The focus of academic studies was seldom on violence and certainly not on nonviolence.

Today, when suddenly there is a spurt of writing about Gandhi, our mind goes back to the abortive period. Gandhi, so near to us, had moved so far away. Rejected by a generation of modern thinkers as a reactionary representative of an antique culture, Gandhi has now finally emerged as a one-man peace brigade who might yet succeed,[2] one fondly hopes, in stemming the dangers of total violence, both of society and of the protests against it.[3] How ruthlessly we dared to ignore his momentous message. He finally had to write it with his own blood, saying out of utter exasperation, 'I shall speak to you, I shall speak to you from my grave.'

But now that Gandhi has become the focus of so much attention, the question arises: why? Why did Gandhi become a forgotten figure then, when his memory was so fresh and alive? And why has he become a subject of contemporary discussion now, when his memory seems blurred?

THE RIGHT TO WRITE

The reason for having very limited writings on Gandhi is easy to understand. Writings on the subject of personalia sociology[4] or political psychology, or whatever one may use to denote the new theme, require four important insights.

First, A writer must necessarily have a deep contextual acquaintance with the area of his or her concern.[5] While writing on Gandhi an author should have a comprehensive knowledge of the various actions that Gandhi took from time to time and under different circumstances.

Second, The terms that Gandhi used such as nonviolence, violence, development, *khadi*, *Samagra Gram Seva*, were all used with specific conceptual connotations which were as alien to the emerging social sciences of the late nineteenth century as they are today in the late twentieth century.[6]

Third, Gandhi's writings were more intuitively analytical than descriptively empirical. While the tools that are required for intuitive analysis are perspectives and visions of a new society, the other set of tools, in great demand by conventional social scientists, are useful only in the study of their intimate acquaintance with the so-called structures and functions of the outercrusts of past and present society.

Finally, there was one other block that prevented many social commentators from writing about Gandhi. It was the absence of a necessary tool of analysis without which studies of political psychology can never receive penetrating treatment. Empathy, if not absolute sympathy with the subject of one's study, provides the best method for understanding it. Several examples will bear testimony to the point.

First there is the story of a pious Muslim who had vast prejudices against the Hindus but had yet wanted to write a book about Hinduism. The pious man went to his Guru, himself a Muslim, seeking the latter's advice about his own desire to write on the life and religion of the Hindus. The Guru agreed to the proposal but imposed a condition on his disciple. It was that the writer would spend a year's time dressed as a Hindu and living all the rituals of the Hindu civilization to gain first-hand knowledge about his theme before he would settle down and write. The writer, after undergoing the test, wrote a piece which was very different from what he had originally intended to write.

Neither can one forget, in this context, the story of John Howard Griffin, a white man who changed his pigment to become black in order to undergo all the vicissitudes of the life of the subject about which he was to write.[7] Such are the prior preparations that endow one with the claim or right to specialize in a subject.

The actor Ben Kingsley, before portraying Gandhi in the motion picture, had apparently taken all of Gandhi's vows.[8] And, as the first prerequisite for study, hundreds of Australians investigating the history of Gandhi's *Dandimardh* have walked the entire distance that Gandhi walked in 1930.[9]

The point that I wish to make, in this regard, is simply that a study of Gandhi in terms of detached, theoretical analysis can only provide a very inadequate treatment of the subject. One can never fully study Gandhi unless the writer comes to know by first-hand experience of the struggles, aspirations and privations that made Gandhi the special person that he became. Some of the baptizing incidents need to be recorded in a writer's own psyche. For Gandhi did not become the Mahatma the day he was born. Neither did he arrive in the world with a *charka* in his hand. He became the Gandhi we know only after he was beaten and left as dead in Pretoria. Hunger, forced marches and thirsts brought out the best in him. He became Mahatma Gandhi only when he had stuck his fingers deep into the wounds of a leprosy patient. He was profoundly influenced by the constructive work that he did in rural areas of India, by his *Go-seva* movement, his getting lost in the village of Sevagram, and by confrontations with the hungry peasants in his day-to-day social work. One cannot adequately write on Gandhi without having participated in at least some of his lifelong struggles.

An intellectual who thinks that he can write on this subject without becoming a part of the subject would be rebuked by no less a person than Gandhi himself. Dr Radhakamal Mukherjee, known in India as the father of social sciences, had, it seems, engaged himself in a study of the working conditions of industrial labor in India. He had come to see Gandhi with this news at a time when Gandhi was extremely busy with the affairs of the nation. Yet Gandhi cancelled all his appointments and came out of his office eagerly to wait on the scientist.[10] His hope was that Dr Mukherjee was living among the laborers and collecting data all by himself. Gandhi quickly turned his back, sorely disappointed, calling off the interview as soon as he found out that Dr Mukherjee did not live in the slums but had collected all his data from investigators appointed by him.

It thus requires both personal and moral preparation to write about Gandhi. A total commitment to the liberation of the poor, the weak and the afflicted is the precondition for earning this right to write. To offer less would be like writing about Christ without feeling in the writer's own palms the piercing iron that nailed Jesus down.

DEVELOPMENT AS VIOLENCE

Two conclusions emerge from this analysis. The first explains why one has to have a special *'adhikar'* or an *a priori* right to write about Gandhi and to capture a glimpse of his main message.[11] The other explains what that seemingly paradoxical message is: that wealth is the greatest handicap of a society and poverty its only wealth.

It was Gandhi's central thesis that the origins of exploitation lie in violence. In fact, violence can be equated with exploitation — exploitation of human beings by one another; of systems by human beings; of humankind by systems; of age, sex, ethnic groups; and of superpowers and competing economic forces; as well as exploitation of non-human nature by humankind. A society that eliminates such exploitation can be called a nonviolent society and the achievement of such a society provides the basic goal of Gandhian social action.

Gandhi assumed that violence and exploitation were connected in a series of fundamental and complementary ways with industrial development. Equating development with exploitation, he found in societal exploitation what could be called the first category of violence.[12] All other incidences of violence including the violence of protests and revolts were reactive violence and could, therefore, be treated as violence of the second category. A word of explanation, at this stage, may help to clarify the full significance of the statements made above.

Gandhi found that development, a product of modern civilization, was based on large industries and megatechnology. Such industrialization drew its resources from an enormous catchment of men and materials. Their outward flow from the colonial world had initially helped the developed countries to become wealthy and powerful. As examples, Gandhi cited the experiences of

England and France. They were at one time the only developed nations with big industries and large colonies propping up their growth. He was of the firm opinion that the developments that took place in these two countries were based on exploitation. The inspiration for such development came, as Gandhi saw it, from the cravings for a false standard of living which provided the mainstay of what is called a modern civilization, and which to Gandhi was a passing phase; a 'nine days wonder' as he put it. Such a civilization was based not only on megatechnology, large industry and exploitative colonies, both internal and external,[13] but also on professions of various types and well-meaning political institutions which served no real purpose.

Gandhi chose the professions of medicine and law as well as the parliamentary institutions as the main targets of his attack. He dubbed them all prostitutes and pleaded for a transfer of professional powers (skills?) to individuals, families and societies, hoping to snatch them away from the wrinkled jaws of ancient, monopolistic, professional groups which drew fresh leases on life from the tools supplied by the industrial revolution. As far as the parliament was concerned, Gandhi supported wider representation of people in a participatory democracy based not on majority rule but on consensus.[14]

If exploitation meant violence, and violence was often another name for development, then a major task for Gandhi was to reform the economic, political and professional institutions that supported destructive forms of development. The whole syndrome of violence, exploitation and development became the target of his attack.

Reduced to a simple formula, the constituents of modern civilization could be expressed as:

$$D=T+I+P+C+LD+E+V$$

where D is development, T is technology, I is industry, P is the professions, C is colonies, LD is limited democracy, E is exploitation and V is violence.

Gandhi saw the vivid profile of this civilization as he came face-to-face with the economic system that was then guiding the social norms of the Indian and the South African nations. There he came in direct confrontation with racism, imperialism, capitalism, repressive technologies, communalism, casteism and other oppressive mechanisms of several kinds. All these innovations by nationalist societies served to extend their long arms of exploitation. Above all, they created violence, societal violence, in abundance. The hard core of Gandhi's thoughts and action aimed at eliminating all such violence. Gandhi sought to eliminate the institutions of violence not by liquidating the leaders of violence, but by helping them to change the rules of their game and their norms of behavior. He had no need for enemies and refused to recognize anyone who opposed him as an enemy. Naturally he did not want to defeat an opponent, his purpose being to win him over. Indeed, Gandhi's contention was that in any struggle of nonviolence there could, in fact, never be an enemy, anywhere. For the enemy, as Gandhi saw it, was lying within each person and needed an attack by his own conscience. This was probably the point that Thomas Jefferson made, when he said that if America ever becomes weak, the seeds of collapse will sprout from within the society itself. Our erroneous reading of history has taught us to fear the powers of an outside invader whom we happily call an enemy. Gandhi's reading of history had taught him a different lesson. It helped him to turn the searchlight inward and to find that the enemy coming from outside can only be a weak contender as against the enemy that lies within.

It was for this reason that Gandhi did not want to fight hatred and cruelty with cruelty and wrath. The weapons he used were love, gentle persuasion and yet an uncompromising struggle against the cause that he wanted to remove. It was struggle that was then the very breath of his life. Struggle for the elimination of violence and for the establishment of a nonviolent society through participatory political battles and processes; these provided the main themes of his unquiet and eventful career.

Nonviolence then provided one vital element in the structure of Gandhi's thinking. The other was struggle. The *modus operandi* of struggle was nonviolence. Hence, if revolution provided the core of the structure, what Gandhi sought to introduce was a revolution in revolutions, which meant that the transformation he tried to introduce was of a fundamental nature seeking to transform the process of transformation itself.

ECONOMICS AND VIOLENCE

Gandhi wanted to change the traditional norms that guided society and to establish moral codes in place of property-serving laws that provided sanction to the society of violence. Before he died in 1948, Gandhi clearly perceived the rise of the superpowers and the eclipse of the ordinary citizens of the world. He, therefore, renewed his plea for (Hind) the attainment of Swaraj for all, which in effect meant self-rule or autonomy for the weak. The latter was meant not only for India or for Indians but for the British, French and everyone else who suffered from the hegemony of modern civilization. The main task was to make the organizations of the weak strong, everywhere, in every nation, and to link them all together through a series of oceanic circles[15] and not by government-to-government linkup.

Gandhi's concept of society was closely linked with the functions of the economic and political systems and of the economic and social man.[16] To him a study of economics could not be differentiated from a study of social and moral issues. It is for this reason that Gandhi's book *Hind Swaraj* (Ahmedabad: Navajivan, 1946) advances the plea for construction of a whole new society. Strangely enough the logic he evolves is based on a fundamental analysis of the economic system of modern civilization. His main attack in this essay was on the narrow understanding of economics so prevalent then, and now.

In the book *Economics of Permanence* by the late Dr J. C. Kumarappa, and in E. F. Schumacher's three interesting works entitled *Routes of Economic Growth*, *Guide for the Perplexed*, and *Small is Beautiful*, a strong case is made for an integrated study of the total society in which human beings live.[17] The Gandhi–Kumarappa–Schumacher continuum decisively establishes the basis for a holistic approach to economics. Schumacher called it the 'economics of nonviolence'. J. C. Kumarappa described it in terms of permanence and peace. For Gandhi, economics was part of a total social system whose goals were guided by values and morals; never by the efficiency of production, profit, technologies or salesmanship.

In a similar vein, Vinoba and Jayaprakash wished to restructure the political society from the bottom up with a new system in which economic activities were to be guided on the basis of 'incentives to goodness' instead of profit or power.

Together, these visions of a new economics helped to lead the way to a sarvodaya society. They called for the uplift of all people. For economic activities were not only to produce goods, but to ensure that those goods met basic needs and were easily available to the weakest and the poorest of human beings. Economics, if it was to be called a science at all,[18] was meant to engineer a process of social growth towards a moral order whose aim was to bring about a nonviolent and non-exploitative society.

Gandhi's economics dealt with two crucial questions: one involved the distribution of poverty among all people in an equitable manner; the other involved the total participation of consumers in the system of production, defying all specialization whatsoever.

The goal, obviously, was communization of resources and creation of a culture of nonpossession that would have no 'mine' and no 'thine'. The message of this kind of economics was that all factors of production belonged to the society at large and not only to a group, coterie or class. Jesus said that it was easier for a camel to pass through the eye of a needle than for a rich person to enter Heaven; Gandhi went even further, describing all property as theft. Any accumulation, be it of surplus production, even if it is to be ploughed back for further growth for the good of the producers, would be considered as violence or exploitation in this context. The methodology of production and the quantitative expanse of participation were the two important tenets to be considered in this regard.

Instead of encouraging sophisticated production of a variety of goods with the help of unlimited technology, Gandhi spoke of production by the masses done with the help of the simplest possible machines – production that led to the minimum displacement of labor and least accumulation of wealth. Gandhi's society of nonviolence was built on the twin crutches of distribution of work, hunger and decision-making on one hand, and of the use of nonviolent technology on the other. What does nonviolent technology mean? It means that forces of production have to draw from the organic energy produced by living beings and be labor-intensive. The insistence is not on upgrading technology or on economics of scale but on the protection of existing skills by offering a reciprocal protection to markets and the tastes of consumers so that the consumer does not usually opt for a different basket of goods than what the natural or unsophisticated systems of production create.

The function of economics, historically, was to create wealth or to secure development; its secondary aim was to eradicate the 'misery–poverty' syndrome and to fight underdevelopment. Whereas the goal of the entire productive system, today, continues to be development and the creation of wealth, the Gandhian goal remains the just distribution of poverty. Bilateral flows of wealth would constantly transfer surpluses wherever they were concentrated in order to create a society in which there would be neither rich nor poor at any point of time. This is called *antadayya*. Surplus, mother of profit, is the source of exploitation and poverty. The aim of economics, therefore, should not be the creation of wealth but the eradication of all surpluses so that what remains in the world is neither poverty nor wealth. Since production is to be consumed by the producer himself, the consumer *is* the producer.

Whereas all economic systems today depend on megatechnology, both capitalistic and socialistic, for the production of a variety of consumer goods to meet the artificially growing needs of an addicted society, the new economics insists that the creation of surplus be restricted in order to ensure that all energies or wealth of the planet are used to produce enough to fulfill the basic needs of all people.

If the political economy, defined by econometrics, is based on the axiom that human demands are insatiable and that the thirst for consumption grows with increasing satisfaction of human beings, the goal of a moral economy, as we have called it, shall be just the opposite. The axiom now is that human wants are limited and satiable. The new economics, of course, does not restrict production. Moving away from conventional notions of productivity and technology it may produce, in total, more wealth than the traditional scheme does. For example, if three multinationals using advanced technology produce enough shoes to be marketed with profit and no more, the total number of shoes will probably be far less than would be produced by the 700,000 villages of India, each person producing one pair of shoes. There will be less variety but more shoes under the new economics.

What is true of shoes shall also be true of many other items of production. The new economics will produce enough for everyone and remove all vestiges of scarcity at the point of consumption. The total quantity of wealth that it allows a few hands to compile will be limited. It shall use scarce resources not at the point of consumption but at the other end. Traditional economics creates wealth but it does not eradicate underdevelopment. The new economics will achieve that end.

It is easy to see now that the two sets of mores of economics are based on two sets of values and that they lead to two different types of social structure. One emphasizes the establishment of communitarian societies that plead for cooperation in place of competition, for stability in place of change, for satisfaction in place of aspiration and for harmony in place of conflict. The new economic system requires a new set of values, as well as a new institutional structure.

The values of economics, society and politics thus all get rolled into one. They form Gandhi's Truth, Gandhi's morals and Gandhi's religion. If any one wishes to separate his Truth from his morals and his economics from his religion the whole exercise will be self-defeating. For Gandhi never worshipped an image, nor separated politics, economics or social movements from religion. He was deeply a-religious and founded no sub-systems of faith. Neither was he an expert on economics or on society building. The poor were his goods, if he had any, and the struggle for their liberation his method of worship. The only time he entered a temple was to defile it.

The society that comprises the poor is naturally more powerful than the economy. For it is the former that has to control the latter and not *vice versa*. When the economy is destined to serve the poor, the power of decision-making, in terms of the preparation of production schedules and technological choices, will be directed at breaking down the walls of inflation and exploitative trade that perpetuate poverty among the poor nations and wealth among the rich.[19] Initially, in fact, the poorer regions may even gain if exchange rates are properly calculated to give them a slight edge over rich communities in terms of production and consumption of services. Every consumer and unit of production will then observe two tenets of economic law, one that emphasizes creation of an environment where demands for luxury goods are curtailed, and the other that ensures an increase in supply of basic goods without the boom-and-bust interventions of unregulated markets or of productivity campaigns.

The profile of the new economy should be summarized at this point. Such an economy depends neither on markets nor on centralized employment. Since the society will, in the new system, determine the goals of production, the basket of consumption will be simple, comprised only of goods that satisfy the basic needs of life.[20] Most of the goods will be produced in cottage industries and by the self-employed. Not wealth or affluence but a subsistence standard of living based on self-sufficiency is the goal of such an economy.

It is speculation, structural unemployment and the need for hunger built into the economic system that keep the traditional economy going. It is their influence more than battle cries that keep people in shackles. The new economy will travel a different path altogether. There shall be no one employed under it and no one unemployed. Fighting material addiction of the buyers, it shall replace their baskets of consumption with a healthier diet where every one will have enough to eat and no one will revel in wealth. The twin weapons of self-employment and curtailment of consumerism will rescue humankind from the psychosis of violence from which it is suffering today. It is only then that our remembrance of Gandhi will gain some meaning.

For the time being, however, the traditional economics will work hard to sustain itself. Thanks to megatechnology, laws of monopoly and specializations in productive relations, only a few – say only a thousand multinationals as we have identified them – will continue to reap most of the wealth from production. This form of production, conducted by the richest few of the richest nations of the world, can only be done with the help of two crutches: first, by the creation of artificial needs through advertisements and marketing schemes, and second, by forms of technology that facilitate large-scale concentration of economic power. The big producers can, through the opiate of consumerism and the bullets of advertisements, rob all the smaller nations of the world of their sovereignty. Just as it happens in the case of a drug addict who loses his freedom to one who controls the drug supply.

The new economics will present a different scenario. As the wealth-addiction factor is withdrawn, people, under the new dispensation, will need only what they require for survival and what can be produced by bread labor. There will then be no question of profits, surpluses, exploitation and lack of autonomy. Happy with what one has, the moral economy will restore swaraj or sovereignty or autonomy to each community or nation.

CONCLUSION

The new environs of economic change envisioned by Gandhi will eradicate unemployment and bring most exploitation and misery to a grinding halt. As the poor, represented by two million villages, assume control over the wealth of nations, the final crusade for liberation will begin. The man who died on the Cross and the one whom bullets tore into pieces will then be vindicated.

Creation of the nonviolent society, not only on a national or a global scale but in the domesticated world of cottages and villages as well, will be possible only when the traditional economy disappears. The hard core of Gandhi's message will then be heard clearly.

Yet, the listener will need to ensure that he or she records no false messages. For Gandhi's central mission seems to have been lost today for want of empathy and direct participation in the struggle for change – which alone could help a person like Gandhi of Porbunder or Jesus of Nazareth to send out their message of love, nonviolence, and struggle around the world. All in a single package.

Notes

1. The Gandhian Institute of studies at Rajghat, Varanasi, was started by the Sarvaseva Sangh in the late 1950s. The present writer joined the Institute as the joint Director together with Shri Jayaprakash Narayan (as Director) in April 1964. A number of social scientists including an internationally known economist who was a close relation of Gandhi advised me at this time that Gandhi could not become a subject of researchable study. Neither did the ICSSR have any provision for Gandhian studies at that time. Funds for Studies started flowing much later. For a fuller treatment of the subject see 'Gandhi for the Youth' (New Delhi, 1973) by the present author.
2. During the time of the Indian partition there were big riots which had flared up in both western and eastern parts of India. While peace was maintained by a full-fledged army in the west, the responsibility of maintaining peace in the east lay with Mahatma Gandhi. Lord Mountbatten had then described Gandhi as the 'one man peace force'.
3. See *Peace Research in the Third World* by Sugata Dasgupta published in New Delhi by Shanti Prakashan (1971). A distinction is made in this treatise between the violence of protest and war, and the violence of the society. The latter produces peacelessness which is

called the antonym of war. This violence is unseen but hurts as much.
4. By combining the two terms I am denoting a new field that deals with sociology and/or psychology of outstanding political individuals such as Gandhi.
5. I am indebted to Dr M. N. Srinivas for helping to clarify this point.
6. For example, nonviolence to Gandhi was a positive term and not a negative one. It was for this reason that he finally abolished the hyphen between non and violence and made it a positive term.
7. John Howard Griffin, *Black Like Me* (Boston: Houghton Mifflin, 1960).
8. Ben Kingsley is the person who acted as Gandhi in Attenborough's film. Shri Morarji Desai told him that Ben had undergone the vows although this author does not understand how one can accept the Gandhian vow and give it up if one's acceptance was ever serious.
9. 'Dandi March' was the long march that Gandhi organized to defy the British law regarding the Salt Act (1930).
10. Dr R. K. Mukherjee related the incident to me.
11. *Adhikari* means a person who has a right to study a particular subject because of his earlier preparation with interconnected subjects and an *ahadhikari* means one who had not acquired this right.
12. For a fuller statement see *Peace Research in the Third World* by Sugata Dasgupta (Santi Prakashan, 1971).
13. The concept of internal colony has come up only now; but Gandhi pleaded for self-rule in Britian itself, i.e., for the liberation of the British citizens from internal imperialism.
14. Gandhi called majority rule 'violence'. He wanted all controversial decisions to be taken by consensus.
15. For a fuller statement of the concept of economic laws see *Panchayat Raj as the basis of Indian Polity*, by Dharampal (New Delhi: AVARD, April 1962).
16. I use the word *man* not to irritate the women's liberation movement but only to clarify a concept without introducing terminological riddles and confusions.
17. Very few people are aware of these two epoch-making contributions in the field of new economics, one by Dr J. C. Kumarappa who was Gandhi's economist and the other by Schumacher. Schumacher's first book should be considered still the best of all that he has written.
18. Commenting on the thesis, Jayaprakash Narayan had said that economics could not be considered a science any longer if it had to be ordered about where to go. Such an area of knowledge could only be treated as a technology. For all sciences were guided by their philosophies.
19. The World Bank in its report submitted in 1984 has stated, among others, two interesting facts. One was that the US domestic prices were kept low only by their artificially maintained high exchange rate. The other that Soviet Russia received more help in terms of liquid assets from Eastern Europe than the aid they offered. Both the

situations remain valid not only in international but also in domestic or intranational thesis contexts in every country.
20. Gandhi in his historic book *Hind Swaraj* which may approximate to Gandhi's manifesto talks of a concept of basic need. Anybody whose intake is higher than their basic need should be considered, according to Gandhi, an expropriator.

13
The Gandhian Movement in India Since the Death of Gandhi

Geoffrey Ostergaard

In the West, the usual response to the mention of Gandhi's name is to place him into one of two boxes. The first, labeled 'Father of the Indian Nation', suggests that his relevance to non-Indians is on a par with that of, say, George Washington to non-Americans. The second is labeled 'Father of satyagraha', a term often translated as 'nonviolent resistance' rather than more literally and accurately as 'holding fast to Truth'. Unlike the first, the use of the second label, which is the one favored by Western pacifists and which has been encouraged by Attenborough's film, has the virtue of pointing to an aspect of Gandhi that has universal relevance. But this label also has the defect of presenting a truncated image of Gandhi. How much truncated may be seen by looking at the experience of those followers of Gandhi in India who, after his assassination, continued to work on Gandhi's grand project. In this project, nonviolence is not simply a technique of conflict resolution but a key concept, along with Truth, its twin, in a complete philosophy of life. The philosophy includes a vision of 'a new society', and the project may be described thus: making a nonviolent social revolution which will lead, first in India but eventually throughout the world, to *sarvodaya* – a society concerned with 'the welfare of all' or, to use the nearest English equivalent, 'the commonweal'.[1]

Since the end of World War II, the term 'nonviolent revolution' has gained a limited currency in Western pacifist circles. Thus, in the United States in 1946, A. J. Muste and others formed 'The Committee for Nonviolent Revolution', and in Britain the journal *Peace News* adopted in 1971 'for nonviolent revolution' as its subtitle. But the term was first coined by Gandhi and it is only in

India (and neighboring Sri Lanka)[2] that a coherent social movement has developed the theory and practice of nonviolent revolution. Gandhi made two statements in which he referred to the novel and, to most people, paradoxical concept. In the first, he said: 'Some have called me the greatest revolutionary of my time. It may be false, but I believe myself to be a revolutionary – a nonviolent revolutionary.'[3] In the second, he wrote: 'A nonviolent revolution is not a program of seizure of power. It is a program of transformation of relationships ending in a peaceful transfer of power.'[4] Both statements require interpretation. In the first, there is no clear reference to *social* revolution. Gandhi may have been claiming no more than that he had pioneered innovations in the *methods* of struggling against oppression: that he had revolutionized the *technique* of struggle. In the second, the context makes clear that the relationships he had in mind were *political*, not social, the transformation to be marked by the transfer of power from British to Indian hands.

However, Gandhi's other writings and his activities provide confirmation that he *was* a social as well as a political revolutionary: he did seek radical changes in the structure of society, the polity and the economy and also in modes of thinking and individual behavior. He was, in a phrase later popularized by Jayaprakash Narayan, a 'total revolutionary'. For Gandhi, the liberation of India from alien rule was merely the first, if essential first, step towards a radical reconstruction of the social order in India and ultimately in all other countries. As far as India was concerned, this involved, once the British had quit, *not* the building of a modern industrialized nation state, relying for its defense, like other nation states, on armed forces, but, rather, the reconstitution of India as a society of village republics. The new India was to remain a peasant society but one in which the basic unit would be the self-governing and largely self-sufficient village. These basic units, cooperating with each other for the purposes of mutual aid and for the provision of services requiring regional and national organization, would together constitute, in Sugata Dasgupta's phrase, 'a great society of small communities'. Radically decentralized and non-pyramidical in structure, the society would be one in which each individual would be at the center, to use Gandhi's image, of 'an oceanic circle' – a circle radiating and receiving in return the love and strength that comes with the adoption of Truth and nonviolence as the principles of both social and individual life.[5]

Gandhi's vision of the new India was not, it needs hardly to be said, shared by the vast majority of his fellow-countrymen. In particular, it was not shared by most of the leaders of the Indian National Congress, including Nehru, who had accepted nonviolence as an expediential policy rather than as a philosophical creed. With some genuflections in the direction of the man they called 'The Father of the Nation', Congress governments proceeded to develop India as a conventional nation state of the social democratic variety. The gap between their thinking and Gandhi's was revealed when they rejected the proposal Gandhi made on the eve of his assassination, January 30 1948, in a document commonly referred to as his Last Will and Testament. The proposal was that Congress should disband as a political party and flower again as a Lok Sevak Sangh or Association for the Service of the People. 'Congress in its present shape and form, i.e. as propaganda vehicle and parliamentary machine', he wrote, 'has outlived its use. India has still to attain social, moral and economic independence in terms of its 700,000 villages as distinct from its cities and towns.'[6] The proposal reflected two related concerns which Gandhi emphasized in his last years. One was his rejection of political power as the means to transform society; the other was his espousal of constructive, as distinct from combative, nonviolence. During the struggle against the British Raj, combative or resistive nonviolence had been in the forefront. But Gandhi had come to the conclusion that he had gotten his priorities wrong: he had not maintained a proper balance between 'civil resistance' and 'constructive work'. The latter was more important than the former and, certainly, now that Independence had been achieved, the emphasis should be placed on it.

Constructive work had always been part of Gandhi's approach, and piecemeal over the years he had developed what he called his 'Constructive Program'.[7] This included a variety of items such as the promotion of *khadi* and other village industries, the achievement of Hindu–Muslim communal unity, and the abolition of untouchability – all designed to create a united and harmonious nonviolent society. Special institutions had been set up and workers recruited to promote various items in the program. The few thousand 'constructive workers' constituted Gandhi's true followers and it was these who comprised the cadres of the Gandhian movement after Gandhi's death – the Sarvodaya movement, as it is generally called. Congress having rejected Gandhi's

Lok Sevak Sangh proposal, these constructive workers in March 1948 at a conference held at Sevagram, Gandhi's last *ashram*, decided to set up Sarva Seva Sangh, the Association for the Service of All. The idea was to bring under one umbrella all the separate constructive work organizations that Gandhi had established. In practice, this idea was only partially realized because some important Gandhian organizations preferred to retain their separate identities. These latter associations have continued and are expressive of what I call 'institutional Gandhism' – essentially reformist social work with a Gandhian provenance and flavor. Sarva Seva Sangh thereupon developed as the organization of 'revolutionary Gandhism' which accepts nonviolent social revolution as its key concept. Both 'institutional' and 'revolutionary' Gandhism should be distinguished from a third type which I call 'political Gandhism', represented in Congress and some other political parties, and which seeks to achieve *some* Gandhian objectives by conventional political action.[8]

For three years after the Sevagram conference, little headway was made towards realizing Gandhi's vision of the new India, although Sarva Seva Sangh did produce a 'Sarvodaya Plan' which was critical of official development thinking expressed in India's First Five Year Plan. However, on April 21 1951, an event occurred which gave a boost to 'revolutionary Gandhism'. In the village of Pochampalli in Telangana, an area where Communists were actively promoting a Maoist type of violent social revolution, Vinoba Bhave, a constructive worker who was touring the area on a peace mission, was offered by a local landlord 100 acres of land as a gift for distribution to the landless laborers in the village. Vinoba saw the gift as a sign from God, indicating the way in which nonviolent social change could and should be pursued. Thus was born the campaign for *Bhoodan* – the voluntary gift of land to the landless. Joined by other constructive workers and with the campaign endorsed by Sarva Seva Sangh, Vinoba set out on his *padayatra* (pilgrimage on foot) from village to village throughout all the major States of the Indian Union. As gift followed gift, even in areas where revolutionary communists were not active, Vinoba proclaimed that a peaceful land revolution was the key to India's nonviolent social revolution. The campaign was supported by the Congress government as a novel method of promoting land reforms which were part of its own program, and the campaign certainly did help to create an atmosphere conducive to the acceptance of these reforms, notably the abolition of intermediary interests standing between the tiller and the State and the introduction of land ceilings. But for Vinoba and his colleagues, revolution, albeit a nonviolent one, not reform was the aim. Calculating that 50 million acres of land gifts would be necessary to abolish landlessness which afflicted roughly one-fifth of the rural population, they set this figure as the target to be reached by the end of 1957. The target was missed by a large margin. By that year, some four-and-a-quarter million acres had been donated, but roughly half of this turned out to be land that was legally disputed or uncultivatable. Distributing the remainder of Bhoodan land also presented problems, notwithstanding help provided by the government to the movement. But in the end some 500,000 landless laborers benefited from this distribution of Bhoodan – no small achievement in a 'land-hungry' country in which land remains a major means of production.

Although the year 1957 did not prove to be the heralded Year of the Land Revolution, it did mark a stage in the development of the Sarvodaya movement. In some villages, all the landowners had donated all their land. This led naturally to the development of a new concept, that of *Gramdan*, meaning literally 'gift of the village' and in practice the vesting of the title to village land in the village community. From 1957 onwards, Gramdan, the voluntary villagization as distinct from nationalization of the land, became the major plank in the movement's program. Gramdan, involving as it did the social ownership of land and community action, underlined that revolutionary Gandhism was a form of communitarian socialism.

Gramdan was not the only plank in the movement's program. There was also *Shanti Sena* – the development of a volunteer Peace Army intended primarily to act in situations of violent conflict between India's religious communities. There was the promotion of khadi and village industries, as well as the other items in Gandhi's original Constructive Program. Further, Vinoba's fertile mind generated new *dan* concepts, such as *shramdan*, gift of labor, *bhuddidan*, gift of intellect, *sampattidan*, gift of income or wealth, and *jeevandan*, gift of an individual's entire life for the cause of nonviolent revolution. The first jeevandani was Jayaprakash Narayan (widely and hereafter referred to as 'JP'), the leader of the Socialist Party and at one time predicted as Nehru's most likely successor. In 1954, JP abandoned party and power politics and joined the

Sarvodaya movement in which he rapidly earned a place second only to that of Vinoba. JP was the most important convert to join the movement in the wake of the initial enthusiasm generated by the Bhoodan campaign. In an open letter to his former socialist colleagues, published in 1957, JP traced his intellectual odyssey from nationalist non-cooperation to Marxism, from Marxism to democratic socialism, and finally, in the words of the title, 'From Socialism to Sarvodaya'. Throughout his journey, JP pointed out, the ultimate goals of freedom, equality, brotherhood and peace had remained constant; but his conception of how to achieve these goals had changed. The way forward, he now saw, was the Gandhian way, which he described thus:

> to create and develop socialist living through the voluntary endeavor of the people rather than to seek to establish socialism by the use of the power of the State. In other words ... to establish people's socialism rather than State socialism.[9]

JP, a Western-educated intellectual, well versed in the literature of modern social thought, helped in the elaboration of the Indian concept of nonviolent revolution which proceeded along with the movement's pursuit of its practical programs. But it was Vinoba, a more traditional figure, cast in the mold of an Indian saint, who was mainly responsible for the form this concept took in the first twenty years following Gandhi's death. In his interpretation of the Gandhian legacy, Vinoba held fast to Gandhi's distinctive doctrine that, in the realm of human action, means are not separable from ends. Means precede ends temporally but the two are morally indistinguishable and, in the last analysis, convertible terms. Or, to put it in another way, means are never merely instrumental and morally neutral: they are always also expressive, end-creating and part of a continuous chain of events infused with values. Nonviolence is thus both means and end: in the former aspect, it is the way to Truth, the supreme value, and in the latter aspect, it is the obverse of Truth. Vinoba did, however, introduce two conceptual innovations or elaborations which reflected his own understanding of the position Gandhi had reached by the time of the latter's death. The first concerns Gandhi's idea of satyagraha. In Vinoba's view, this should be interpreted positively to mean nonviolent *assistance* in right thinking, rather than negatively as nonviolent *resistance* to evil. The hallmark of genuine satyagraha, Vinoba argued, is its non-coercive quality, its capacity to convert the opponent without arousing his fears. The satyagrahi 'holds fast to Truth' but is mindful that the truth he expresses is only relative, never absolute, and that his opponent may also express a part of the truth. So, there is no insistence on the satyagrahi's side: he leaves it to Truth itself to make its presence felt. The direction of nonviolence, Vinoba further argued, is directly opposite to that of violence. In the domain of violence, people usually employ the least harsh violence. If that fails to secure their objective, they then employ harsher and, finally, the harshest violence. But in the domain of nonviolence, if people find that gentle methods do not produce the desired result, they should infer that there is something wrong in their choice of methods. They should then proceed to substitute gentler and, if necessary, the gentlest methods. Vinoba did not rule out entirely the use of 'negative' satyagraha, but he argued that in a democratic country – such as India had become since Independence – the occasions for its use were very rare. The accent should, therefore, be on 'positive' satyagraha, peaceful, loving persuasion to induce right thinking.

Vinoba's second innovation concerns politics. In current orthodoxy, politics is defined in terms of power, the ability to get one's way despite resistance, using methods ranging from subtle pressures through force ('legitimate violence') to naked violence. Such a conception, Vinoba argued in effect, can have no place in a society which accords primacy to Truth and love. The nonviolent revolution must, therefore, develop a new kind of politics – the politics of Truth and love. This new politics he called *Lok-niti*, the politics of the people, in contrast to *Raj-niti*, the old politics of the state, of power and of parties. The hallmark of the new politics, Vinoba suggested, is consensus. Since all men and women can be deemed to express part of the truth, decisions arrived at by consensus carry with them the surest guarantee that the politics of Truth and love, not the politics of power, is being practiced. In developing the new politics, Vinoba's attitude was that 'we should keep ourselves aloof from the old kind'.[10] This was in line with the advice Gandhi had given to constructive workers in 1947 when he said: 'Politics have today become corrupt. Anybody who goes into them is contaminated. Let us keep out of them altogether. Our influence will grow thereby.' The role of constructive workers, Gandhi had added, was to guide political power and to mold the politics of the country without taking power themselves: 'Banish power and keep it on the right path.'[11] Keeping aloof from the old politics did not mean, in Vinoba's view, that nonviolent revolutionaries should not seek the cooperation of everybody, including political parties and the state authorities, in promoting the movement's programs, even though, when the new society was fully developed, there would be no place in it for either political parties or the state. It also did not imply that nonviolent revolutionaries should ignore elections. Their intervention in them, however, should be strictly non-partisan and educational, informing voters of their rights and duties, and, beyond that, trying to persuade them to practice the new politics – for example, by getting *gram sabhas* (the village assemblies, the organs of direct democracy in Gramdan villages) to put up in a constituency a single agreed candidate who would then be returned unopposed. Vinoba, it may be noted, was an anarchist, but of the distinctively Indian kind. Unlike mainstream Western anarchism, Indian anarchism is not only spiritual and nonviolent but also gradualist rather than 'immediatist', and non-statist rather than anti-statist. Like all anarchism, it rejects the state as 'organized violence' (Gandhi), but it believes that those who rule in democratic states can be persuaded to cooperate in making themselves redundant. The state, therefore, is not to be abolished, as Bakunin advocated; rather, to use Engels' phrase, it will 'wither away'. According to Vinoba, it will progressively 'wither away' as the people, practicing the new politics, proceed to build up the nonviolent alternative culture and institutions which make the state unnecessary.[12]

Turning from such theoretical to more practical matters, we must now note the progress made after 1957 in the campaign for Gramdan. For various reasons, one being that Gramdan was patently more radical than Bhoodan, the progress was disappointing. The six fat years of the movement's Bhoodan phase, 1951–57, were succeeded by six rather lean years. In this latter period, villages continued to declare for Gramdan and by 1963 their number totalled over six thousand. But this figure represented only a tiny fraction of India's half-million villages and, moreover, the distribution of Gramdan villages was much less even than had been the case with Bhoodan. The villages concerned were generally very small, very poor, and concentrated in low caste and tribal areas. By 1963 it was evident that the pace of the movement had slackened considerably. In this situation, applying Vinoba's 'gentle, gentler, gentlest' approach, it was decided to revise the concept of Gramdan. Under the revised concept known as simplified or *Sulabh Gramdan*, participants agreed to surrender to the village community the ownership of their land in the village but were allowed to retain possession of 95 per cent of it, the remaining 5 per cent being distributed to the landless. In addition, although donors were allowed to transfer land in their possession only to other persons who had joined the Gramdan, they continued to enjoy other rights, including the right to pass on the land to their heirs. Sulabh Gramdan thus retained the principle of villagization of land but was much less radical and egalitarian than the original concept.

Armed with the revised concept, the movement proceeded in 1965 to launch a *toofan* or whirlwind campaign to spread the message of Gramdan, the hope being that in the process the movement for nonviolent revolution would reach the take-off point at which it would be transformed from a movement of workers *for* the people into a real 'people's movement' expressive of 'people's power'. The new campaign was largely concentrated in, but not confined to, JP's home State of Bihar. The campaign appeared to make spectacular progress. Within the next few years, the majority of villagers in thousands of Bihar's villages had signed, or put their thumbprint on, pledges in favor of Sulabh Gramdan; and for the first time villages in large contiguous areas opted to enter the Gramdan fold, thereby generating the new *dan* concepts of blockdan,[13] districtdan, and provincial Statedan. October 2 1969 marked the centenary of Gandhi's birth, so the movement set itself the target of achieving Bihardan by that date. This objective was virtually achieved. On Gandhi's birthday, at the Sarvodaya conference, attended by 22,000 delegates and ten times that number of invitees and spectators, including the President of India and the Dalai Lama, it was announced that 60,000 of Bihar's 67,000 villages had declared for Gramdan, and that the number of such villages throughout the country was 140,000 – approximately one-quarter of all the villages in India. These figures, however, relate to pledges in favor of Gramdan. In the course of the campaign, the concept of Sulabh Gramdan, considered as a process, had been clarified. Three stages had been distinguished: first, *prapti*, in which not less than 75 per cent of the adults in a village owning at least 51 per cent of the land sign a document indicating their willingness to transfer to a village assembly the ownership of their land; secondly, *pushti*, in which the main conditions of Gramdan are implemented – the gram sabha and a village fund established, the land gifts verified, the legal titles transferred, and the one-twentieth part of the donated land distributed among the landless; and thirdly, *nirman*, the stage in which, through the gram sabha, resources are mobilized and a program of reconstruction and development in the village begins. By October 1969 only the first stage had been completed in the bulk of the 140,000 villages. Nevertheless, as JP put it at that time, it seemed 'reasonable to hope that in the Gramdan states, such as Bihar, the entire social, economic and political picture might be transformed in the next five years'.[14]

This hope was not realized – at least not in the way JP had expected. The declaration of Bihardan was soon shown to be largely symbolic or a pious fraud. After the declaration, Vinoba, then aged 74, returned to his ashram at Paunar in Maharashtra to enjoy a well-earned period of semi-retirement in which he devoted himself mainly to the spiritual matters that had always been his deepest concern.[15] Before leaving, he exhorted the Sarvodaya workers to complete the task of implementing Gramdan in Bihar within twelve months. Although they were exhausted by the efforts made during the whirlwind campaign, the workers took up the task, but in doing so they soon came 'face to face' with the harsh realities of Indian rural life.[16] They found that many of the pledges had not been properly executed and that, even where this was not the case, many villagers were reluctant to fulfill their promises. The attempt to implement Gramdan revealed a major flaw or problem in Vinoba's approach to social change.

Gramdan, even in its modified form, implied radical changes in the power structure of the villages. Instead of power being monopolized typically by the larger landowners and richer peasants, all villagers were to have an equal voice in the gram sabha or village assembly. This change, Vinoba insisted, should be achieved by consensus – the hallmark of the new politics. In other words, he was insisting that members of the dominant class in the villages should voluntarily relinquish the power on which their dominance as a class rested. Not surprisingly, when it came to the point of real action, many of the dominants drew back; and, even when gram sabhas were set up, they often subverted their effective operation by exercising the veto power which was inherent in the principle of consensus.

The movement's workers soon gave up the idea of implementing Gramdan in the whole of Bihar in the immediate future; instead, they concentrated their activities in two areas – the small district of Saharsha and the Musahari block. Some success was achieved in both areas but it was not commensurate with the efforts involved: in neither area was there any real sign that it was developing as a model of nonviolent social revolution or that the movement was becoming a 'people's movement'. By 1971 it seemed that the movement was in danger of running into the sands and disappearing without visible trace. Realization of this danger sparked off what was in effect a protracted debate over the movement's strategy. In this debate, JP, by now the effective if not universally acknowledged leader of the movement, took a line which increasingly diverged from that previously laid down by Vinoba.

By the end of 1973, re-thinking of the Sarvodaya movement's strategy had embraced seven main points. (1) It was necessary to adopt on a much larger scale than hitherto resistive or 'negative' satyagraha of the kind used by Gandhi in the struggle to oust the British Raj. (2) The existing cadre of revolutionaries, still only a few thousands in number, had to be enlarged. The main source of new recruits was identified as rebellious students and idealistic youth, the group that had constituted the 'revolutionary vanguard' in other countries. (3) It was also necessary to enlist the active support of concerned but politically uncommitted citizens, especially middle-class professionals and intellectuals, who hitherto had been notably skeptical about the movement. (4) In order to mobilize wider popular support than the program of Gramdan had achieved, it was essential for the movement to take up, articulate, and seek to solve the current problems that affected the masses, such as inflation, unemployment, corruption, and the evasion of the government's land reforms. (5) The movement, hitherto centered on the villages, should advance into the cities and towns, developing programs and institutional forms appropriate to both rural and urban areas. (6) At the same time, the movement should take a more active interest in what was happening in the arena of conventional power and party politics. Without abandoning its non-partisan stance, it should apply more resolutely Gandhi's Lok Sevak Sangh idea of constructive workers guiding political power and molding the politics of the country. And finally, (7), the movement should intervene more actively in elections; instead of restricting itself to educating voters, it would proceed to promote non-party 'people's candidates'.

The revised strategy implied what those workers who opposed it called 'the politicalization of the movement' which they contrasted with Vinoba's attempt at 'the spiritualization of politics'. The new strategy was never formulated in a document and adopted by the movement – a procedure which would not have been possible since Sarva Seva Sangh itself took decisions by unanimity or consensus, so that those who opposed the strategy could have vetoed it. However, the majority of the Sangh's executive group were thinking along the lines I have indicated. It is also important to note that one of the factors prompting the idea that the movement should take a more active interest in happenings in the conventional political arena was the belief that Indian democracy under Mrs Gandhi's leadership was moving rapidly in the early 1970s in an authoritarian, if not indeed totalitarian, direction.

In January 1974 the students of Gujarat rose in revolt and within two months had forced the resignation of their corrupt State government and the dissolution of the State assembly. Their revolt sparked off a similar student agitation in Bihar in the following March. These events convinced JP and most of his Sarvodaya colleagues that a revolutionary situation was developing in the country. They concluded that their years of hard labor in the field were at least beginning to bear fruit and that an unforeseen but unparalleled opportunity had arisen whereby the nonviolent revolution could take a great leap forwards. JP, although by that date aged 72 and in poor health, was invited by the Bihar students to guide and lead their agitation. He accepted the invitation and the majority of the Sangh's workers, both in Bihar and elsewhere, supported his action, although the Sangh as an organization was not officially involved. Under JP's leadership and with the aid of Sarvodaya workers, what might otherwise have been one more ephemeral student agitation was transformed, over the next fifteen months, into the most serious effort so far made to carry through what JP came to call a 'Total Revolution' – in effect, his version of the sarvodaya nonviolent social revolution.

In the course of what was variously referred to as 'the Bihar movement' and 'the JP movement', further elements were added to the revised strategy. The most significant of these was the challenging of 'state power'. Manifested originally in the demand of the Students' Struggle Committee for the resignation of the Bihar government and the dissolution of the Bihar assembly, the challenge deepened as the movement developed. With the Bihar government propped up by the Union government, it soon became clear that the challenge had to be directed against the latter also. The challenge became more significant when, following the success of a three-day general strike and shut-down in Bihar in early October 1974, plans were announced to set up a system of *Janata Sarkar* or People's Government at the local levels and to establish at the State level a People's Assembly. These plans could be interpreted as providing for 'parallel government' as the revolution entered the crucial stage of 'dual power' in which the established government competes for legitimacy with the alternative revolutionary government. The challenge to 'state power' was in marked contrast with the strategy pursued under Vinoba's leadership. The latter strategy had assumed that the state was neutral as between different sections of society and that 'state power' would not be used to crush the nonviolent revolution but, somehow, would dissolve as 'people's power' was generated. Now, JP admitted that it was 'glaringly apparent' that 'the state system was subservient to a variety of forces with their interests entrenched in keeping it a closed shop'.[17] And, faced with the state's attempt to repress the revolutionary movement, he was proposing in effect that the people, through the popular institutions thrown up in the course of the struggle, should transfer 'state power' to themselves, in much the same way as had happened in the early stages of the Russian Revolution.

JP did in fact see the students' and the people's struggle committees and the organs of Janata Sarkar as the embryonic equivalents of the Russian Soviets. If he had developed this idea and, more importantly, succeeded in giving substance to it, the Bihar movement would have moved very clearly in a revolutionary direction. Unfortunately, another new element injected into the strategy, the attempt to mobilize the opposition parties in support of the movement, ran in a counter, essentially reformist, direction. At the outset and in accordance with the sarvodaya idea of people's and partyless, as opposed to party, democracy, he made determined efforts to ensure that the movement was as non-partisan as it could be in the circumstances where it was confronting a Congress government supported by its ally, the Moscow-oriented Communist Party of India.[18] In Bihar these efforts were largely successful. But, at the same time, when he saw that the opposition parties could not be kept out of a people's movement and that they added dynamism to it, he positively solicited their support. Moreover, as the agitation in Bihar developed into a national movement, JP threw his moral weight behind moves to unite the four main non-communist opposition parties so that, as a single party, they would provide a viable alternative to Mrs Gandhi's Congress. The real and fatal turning point in JP's movement came, however, in November 1974 when he accepted Mrs Gandhi's challenge to decide the issues between them at the next election. JP argued that by by bringing elections into the arena of struggle Mrs Gandhi had made 'a great mistake'.[19] But in fact it was he who made the bigger mistake, since the decision propelled the movement in the direction of conventional politics and meant that henceforward the emphasis would be on parliamentary action rather than nonviolent direct action. Thus, in the first six months of 1975, although in some ways – such as the setting up of the Bihar Vahini, a non-party youth corps dedicated to nonviolence[20] – the revolutionary character of the movement deepened, in other and more important ways it became increasingly liberal and reformist.

Two events then supervened to bring the confrontation between 'state power' and an increasingly ambiguous 'people's movement' for 'total revolution' to a disastrous climax. The Congress Party was defeated by the People's Front[21] in the Gujarat State elections and the Allahabad High Court found Mrs Gandhi guilty of malpractice in the previous general election. The first indicated clearly that Congress might well be defeated nationally at the next general election; the second threatened Mrs Gandhi's personal position as Prime Minister and leader of Congress. So, on June 26 1975 Mrs Gandhi delivered a stinging pre-emptive strike: she imposed a draconian state of emergency[22] on the country and jailed JP and many other opposition leaders and workers.

Even before the emergency had been imposed, JP's revised strategy had led to serious divisions within the Sarvodaya movement. He was accused by some workers of contravening Gandhian principles of nonviolence and of countenancing coercion. The charge was to some extent justified, and certainly JP's attitude toward nonviolence became increasingly pragmatic.[23] JP's Sarvodaya critics, however, closed their eyes to the violence used by the state authorities which resulted in the death, by police firing, of over one hundred demonstrators, the bulk of whom had eschewed violence themselves. To indicate his disapproval of the course the movement was taking, Vinoba on Christmas Day 1974 embarked on a year of self-imposed silence. When the emergency was declared six months later, the Sarvodaya movement, therefore, found itself in serious disarray. A small minority of its workers actively supported Mrs Gandhi's action and rushed to help implement her 20-point program, the sweetener which followed her administration of the bitter pill.[24] The majority of the Sangh's workers opposed the emergency, and the most active of these soon found themselves in jail. Others, including many in the Gandhian institutions, tried to adopt a neutral stance – neither opposing nor supporting the emergency. Vinoba himself took this line, but he did not protest when an ambiguous written comment he had made was seized on by the government to suggest that he endorsed Mrs Gandhi's imposition of 'an era of discipline'.[25] The incident resulted in Vinoba, the philosophical anarchist, being hailed, ironically, as 'the Saint of the Government'. After the end of his year of silence, he explained his comment and took steps designed to reconcile the government and the opposition;[26] but until the end of the emergency his position remained exceedingly ambiguous.

The emergency effectively put an end for the time being to any people's movement for nonviolent revolution. In some sense, the movement continued and there was widespread, largely unpublicized, resistance. But the overriding objective was no longer radical social change but restoration of the status quo ante. JP, released from jail a seriously sick and dying man, became the symbol of the resistance; but his situation and his feeling of guilt at having led the movement into a disastrous confrontation with the government impelled him still further in the direction of conventional politics. Believing that earlier he had overstressed nonviolent direct action, he now put most of his weight behind uniting the opposition parties.

Meanwhile, Mrs Gandhi had drastically amended the Constitution so as to institutionalize a system of near-autocratic power. She then decided, in January 1977, that it was safe to hold the postponed general election. But, to her great surprise, when the electorate went to the polls in the following March, Congress was roundly and soundly defeated. As soon as the election was announced, the opposition parties, cajoled by JP, speedily united to form the Janata (People's) Party. Aided by defections from Congress, the new party swept the board in the Hindi-speaking heartland, including Bihar, where every Congress candidate lost. Under JP's guidance, the Janata Party adopted a program of 'Gandhian socialism'; and JP and other Sarvodaya leaders, notwithstanding their self-imposed pledge as Sarvodaya workers to remain non-partisan,[27] actively campaigned for Janata candidates.

The Janata Government, headed by the veteran 'political Gandhian', Morarji Desai, was installed in office in a euphoric atmosphere reminiscent of the days immediately following Independence. There was much heady talk which fostered the illusion that 'people's power', which had burgeoned in Bihar in 1974–75 only to be repressed, had manifested itself again in a spectacular fashion. Mahatma Gandhi, it was said, had been the architect of the first nonviolent revolution which had ousted the British Raj, and now, thirty years later, a second Gandhi in the person of JP had inspired and led 'a second nonviolent revolution' which had ousted 'the Indira Raj'. The illusion that dramatic changes were in the offing was encouraged when, on the day the new Prime Minister took office, all the Janata MPs assembled at Gandhi's *samadhi* (shrine) at Rajghat in Delhi and solemnly swore 'to complete the work initiated by the Mahatma'. In practice, the illusion was rapidly and cruelly exposed. The Janata Government was equipped to perform only a limited historical role – that of dismantling the structure of 'the Indira Raj'. For most of its leaders, 'Total Revolution' had been little more than a slogan – as JP had openly suspected before the emergency – and it was effectively over once they had achieved political office. Within less than three years, amidst prolonged and unedifying bouts of politicking, the party assembled by JP had fallen apart, the Janata Government had resigned, and JP himself had died in October 1979 a sadly disillusioned man. Meanwhile, Mrs Gandhi had staged a remarkable political comeback which, interestingly enough, began with a well-publicized visit to the aging Vinoba in his ashram.[28] In the mid-term general election of January 1980, the electorate passed a decisive verdict on the political antics of the Janata Party and voted Mrs Gandhi's Congress back into office with a commanding majority. Thus the political wheel which JP had begun to turn in 1974 finally came full circle; and Vinoba, who in 1974 had predicted that nothing would come out of the Bihar agitation, was at last, in some sense, proven right.

In March 1977, it must be said, the cadre of total revolutionaries – those Sarvodaya workers who had accepted JP's revised strategy and his youthful followers who proceeded to relaunch the Vahini as a national organization – had understood that the election of a Janata Government was only a step on the road to nonviolent revolution. But it was a step involving consequences they had not foreseen. It was precisely at the point when 'state power' came into the hands of an apparently sympathetic government that the ambiguous nature of the relationship between 'state power' and 'people's power' in JP's thinking was revealed. In Bihar in 1974–75, the generation of 'people's power', which had eluded the Sarvodaya workers in their campaign for Gramdan, was achieved – to the extent that it was achieved at all – through a struggle *against* 'state power'. The confrontation provided the dynamism necessary for the constructive work of institutionalizing 'people's power' in the form of the embryonic system of 'people's government' at the local levels. But JP's strategy had been predicated on the assumption that confrontation between 'state power' and 'people's power' was only a passing phase. In principle, he did not believe in such confrontation. Except for the important difference that JP recognized that *sometimes* (when the government was obdurate) confrontation with the state was inevitable, his position was not all that far removed from the position of Vinoba who sought the cooperation of the state in achieving nonviolent revolution. In JP's view, the Janata victory of March 1977 had set the stage for a period not of confrontation but of cooperation between 'state power' and 'people's power'. What he did not explain was how, in the absence of confrontation and struggle, 'people's power' could be generated or, if it can be supposed to have been manifested in the election of 1977, sustained after the votes had been cast.

That this was a major problem was shown when the total revolutionaries tackled the task of setting up 'People's Committees'. These committees, which were to be formed at every level from the local to the national, were intended by JP to act as watchdogs over the government and the administration, to ensure that the election pledges were honored, and that the elected representatives were accountable to the people between elections. As such, they had a vital role to play in transforming the political system into a radical, participatory democracy. But, in the absence of combative struggle after March 1977, these (diluted) successors to the organs of self-government that had begun to emerge in Bihar in 1975 proved difficult to set up. By the summer of 1980, only some 10,000 had been formed and, although in a few areas local people's committees have been active, in general they have not fulfilled the role assigned to them.

As the Janata Government stumbled towards its final fall, Sarva Seva Sangh, which in May 1977 had been re-activated as the organization representing JP's, as distinct from Vinoba's, version of nonviolent revolution, began to distance itself from the new ruling party. Rather surprisingly, in view of the rhetoric about 'a second nonviolent revolution', the Sangh showed few signs of developing into an influential and broad-based organization. As the realization dawned that the new society was 'still far off', the Sangh decided, therefore, in 1978 to select about a hundred areas for intensive work. The idea is that key workers should 'bury' themselves for a decade in the countryside and, by blending constructive work with combative struggle over local issues, help the people to build the bases of the 'total revolution'. As part of this program, the Sangh has also revived the idea of promoting in future elections non-party 'people's candidates', nominated by and accountable to the 'people's committees' or, in the absence of the latter, to 'voters' councils'.

Armed with the new program, which also included implementing where possible the old program of Gramdan, the Sangh's workers became visibly more active after Mrs Gandhi's return to power in January 1980. Prior to the assassination of Indira Gandhi there was no return to emergency rule, but a sharper edge was given to the activities of India's nonviolent revolutionaries by the creeping authoritarianism of the new Congress government, accompanied as it has been by diminishing popular support for the government. In May 1982 the Sangh issued an important policy statement, 'A Call to the Nation', in which it observed that, although some positive results had been achieved since Independence, the hopes of the people for an end to their hardships had not been realized.[29] Because the direction and the priorities of the plans and policies actually adopted were wrong, only a small section of the people had benefited from development while the common people had still to be provided with the basic necessities. Further, there had been 'a cultural degeneration' and 'the entire social structure has become both hollow and fragile because of the rampant corruption in every sphere of life'. This outcome was ascribed to the failure to heed Gandhi's advice:

> Independence must begin at the bottom. Thus every village will be a republic or panchayat, having full powers. It follows, therefore, that every village has to be self-sustained and capable of managing its own affairs ... Real swaraj will come, not by the acquisition of authority by the few but by the acquisition of the

capacity by all to resist authority when it is abused.

The policy statement provided the intellectual basis for the Sangh's taking the initiative in attempting to mobilize popular support for what it refers to as 'The Non-Party Alternative'. A program of 'national regeneration' was chalked out which included a drive to recruit new workers, renewed efforts to form people's committees, and a call to gram sabhas to begin the task of managing their own affairs without waiting for the government to introduce the desired constitutional changes. Satyagraha on both local and *national* issues was envisaged. The issue favored for a nation-wide satyagraha was one which strikes at the root of the exploitation of the villages by the cities. With like-minded organizations, the Sangh and its associated bodies should create a joint front to campaign for 'fair prices to farmers' and 'just wages to agricultural workers'. Preparations should also be made to field a significant number of 'people's candidates' at the coming general election. To oversee the mobilization of support for 'The Non-Party Alternative', the Sangh, together with certain Gandhian and kindred organizations, proceeded to set up a 'national collective' known as the Swaraj Sangam. What success this new body will have, in the absence of a charismatic leader of the stature of JP, remains to be seen.

Not all Sarvodaya workers, it should be said, are happy about the oppositional role that the Sangh is now playing. The divisions within the Sarvodaya movement which first manifested themselves in 1974 remain. The Sangh's workers, numbering in 1982 about 8,000, along with the youth corps, the Vahini, remain as the vanguard of the Indian movement for nonviolent revolution. But a vocal minority, while claiming to be 'non-political', remained firmly attached to the government. A larger number, more genuinely if also more naively 'non-political' – mainly those involved in 'institutional Gandhism' – have still not embraced JP's revised version of nonviolent revolution.

There have been some efforts to heal the divisions within the Sarvodaya movement. The various factions, or parts of them, joined together in campaigning for a ban on cow slaughter. This is an issue which Vinoba first raised in 1976 during the emergency. He raised it again in 1979 during the Janata regime, and for the third and last time in 1981. To Westerners it may seem an odd issue for nonviolent revolutionaries to raise. The cow, of course, is a sacred Hindu symbol – and because of that an issue which divides India's religious communities. But cow protection also has a distinctively Gandhian symbolism – signifying the importance of the agrarian economy in which the cow and the bullock play a vital part, and beyond that the cosmic unity which binds animals to humans and all things to God. One point of interest is that, on this issue at least, Vinoba was prepared to countenance resistive satyagraha. With his active encouragement a fairly large-scale satyagraha, directed principally against the slaughterhouses in Bombay, was going on when he died on November 15 1982. In the last years of his life, so it would seem, Vinoba moved closer to JP's way of thinking about the need on occasions for a kind of satyagraha that goes beyond peaceful, loving persuasion. To the end, however, he remained non-approving of the Sangh's current political line, as was shown by his insistence that members of the new Shanti Sena which he formed in 1980 should pledge themselves not to vote in elections, not even for 'people's candidates'.

This brief review of the experience of the Gandhian movement in India since Gandhi may not make encouraging reading for those in the West who are beginning to look to Gandhi as a source of inspiration for their own efforts to bring about radical but nonviolent social change. With some reservations, it may be said that nonviolence, under Gandhi's direction, did play a large part in achieving the national liberation of India from alien rule. But that objective, as we have noted, was only an essential first step towards Gandhi's larger and much more ambitious project: the attainment of what he termed 'real Swaraj'. In the person of Vinoba, recognized by Gandhi as his 'true son' and as a man of great spirituality, a worthy successor emerged to carry on Gandhi's project beyond the purely political revolution that Independence involved. Through Bhoodan and Gramdan, Vinoba did succeed in mobilizing and inspiring a small but significant social movement directed towards the Gandhian ideal of *Gram-swarajya*. In the process, much practical good was done and there are thousands of villagers in India who have cause to be grateful for Vinoba's work. But the hope that the foundations of a sarvodaya society in India would be laid by the time of Gandhi's birth centenary in 1969 was not realized. Vinoba's strategy for nonviolent social revolution, it appeared, had failed. In this situation, JP, with his rather different interpretation of the Gandhian legacy, developed a revised strategy in which nonviolent struggle played a more important part than the loving persuasion favored by Vinoba. For a brief moment in the mid-1970s, it seemed that, led by JP, a mass movement was developing which could bring about a 'total revolution' along Gandhian lines. But JP's strategy, involving as it did head-on confrontation between 'people's power' and 'state power' also failed, and in the end provoked the disastrous imposition of emergency rule, 1975–77. Subsequently, Mrs Gandhi and her Congress suffered a political set-back, albeit only temporarily, but the Janata experiment of 1977–79 did little more than underline the failure of JP's strategy. Upon Mrs Gandhi's return to power and subsequent assassination, the Sarvodaya movement, or more accurately Sarva Seva Sangh, had to re-think its strategy in a way that went beyond the thinking of both Vinoba and JP, the two intellectual giants who emerged as Gandhi's successors in India. As the crisis in India continues, opportunities for a new initiative by Gandhians to mobilize support for a Gandhian resolution of the crisis exist, but whether the opportunities can or will be seized remains problematical.

There are many, and they include Marxists in all their various hues, who will draw the conclusion that the Gandhian project of nonviolent social revolution is an illusion. An overtly violent revolution, they will argue, may not be inevitable, but no social revolution can be achieved without capturing and making use of the covert violence represented in 'state power': a nonviolent revolution is a sheer impossibility. They may be right, but no Gandhian is likely to accept such a conclusion readily. He is more likely to recall, as I do, the wise words of Gandhi: 'Our task is to make the impossible possible.' Prizing open the limits of the possible is, in my view, what politics – and much else in human life – should be about. In this connection, it is worth remembering that Max Weber, the sociologist who coined that very unGandhian dictum, 'The decisive means for politics is violence', also made much the same point as Gandhi: 'All historical experience', he wrote, 'confirms the truth that man would not have attained the possible unless time and again he had reached out for the impossible.'[30]

Notes

* This essay draws on material used in my book, *Nonviolent Revolution in India* (New Delhi: Gandhi Peace Foundation, 1985).
1. The term 'Sarvodaya' was first used by Gandhi as the title of his translation of John Ruskin's *Unto This Last* and since Gandhi's death has become the preferred term to describe Gandhi's social ideas.
2. For an account of the Sri Lankan movement which makes interesting comparisons with the Indian, see Detlef Kantowsky, *Sarvodaya, The Other Development* (New Delhi: Vikas, 1980).
3. Quoted as an epigraph to an article by Jayaprakash Narayan in *The Times* (London), October 13 1969.
4. *Harijan*, February 17 1946.
5. For Gandhi's image of 'an oceanic circle', see M. K. Gandhi, *Sarvodaya* (Ahmedabad: Navajivan, 1954) pp. 70–1.
6. Pyarelal, *Mahatma Gandhi: The Last Phase* (Ahmedabad: Navajivan, 1956) vol. 1, p. 44.
7. See M. K. Gandhi, *The Constructive Program* (Ahmedabad: Navajivan, 1945). This was a revised edition of a pamphlet first published in 1941 and lists eighteen items of social work.
8. For an elaboration of my typology of 'Gandhism', see G. Ostergaard and M. Currell, *The Gentle Anarchists* (Oxford: Clarendon Press, 1971) pp. 6–7.
9. Jayaprakash Narayan, *Socialism, Sarvodaya and Democracy* (Bombay: Asia, 1962) p. 161.
10. Vinoba Bhave, *Democratic Values* (Kashi: Sarva Seva Sangh Prakashan, 1962) p. 56.
11. See Pyarelal, *Mahatma Gandhi: The Last Phase*, vol. 1, pp. 664–6.
12. For a more extended discussion of Vinoba's anarchism, see my contribution to the symposium on Vinoba, 'Vinoba: Anarchist or Saint of the Government?' *Gandhi Marg*, November–December 1983.
13. A 'block' is about 100 villages, considered as a group in the Government's Community Development Program.
14. *The Times* (London), October 13 1969.
15. These include the synthesizing of science and spirituality. See G. Ostergaard and M. Currell, *The Gentle Anarchists*, pp. 118–23.
16. The phrase is taken from the title of JP's interim report on his attempt to implement Gramdan in the Musahari block. The report is republished in B. Prasad, *A Revolutionary's Quest* (Delhi: Oxford University Press, 1980), Ch. 25.
17. *Everyman's*, April 27 1975.
18. The other main Communist party, the CPI (Marxist), gave critical support to the movement, while refusing to associate too closely with the other opposition parties, particularly the Jana Sangh.
19. *Everyman's*, November 23 1974.
20. The Chhatra Yuva Sangharsh Vahini was launched in January 1975 and was set the target of enrolling within six months 100,000 volunteers in the 14–30 years age group.

21. The Janata (People's) Front was an electoral alliance of the four non-Communist parties which later joined to form the Janata Party.
22. More accurately, Mrs Gandhi declared a second state of emergency for 'internal' reasons. A state of emergency, declared for 'external' reasons, had existed since the Bangladesh crisis of 1971: its perpetuation was one sign of Mrs Gandhi's penchant for authoritarian rule.
23. The 'silent march' in Patna, led by JP on April 8 1974, was an impressive example of Gandhian nonviolent protest. Subsequently, JP countenanced the use by students of coercive methods, including the *gherao*, in an effort to 'persuade' members of the Bihar Legislative Assembly to resign. He then tended to describe the agitation as 'peaceful' rather than as 'nonviolent' according to the canons laid down by Gandhi.
24. The 20-point program gave priority to curbing inflation but several items were particularly concerned with the other problems of those living in the rural areas, including the distribution 'with redoubled zeal' of surplus land to the landless. With Vinoba's blessing, the remaining Bhoodan land was included in the program of distribution as part of the official celebration of the Bhoodan Silver Jubilee Year.
25. In a written comment to a visiting Congress MP, Vinoba, soon after the emergency was declared, used the phrase *anushasan parva*. In breaking his silence on December 25 1975, he explained that the phrase was from the *Mahabharata* and referred to the discipline laid down by the *acharyas* (traditional teachers) in ancient times to guide their pupils. It was to be distinguished from *shasan* or rule enforced by the state.
26. In January 1976 Vinoba sponsored a conference of acharyas which called for a speedy return to 'normality', but the call was ignored by Mrs Gandhi.
27. One of the pledges taken by the Sangh's workers was not to take part in party or power politics. A few Sarvodaya workers did join the Janata Party but most, including JP – 'the Father of the Janata Party' – did not. They argued that the general election was in effect a referendum on the emergency.
28. From early 1974 onwards Mrs Gandhi had paid periodic visits to Vinoba whom she hailed as a true votary of nonviolence in contrast with those who followed JP's 'new line'.
29. *Vigil*, July 9 1982.
30. H. H. Gerth and C. W. Mills, *From Max Weber* (London: Kegan Paul, 1947) p. 128. For the dictum, see p. 121.

14

Gandhian Feminism

Sushila Gidwani

Modern feminism is a struggle by women to liberate themselves from the shackles of forced domesticity and motherhood, to rid themselves of the evils of sexism, to gain an equal share of economic and political power and to acquire full control over their bodies and destinies. It is a demand for a right to seek self-fulfillment in the same manner as men: social recognition, political power, economic independence and material enjoyment. In identifying the institution of private property and capitalism as the root of sexism, many feminists see the solution in socialism but fail to separate it from a more basic problem – industrialism.

The continued existence of the industrial system depends upon the increasing devotion of participants to materialism. Material success becomes the measure of achievement and a prime source of self-fulfillment, consuming enormous amounts of human energy and occupying a major part of daily life. As a result, the system subordinates other human aspirations to the dictates of organized and stranger-defined (Diwan, 1985) economic pursuits.

Industrial capitalism causes production for the sake of production and demands devotion to materialism. The source of national power is not people but production; profits are the motive force, and competition and technology are the weapons of choice in the war for market shares. Home based production and self-sustaining non-market sectors become targets of economic monetization, and conspicuous consumption becomes an economic necessity. The system thrives upon the promotion of socially harmful human qualitites: greed, possessiveness, vanity, selfishness, indulgence, impatience and carnal pleasures.[1] It employs exploitative and manipulative techniques, hence it is discriminatory; it is ruthlessly competitive, hence, covertly violent. Even though economically efficient in terms of productive capacity, it incorporates many socially unjust elements. It is profit- and not people-oriented.

The modern feminists – reformists, liberal or radical – while challenging the sexual division of labor have rarely voiced opposition to the system itself. They desire their part of the benefits. Modern feminism is therefore women's struggle for the right of equal participation in the honors and spoils of the ruthless economic wars waged traditionally by men for market power and led by men imbued with strong competitive spirit, expert in manipulating technology with powerful masculinity. To fight men's wars with men's weapons, successful modern women are anxiously discarding their femininity in favor of masculinity. The goal is to achieve gender neutrality of sex roles at home and in the labor markets. Therefore, modern feminism as a theory and as a movement ultimately is anti-feminine in character. In Gandhi's words modern women are attempting to 'ride the horse that men ride'.[2]

Upon gaining equality, many successful women would be indistinguishable from successful men, and once their economic interests become vested in the system and crucial to their power, the exploited will become the new exploiters.

GANDHIAN SOCIETY

In the Gandhian society the ideal political state is *swaraj* – a state of enlightened anarchy where every one is his or her own ruler.[3] Here the ideal social system is devoid of privileges while the fulfillment of duties is the source of rights.[4] The Gandhian economic system and the role of the participants in it also follow from his main theme, *ahimsa* and service.

Feminism and economics are closely related. Hence, it may be helpful to compare the economic assumptions of Gandhian feminism with those of modern feminism.

Until recently, Gandhian economic thought remained unexplored and even rejected as a backward movement by the modern thinkers in his own country. The inability of the modern economic system to eliminate poverty, instead widening international and national disparities of wealth, together with rising environmental concerns, have led a small but growing number of economists to explore Gandhi's economic ideology.[5]

A Gandhian economic system requires six interrelated principles: (1) non-exploitation or nonviolence, (2) equality, (3) *apigrah* or nonpossession (trusteeship), (4) *wadeshi* or self-reliance, (5) *sarvodaya* or service, and (6) bread labor.[6]

In the self-reliant, need-based, non-possessive and non-exploitative Gandhian economic system, guided by service and ahimsa, production will take place, not on a mass scale, but mostly for self-use, necessarily by use of one's own physical labor, in the spirit of duty and service rather than self-interest and for the satisfaction of basic needs. Unlike the modern complex system striving to serve the simple needs of human beings through material self-interest, it is a simple system striving to serve the basic human aspiration, self-realization, through selflessness, service and duty. Its goal is not to promote material wealth but to promote health: a healthy body, a healthy mind and a healthy soul. It promotes the higher human qualities: love, sharing, caring, self-sacrifice, service, humility, self-discipline, equity, justice, non-violence, cooperation and non-competition. These being the qualities most often found in women, the Gandhian economic system can rightly be labeled a feminine system. In a rapidly shrinking world faced with glaring inequalities and poised for nuclear war, it is a futuristic rather than a backward system.

Equality and non-exploitation imply equality of men and women in all aspects of life. In Gandhi's view, men and women, being the same in the essence of life, are equal: yet being different in form, they should perform functions suited to their abilities.[7] Hence, equality does not exclude division of labor between the sexes. In the Gandhian economy, men and women will perform their equally valuable and equally respected traditional roles. In fact, women's traditional role being more service-oriented, they will derive greater satisfaction from it.

The Gandhian society was the ideal of an enlightened man who was well aware of its unattainability. However, he believed that it is 'our bounden duty to set about reducing it to practice to the extent of our capacity'.[8] What will the women's role be in this transition from the present unequal state towards the Gandhian state?

GANDHIAN FEMINISM

Gandhi viewed women as a positive and powerful force for change toward his ideal society. He viewed the female sex not as a weaker sex but as the stronger of the two. It is 'The nobler of the two, for it is even today the embodiment of sacrifice, silent suffering, humility, faith and knowledge.'[9] Ahimsa means infinite love and it demands infinite capacity for suffering and being mothers, women posses it in the large measure.[10] Unlike modern feminists, Gandhi viewed the traditional role of women not as inferior, discriminatory and confining, but as a noble calling for women, demanding in time and energy.[11] Man is the breadwinner, women the keeper and distributor of the bread. One is led to conclude that production is necessary but that distribution, by calling upon a human being's sense of justice and fairness, is more challenging and more morally and spiritually satisfying. Movement towards a Gandhian society necessitates the shedding of aggressiveness, assertiveness, egoism, greed, possessiveness, competitiveness – in short, conventional masculinity – and the promotion of nonviolence, courageous passivity, selflessness, humility, service, sacrifice, high sense of duty, cooperation, and all the other traits associated with femininity. Women's femininity makes them natural leaders of *satyagraha* and the Gandhian revolution in the same way that masculinity made men the leaders of the industrial revolution. 'If non-violence is the law of our being, the future lies with women ... they can make better appeal to the heart than men.'[12]

Drawing upon Hindu views regarding sex roles, complementarity, equality in diversity and sanctity of *varna*, Gandhi viewed the sexual division of labor as natural yet as equal in value and in dignity. Hence functional diversity does not connote inequality.[13] The roots of the existing inferiority of women lie in 'man's interested teachings'[14] and in the reliance of societies upon brute force for survival.[15] Woman is viewed as superior to man in moral strength; she possesses greater powers of intuition, endurance, moral courage and faith.[16]

The power to eradicate sexual and social discrimination and to rid themselves of inferiority complexes, and men of superiority complexes, lies within women themselves. Moral courage, self-confidence and ability to face the world, self-discipline, self-dignity, continence, 'useful' education, nonviolence and, if necessary, economic independence are her means to achieve equality of respect with men. She must shed false modesty, vanity and exhibitionism.[17] Male cooperation[18] and political will are necessary complements.

Gandhi lays out a clearly defined path for women and men to follow towards satyagraha.

Gandhi on Division of Labor

In my opinion it is degrading both for man and woman that woman should be called upon or induced to forsake the hearth and shoulder the rifle for the protection of the hearth. It is a reversion to barbarity and the beginning of the end. In trying to ride the horse that man rides, she brings herself and him down. The sin will be on man's head for tempting or compelling his companion to desert her special calling. There is as much bravery in keeping one's home in good order and condition as there is in defending it against attack from without.[19] The care of the children and the upkeep of the household are quite enough to fully engage all her energy. In a well-ordered society the additional burden of maintaining the family ought not to fall on her. The man should look to the maintenance of the family, the woman to household management; the two thus supplementing and complementing each other's labors.[20]

Gandhi on the Power of Motherhood

Theirs (women's) must be the strong, controlling, purifying, steadying hand, conserving what is best in our culture, and unhesitatingly rejecting what is base and degrading. Economic and moral salvation of India rests on your knees, for you will nurture the future generation. You can bring up the children of India to become simple god-fearing and brave men and women, or you can coddle them to be weaklings, unfit to brave the storms of life and used to foreign fineries which they would find difficult in after-life to discard.[21]

Gandhi on the Power of Simplicity

The real ornament of woman is her character, her purity. Metal and stones can never be real ornaments. If she wishes to be an equal partner with man, she must refuse to adorn herself for men. Refuse to be the slaves of your own whims and fancies, don't go in for scents and lavender waters; if you want to give out the proper scent, it must come out of your heart, and then you will captivate not man, but humanity. It is your birthright.[22]

Gandhi on Duty and Equality

No one can divest us of our duty, unless we ourselves choose to shirk it. The woman who knows and fulfills her duty realizes her dignified status. She is the queen, not a slave, of the household over which she presides.[23]

Man has no right to touch his wife so long as she does not wish to have a child, and the woman should have the willpower to resist even her own husband.[24]

Woman is man's equal and can even be superior. Care of children and the home is a joint responsibility. Woman is the mother, but her own motherly tenderness should extend beyond her own children and, therefore, her sphere must also extend beyond the home.[25]

I wish to see woman as man's equal and even their superiors. I would like you to occupy all posts of responsibility. But that does not mean that I would like you to occupy them without possessing the capacity.[26]

In the new order of my imagination, all will work according to their capacity for an adequate return for their labor. Women, in that new order, will be part-time workers, their primary function being to look after the home.[27]

Equality must not mean copying men's shortcomings. Smoking and drinking, for instance, are common amongst men. You are not to descend to their level. You are to set an example in purity, renunciation, selfless love and service.[28]

Gandhi on Women and War

Military training, which disciplines them (women), which teaches them cooperative endeavor, which gives them lessons in first aid and ambulance work in the field, which will make them self-reliant and fearless is all to the good. But for women to want to learn the use of firearms goes against the best traditions of all that the ancient culture and civilization of womankind of every land have stood for.[29]

Gandhi on Feminist Activities

My appeal to women, therefore, is that they should intelligently become the personification of renunciation and, thereby, not only adorn but raise the status of sex and the nation.

So long as consideration of caste and community continue to weigh with us and rule our choice, women are well advised to remain aloof and thereby build up prestige. The question is as to how best this can be done ... Women workers should enroll women as voters, impart to them (women) practical education, teach them to think independently, release them from the chains of caste that bind them so as to bring about the change in them which will complement efforts to realize woman's strength and capacity to sacrifice and give her places of honor. If they do this they will purify the present unclean atmosphere.

As to men they should consider it their duty to come out of the impure atmosphere wherever it exists ... Where capable women are left out men should make amends. It is their duty to give such encouragement to women as will enable them to outshine men. If both parties act as suggested the atmosphere will soon become pure.[30]

Therefore, I advise women to resort to civil rebellion against all undesirable and unworthy restraints. All restraints to be beneficial must be voluntary. There is possibility of harm resulting from civil resistance.[31]

These views leave no doubt as to the ideological biases, the goals, the methodology and the means of Gandhian feminist theory. Accordingly, Gandhian feminism can be defined as in (1)–(3) below.

(1) The theory of religious, social, political, economic and moral

equality of sexes aiming at equality of dignity, of sexual division of labor incorporating femininity as a guiding principle to move toward satyagraha: a path of ahimsa, service, self-reliance and simplicity.

(2) The movement to remove all kinds of discrimination and to transform the present religious, social, political and economic structures into new forms incorporating equality, social justice, nonviolence, self-reliance, bread labor and trusteeship (nonpossession) as guiding principles.

(3) The use of educative, nonviolent and moral means to raise awareness among men and women of the need for the feminine qualities: gentleness, moral strength, love, humility, nonviolence, endurance, sacrifice, suffering, cooperation, etc., as the building blocks of a Gandhian society.

Gandhian feminism is pro-feminine as modern feminism is pro-masculine; Gandhian feminism aims at changing men to become qualitatively feminine while the modern feminism aims at changing women to become qualitatively masculine. Gandhian feminism challenges the ideological frameworks of modern societies and aims at revolutionizing them while modern feminism accepts them as given. Gandhian feminism concentrates upon selflessness, simplicity, humility and human needs while modern feminism promotes self-interest, self-indulgence, vanity, and wants. And, lastly, the subject range of Gandhian feminism is the whole of humanity while that of modern feminism is women.

Notes

1. J. Mitchell, *Woman's Place*, pp. 94–5.
2. M. K. Gandhi, *Harijan*, February 24 1934, p. 13.
3. M. K. Gandhi, *All Men Are Brothers*, ed. by K. Kriplani, pp. 127–8.
4. M. K. Gandhi, *Young India*, January 8 1925.
5. R. Diwan and M. Lutz (eds), *Essays in Gandhian Economics*, 1985.
6. R. Diwan and S. Gidwani, 'Elements of Gandhian Economics', *Gandhi Marg*, August 1979, p. 250.
7. M. K. Gandhi, *Harijan*, February 24 1940, pp. 12–14.
8. M. K. Gandhi, *Economic and Industrial Life . . .*, ed. by V. B. Kher, p. xix.
9. M. K. Gandhi, *All Men Are Brothers*, p. 147.

10. M. K. Gandhi, *Harijan*, February 24 1940, pp. 12–14.
11. M. K. Gandhi, *Harijan*, October 12 1934.
12. M. K. Gandhi, *All Men Are Brothers*, pp. 146–52.
13. M. K. Gandhi, *Harijan*, December 2 1939, p. 359.
14. M. K. Gandhi, *Harijan*, February 24 1940, pp. 12–14.
15. M. K. Gandhi, *All Men Are Brothers*, pp. 94–6.
16. M. K. Gandhi, *Young India*, April 10 1930.
17. M. K. Gandhi, *Harijan*, April 4 1936; May 23 1936; September 5 1936; December 31 1938; March 8 1942; February 10 1946.
18. M. K. Gandhi, *Harijan*, November 5 1938, p. 317.
19. M. K. Gandhi, *Harijan*, February 24 1940, p. 13.
20. M. K. Gandhi, *Harijan*, October 12 1934.
21. Ibid.
22. Ibid., p. 13.
23. M. K. Gandhi, *Harijan*, October 12 1934.
24. M. K. Gandhi, *Harijan*, May 5 1946, p. 118.
25. Ibid.
26. Ibid.
27. Ministry of Education and Welfare, Government of India, *Mahatma Gandhi: Views on Women*, 1975, p. 17.
28. Ibid.
29. M. K. Gandhi, *Harijan*, May 9 1948, p. 93.
30. M. K. Gandhi, *Harijan*, April 21 1946, p. 96.
31. Ministry of Education and Welfare, Government of India, *Mahatma Gandhi: Views on Women*, p. 18.

Select Bibliography

Modern Feminism

Beauvoir, Simone de, *Force of Circumstances* (André Deutsch, 1965) p. 192.
Boserup, Ester, *Women's Role in Economic Development* (New York: St. Martin's Press, 1970).
Epstien, Cythia, *Woman's Place* (Los Angeles: Univ. of California, 1970).
Firestone, Shulamith, *The Dialectic of Sex* (New York: William Marrow and Co., Inc., 1970).
Gidwani, Sushila, Economic Origins of the Women's Liberation Movement (Unpublished paper, 1981).
——, Impact of the National and International Monetary and Financial Policies upon Women (Unpublished paper, 1984).
——, *Impact of Monetary and Financial Policies upon Women* (INSTRAW, United Nations, 1985).
Letourneau, CH., *Property, its Origin and Development*, The Contemporary Science Series (London: Walter Scott, Ltd., 1892).
Millet, Kate, *Sexual Politics* (New York: Avon Books, 1970).
Mitchell, I., *Woman's Place* (New York: Pantheon Books, 1971).
Morgan, Robin (ed.), *Sisterhood Is Powerful* (New York: Random House, 1970).
Reevs, Nancy, *Womankind: Beyond the Stereotypes* (Chicago: Aldine, 1970).
Stanley, Autumn, 'Daughters of Isis, Daughters of Demeter: When

Women Sowed and Reaped.' In *Women, Technology and Innovation*, ed. by Joan Rothchild (New York: Pergamon Press, 1981).

Thompson, Mary (ed.), *Voices of New Feminism* (Boston: Beacon Press, 1970).

Ware, Cellestine, 'New York Radical Feminist Manifesto', in *Woman Power* (Tower Public Affairs Books, 1970).

Gandhian Society

Diwan, Romesh and Gidwani, Sushila, 'Elements of Gandhian Economics', *Gandhi Marg* (Journal of the Gandhi Peace Foundation, New Delhi), August 1979.

Diwan, Romesh and Lutz, Mark (eds.), *Essays in Gandhian Economics* (New Delhi: Gandhi Peace Foundation, 1985).

Gidwani, Sushila, *Gandhian Economics and the Conventional Labor Economic*. Paper presented at the 96th ASSC, December 27–30 1983.

Gandhi, M. K., *Economic and Industrial Life and Relations*, ed. by V. B. Kher (Ahmedabad: Navajivan Publishing House, 1957).

——, *All Men Are Brothers*, ed. by Krishna Kriplani (New York: Continuum, 1982) pp. 146–52.

Koshal, Rajinder and Koshal, Manjulka, 'Gandhian Economic Philosophy', *The American Journal of Economics and Sociology*, 1976, pp. 191–209.

Gandhian Feminism

Harijan
  1934: Sept. 28; Oct. 12; Oct. 19
  1936: April 4; April 25; May 23; Sept. 5
  1938: Nov. 5; Dec. 31
  1939: December 2; December 9
  1940: Feb. 24
  1942: March 8; March 15
  1946: Feb. 10; Feb. 17; April 7; April 14; April 21; May 5; June 9; Nov. 3
  1947: Feb. 9; Sept. 7
  1948: May 9; July 11
  1949: April 17; June 19; Sept. 11
  1952: March 22; March 29; May 10

Ministry of Education and Welfare, *Mahatma Gandhi: Views on Women* (Government of India, 1975).

Gandhi, M. K., *All Men Are Brothers*, ed. by Krishna Kriplani (New York: Continuum, 1982) pp. 146–52.

15

The Influence of Gandhi on Martin Luther King, Jr.

Thomas Kilgore, Jr.

Four years before the death of Martin Luther King, Jr. Lerone Bennett, Jr. wrote *What Manner of Man*, a clear and perceptive biography of King.[1] This book, which highlights in words and pictures the major activities of King's life, ends with this statement:

> It was true, as Carl Sandburg has so eloquently said, that 'A tree is measured best when it is down,' but it is also true that standing trees can tell us things that fallen trees cannot. To an almost unprecedented degree, perceptive persons have recognized the worth of a tall, young tree still standing among us ... Beyond race, civil rights and religion, King must be seen and confronted finally as a man who bypassed cerebral centers and attacked the archetypal roots of man. His grace, like Gandhi's, grows out of a complicated relation not to oppression but to ancient scourges of man to pain, to suffering, to death. Men who conquer the fear of these things in themselves acquire extraordinary power over themselves and over others.

Martin Luther King, Jr. was born January 15 1929, in Atlanta, Georgia, a city haunted by the Negro and the Negro cause. The grandson and son of Baptist preachers, King was reared in the fundamentalist, simplistic piety of Black Baptist Protestantism in the South. This fact almost dissuaded him from going into the Christian ministry. But the love and care of a strong Black family gave him a sense of security and balance that added greatly to his ability in choosing priorities and making important decisions as he matured.

Beyond the profound influence of his immediate family and his early church experiences, King's thought was framed in large part by his education at Morehouse College and at Crozier Theological Seminary. King said, 'I gained my major influences in philosophy, theology, and ethics from Morehouse and Crozier. And I am greatly indebted to them. They gave me the basic truths that I now believe ... and the world view that I have ... the idea of the oneness of humanity and the dignity and worth of all human personality.'

It must be emphasized that King's concern for social justice and the employment of nonviolent direct actions were rooted in his theology and ethics. His theology, in turn, was largely shaped prior to his encounter with Gandhi's teaching. Thus, when considering the influence of Mahatma Gandhi upon King's thought and action, one must never ignore the distinctly Christian roots of King's theology and ethics. Many of the concepts attributed to Gandhi are perhaps better attributed as cardinal tenets of a school of Christian theology already alive in King's thought.

How did King first become acquainted with Gandhi? When did he actually embrace nonviolence as a way of life to effect creative social change? There has been much speculation. King relates in his book, *Strength to Love* that he was exposed for the first time to the pacifist position by Dr A. J. Muste, a speaker at Crozier.[2] King was moved by his presentation, but doubted the practicability of the position. He felt at that time that while war could never be a positive or absolute good, that it could serve as a negative good to halt the spread of evil forces. King states that during this period he had almost despaired of the power of love in solving social problems. This may have been influenced by his reading of Nietzsche's *Will to Power* and *The Genealogy of Morals*.[3]

Shortly after Muste's presentation, King and several other students from Crozier went to a meeting at Fellowship House in Philadelphia to hear Dr Mordecai Johnson, President of Howard University, who had just returned from India. Dr Johnson spoke on the life and teachings of Gandhi. His message electrified King to the extent that the next day he purchased a half-dozen books on Gandhi's life and works.

As he read, King became deeply fascinated by Gandhi's campaigns of nonviolent resistance. He was particularly moved by the Salt March to the sea and the numerous fasts. The whole concept of *satyagraha* was profoundly significant to him.

In his use of *satyagraha* and *ahimsa*, Gandhi revealed the two major philosophical and religious concepts that lay behind his actions. But what is this 'Truth' which Gandhi incorporated as the essential element of his premier technique? How does it become a force, and how does it relate to man's action in the field of conflict? For Gandhi, it excluded the use of violence, because man is not capable of knowing the Absolute Truth and therefore not competent to punish. Even so Gandhi's search for more comprehension of Truth continued.

> ... I am but a seeker after Truth. I claim to have found the way to it. I claim to be making ceaseless efforts to find it. But I admit that I have not yet found it. To find Truth completely is to realize oneself and one's destiny, that is to become perfect. I am painfully conscious of my imperfections, and therein lies the strength that I possess, because it is a rare thing for a man to know his own limitation.
>
> (*Young India*, 1921)

Therefore, as Gandhi pursued his experiments with satyagraha, the relative character of Truth as an operative principle became increasingly visible. So satyagraha developed as both the tool whereby Gandhi dealt with practical, social and political problems, and as the foundation of his philosophical beliefs. But how does one proceed to know and hold to Truth? If striving after Truth differs with every case, how can confusion be avoided? Gandhi's answer lay in the further precept that Truth is *inseparable* from 'ahimsa'. Ahimsa expressed the ancient Hindu, Jain and Buddhist ethical precept. The negative prefix *a* plus *himsa*, loosely meaning 'inquiry', make up the word which is usually translated 'nonviolence'. But ahimsa is eminently more than a negative action. The full force of ahimsa explicitly stated means 'action based upon the refusal to do harm'. Etymologically, ahimsa is the desiderivative form of *han*, meaning to kill or to damage. Ahimsa means the renunciation of the will to kill or damage.

To Gandhi ahimsa was not just a negative state of harmlessness, but it was also a positive state of love, of doing good even to the evil-doer. But it does not mean helping the evil-doers to continue to do wrong, or to tolerate wrong by quiet acquiescence. On the contrary, love, the active state of ahimsa, requires you to resist the wrong-doer by disassociating yourself from him even though it may injure him or offend him. Finally, ahimsa means putting one's whole soul against the will of the tyrant, and never submitting to the will of the evil-doer. But to Gandhi, suffering injury to one's person is the essence of nonviolence and is the consciously chosen substitute for violence to others.

King was impressed by the amazing results of Gandhi's campaign to find and live Truth, and his campaign for Independence for India. He commented after his own trip to India that he saw no evidence of the hatred that ordinarily follows a violent victory. Rather, he saw a large measure of mutual friendship based upon an equality of Indians and British. King called this a victory of love, and called Gandhi one of the half-dozen greatest men of history. In his many fiery speeches he encouraged his followers, including me, to emulate Gandhi's methods of employing the weapon of Truth, along with his inspiring courage and soul-force, in combating the evils of segregation and discrimination.

Like Gandhi, King stressed that nonviolence is not passive, but active resistance. Gandhi strengthened King's belief that there is a moral obligation to resist evil. When the Supreme Court decision integrated the Montgomery buses, King said to his followers, 'Be loving enough to absorb evil, and understanding enough to turn an enemy into a friend.' King, like Gandhi, clearly declared that his nonviolent protests were directed against the forces of evil at work in the unjust systems, and not against the persons at work in the systems. Like St. Augustine, he said, 'Hate the sin, but love the sinner.' To him the Montgomery bus boycott, the struggle in Birmingham, the march on Washington, and the march from Selma to Montgomery were not struggles of racial tension, but conflicts between justice and injustice. Victory was never his aim – justice and freedom were.

King shared Gandhi's vision of the value of unearned suffering. He believed that the willingness to suffer could arouse the conscience of the opponent. He often warned his followers that their participation could mean jail or death. He urged all to meet hate with love, and to confront physical force with love force.

John J. Ansbro, in his book, *Martin Luther King, Jr.: The Making of a Mind* recognized the profound influence that Gandhi had on King, but points up three ways in which King differed from Gandhi.[4]

First, Gandhi acknowledged that he had not found the Truth he sought. He had no fixed and final theological or philosophical system apart from his commitment to the principle of nonviolence. This allowed him to choose insights from several creeds and philosophical systems, and this caused him to constantly have to change his actions and strategies, so as to respond to the actions of his opponents. Said Gandhi, 'We will never all think alike, and we will see Truth in different angles of vision, and in fragments.' In contrast, King arrived at a system of definite philosophical and theological convictions about the nature of God, human nature, the direction of history, the mission of the Christian Church, and the role of the state in social reform. After his formal studies, King did not pursue answers to the ultimate questions, but rather sought the implementation of the ultimate Truth he had already accepted. He, like Gandhi, could revise his tactics in the course of the campaign,[5] but he was more interested in securing concession, and was not as willing as Gandhi to alter his strategies and basic goals in response to the reactions of the opponent.

In *Stride Toward Freedom*,[6] King says, 'For while the nonviolent resister is passive in the sense that he is not physically aggressive toward his opponent, his mind and emotions are always active, constantly seeking to persuade the opponent that he is wrong.' This inflexibility of King enhanced appreciation for King's adherence to his announced goals and to the basic principles of his philosophy of nonviolence.

Second, King disagreed with Gandhi on the degree of emphasis on self-help programs. With all of Kings' advocacy of Black self-help programs he maintained, 'The ultimate way to diminish the problems of crime, family disintegration, illegitimacy and so forth, will have to be found through a government program to help frustrated Negro males to find true masculinity.' Gandhi had no faith in a non-Indian government. King believed that there was the possibility of change in the governmental structures of the United States. In this he understood full well that Blacks were a vast minority in American while Indians were a vast majority in India.

Finally, King did not share Gandhi's conception of the role of asceticism in the practice of nonviolence. Gandhi made a definitive connection between the purification brought on by fasting and ascetic living and adherence to nonviolence. If attachment to the flesh and the world is cut, Gandhi believed that nonviolence was more powerful. Then fear of loss would not indirectly breed violence. He believed further that in self-purification one could feel, think, and better aim for the good of others. He regarded renunciation as the highest form of religion, and he used the ascetic disciplines from the tradition of the Hindu sage Patanjali: self-control over mind, spirit, and body; adherence to the five precepts of non-injury, Truth, non-theft, continency, and non-covetousness; and the adoption of austere diets, poverty, a loin cloth, and sexual abstinence.

King agreed with Gandhi on the value of unearned suffering, but he never emphasized asceticism as necessary for nonviolence. On occasions he took rest periods for reading, prayer and rejuvenation. The Montgomery boycott was an example of a successful nonviolent movement without asceticism.

Still, King's life was to a degree ascetic in spite of the fact that he did not make asceticism an explicit goal for his movement. This became evident through his tireless efforts in Montgomery and as an organizer, speech maker and fund raiser, where he insisted on a small salary. It is also apparent in his way of coping with life in the Chicago slums and in jail. Like Gandhi, at times he needed to get away from it all. In a 1965 interview he said: 'I subject myself to self purification and to endless self-analysis; I question and soul search constantly into myself to be as certain as I can that I am fulfilling the true meaning of my work, that I am maintaining my sense of purpose, that I am holding fast to my ideals, and that I am guiding my people in the right direction.

A COMPARISON OF GOALS AND PROGRAMS ADVOCATED BY GANDHI AND KING

Gandhi – Self-purification as a condition for achieving political independence (e.g. fasts)
– Development of village industries and sanitation
– Adult education and health programs
– Elimination of liquor
– Use of a spinning wheel in every home
– Organization of Labor satyagrahas (e.g. Ahmedabad in 1918)

King – Federal grants for housing, employment, and education
– 1963 Bill of rights for the disadvantaged
– Government-guaranteed income
– Development of Black co-ops
– Breadbasket program
– Organization of unions

In King's mind and spirit, Gandhi's thought struck a responsive chord. The fact that Gandhi refused to separate the spiritual and the secular, the religious and the ethical, and the individual and the social, influenced King. King perceived that Gandhi was completely absorbed in the attempt to meet the needs of the people and to render unselfish service to all humanity.

Although King's religious presuppositions were drawn from Christian theology and ethics, his movement of nonviolence drew freely from both the thought and example of Gandhi at the level of strategy and tactics. For oppressed people, King saw three possible options as they faced the opponent: (1) resignation, which was the way of the coward, and worse than violence; (2) violence, which was counterproductive and only bred more violence; and (3) nonviolent resistance, which involved soul-force rather than stagnant passivity. Clearly, the third type was not for cowards. Those who adopted it did not seek to humiliate their opponent. They sought to attack evil systems, not persons; to accept suffering without inflicting suffering; to see the universe as being on the side of justice; and to avoid internal violence to the human spirit. Drawing heavily on Gandhi's 'Truth-force' and ahimsa as means of strategy and tactics, King added his own concept of 'Love Force'.

In agape there are no boundaries that separate us. No fences that divide us. The beloved community is the universe and agape is redeeming goodwill for all people in that community.

In King's prophetic words:

Agape is disinterested love. It is a love in which the individual seeks not his own good, but the good of his neighbor (I Cor. 10:24). Agape does not begin by discriminating between worthy and unworthy people, or any qualities people possess. It begins by loving others for their sakes. It is an entirely 'neighbor regarding concern for other,' which discovers the neighbor in every man it meets. Therefore, agape makes no distinction between friend and enemy: it is directed toward both.

Indeed it is the keystone of my faith in the future that we will someday achieve a thoroughly integrated society. I believe that before the turn of the century, if trends continue to move and develop as presently, we will have moved a long, long way toward such a society.

Notes

1. Lerone Bennett, Jr., *What Manner of Man* (Chicago: Johnson, 1968).
2. Martin Luther King, Jr., *Strength to Love* (New York: Harper & Row, 1963).
3. Nietzsche, *The Genealogy of Morals* (New York: Macmillan, 1924).
4. John J. Ansbro, *Martin Luther King, Jr.: The Making of a Mind* (Maryknoll, NY: Orbis Books, 1982).
5. See, for example, King's strategy at the Pettus Bridge.
6. Martin Luther King, Jr., *Stride Toward Freedom* (New York: Harper & Row, 1958).

16

An Anti-Secularist Manifesto

Ashis Nandy

I

Gandhi said he was secular. Yet, he thought poorly of those who wanted to keep religion and politics separate. Those who believed in such separation, he said, understood neither religion nor politics.

This contradiction has its roots in two meanings of secularism current in contemporary India. The first meaning is known to every modern Westerner; the second is an Indianism which has no place either in the *Oxford English Dictionary* or in *Webster's Dictionary*. According to the first, religious tolerance could come only from the devaluation of religion in public life and from the freeing of politics from religion. The less politics is contaminated by religion, this argument goes, the more secular or tolerant a state you will have. The word 'secular' here is the opposite of the word 'sacred'. (I shall use the words 'religion', 'culture' and 'ethnicity' loosely and often interchangeably in this chapter, for the political problems which religions face or pose today are a part of the problem of cultural survival in India and yet, to understand the problem of this survival in all its complexity, one must first learn to state it in terms of religious conflicts.)

According to its second meaning, 'secularism' is not the opposite of the word 'sacred' but that of 'ethnocentrism', 'xenophobia', and 'fanaticism'. One could be a good secularist by being equally disrespectful towards all religions or by being equally respectful towards them. And true secularism, the second meaning insists, must opt for respect. It is this non-modern meaning of secularism which anti-colonial India stressed, given its concern with mass mobilization and a broad consensus against British rule. The meaning recognizes that even when a state is tolerant of religions, it need not lead to religious tolerance in a society. For tolerance by the state cannot guarantee tolerance by the society. State tolerance may ensure, in the short run, the survival of a political community; in the long run the community must go beyond it. This meaning of secularism recognizes covertly what we are now finding painfully, namely that the growth of vested interests in a secular public sphere is an insufficient basis for the long-term survival of a political community. Otherwise the Scots and the Welsh or, for that matter, the Sikhs and the Assamese would not be creating so many problems for their countries.

Previously, thanks to a number of fortunate circumstances, one could follow the logic of the second, more local, meaning of secularism in Indian politics while paying lip-service to the first. In recent years, the nature of the democratic process in India has been forcing the political actors to choose between the two meanings. First, the condition of the Indian state today is such that to advise the religious traditions to abide by values derived from the Indian state is likely to fall on deaf ears. Few will believe that Hinduism, Sikhism or Islam have any moral lesson to learn from the Indian state. For the same reason, the hope that the state can be an impartial arbiter among different religious communities in its present situation appears a rather pallid one. Second, in spite of the tremendous growth in the power of the state in India, sensitive political analysts as well as activists are in no doubt as to who or what will be abolished if the Indian nation-state today takes on the task of abolishing religious and ethnic identities. The secularization of the Indian state has gone far but there are limits to its capacity to secularize the society. (As I am primarily writing for the modern English-speaking person, I shall use the word 'secularism' in its proper English sense in the rest of this chapter and forget the other secularism as an improper Indianism.)

The awareness of these issues has created problems for our concept of the state in India. Since about the seventeenth century, the modern ideology of the state has wanted the state to be secular by separating religion and politics. Since we first began to borrow the ideology in the third decade of the last century, it has also dominated the modern Indian consciousness. And we, too, have systematically tried to separate religion from politics. Now we suddenly confront the embarrassing fact that not only many Indians but a significant proportion of humankind have become suspicious of the Western concept of secularism and have become receptive to a non-secular concept of religious and ethnic tolerance.

To understand the nature of this response we have to first recognize that modern nation-states, being by definition suspicious of the presence of culture in politics and trying to carve out a sphere of the state where only the values of statecraft will rule, work with the following ordering of the citizen (I also give examples from Indian public life):

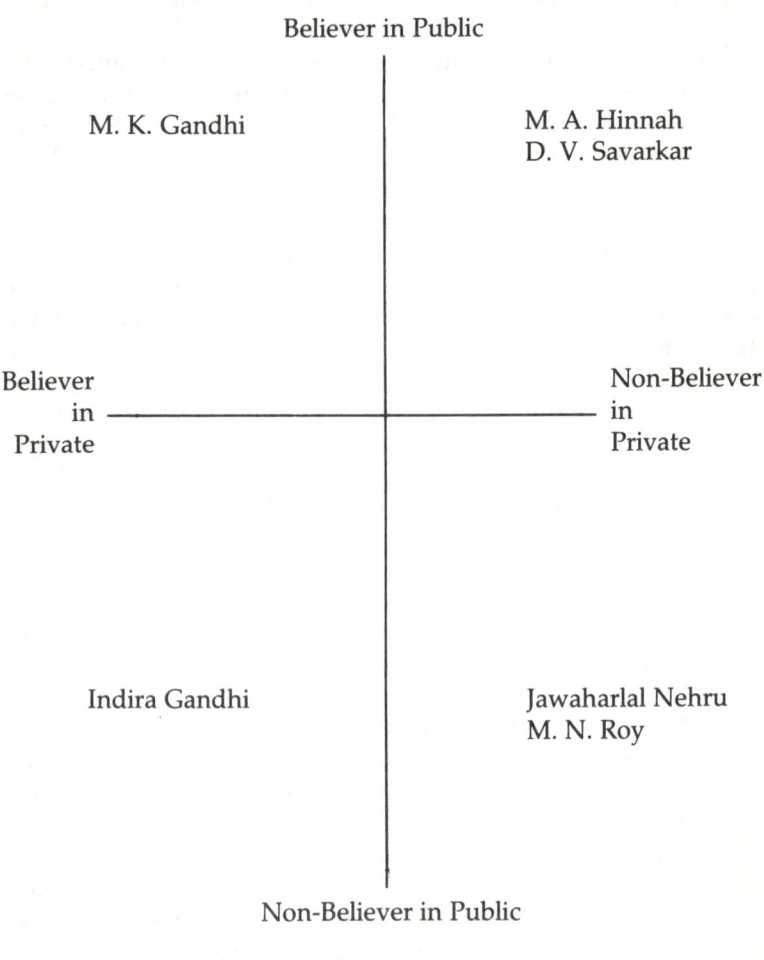

Believer in Public

M. K. Gandhi   M. A. Hinnah
                                D. V. Savarkar

Believer   Non-Believer
in ——————————————————— in
Private   Private

Indira Gandhi   Jawaharlal Nehru
                                M. N. Roy

Non-Believer in Public

Figure 1.

In other words, to the ideologues of the modern state system, the ideal political man is someone like Nehru or Roy. And they believe that, given the ineluctable laws of social progress, more and more citizens will enter the first category, to shed, as a first step, their religious beliefs in public and, then, as a second step, their beliefs in private. This hierarchy of citizens, which persists in spite of the official and unofficial veneration of Gandhi as the 'father of the Indian Nation', follows naturally from the modern ideology of secularism and provides the basis of the Indian state's claim to a monopoly on religious and ethnic tolerance. At the level of the person, such tolerance is definitionally the prerogative of one who has some Western education and some exposure to the modern culture and the modern idiom of politics.

A Gandhian criticism of the approach could be threefold. First, that the approach ignores the finer differences within traditions, while playing up such differences within the modern culture. It ignores the fact that some forms of religion do lead to intolerance, other forms do not. Thus while the approach draws a line between vulgar Marxism and nonvulgar Marxism and one between a vulgar West and a nonvulgar West, it refuses to draw a line between vulgar religion and nonvulgar religion or between tolerant and intolerant forms of culture. Often such secularism – I shall call it official secularism – goes farther. It compares the ideals of modernity with realities of religions and cultures. Thus, the ideals of modern politics are compared with the realities of the caste system (to show how bad the latter is) the way many zealous apologists of Hinduism compare the ideals of the caste system with the realities of hierarchizing modern bureaucracy (to show how good the former is).

Second, official secularism tries to limit the democratic process by truncating the political personality of the citizen. While the personality of those within the fully secular, modern sector is well-represented in the democratic order, those outside the modern sector have only a part of themselves represented in politics. The other part they have to keep carefully outside the public sphere. This of course means that the creative role which politics might play within a religious or cultural tradition, by playing up some sub-traditions against the others or by reordering the hierarchy of sub-traditions, is pre-empted. Instead of a dialogue between the public and the private within a person – and between politics and culture – the two spheres are rigidly separated and the latter is frozen in time. As a result, the religious and cultural traditions are forced to become, as the modernists invariably accuse them of being, status-quo-ist. That does not of course keep religion out of politics; it only means politics enters it by a different route. We shall return to this point.

Third, official secularism fails to take into account the politics of cultures today. It sees the believer as a person with an inferior political consciousness and it celebrates the fact that we live more and more in a world where all faiths and cultures, except modernity, are in recession. Such secularism fails to sense that critical social consciousness, if it is not to become a reformist sect within modernity, must respect and build upon the faiths and the visions that have refused to adapt to the modern worldview. For one cannot any more venture a basic criticism of a modern society from within the modern tradition; at best, one can provide an internal criticism palatable to the Third World elites living in the modern sectors of their societies.

I have spoken of the growing marginalization of religions, cultures and visions. This may seem odd at a time when the secularists are obviously having difficulties. In Lebanon, Quebec, Scotland and the Basque region – and in Punjab, Assam, Sri Lanka and Sind in the Indian subcontinent itself – ethnicity is challenging established modern nationalism; racism is on the rise in parts of the liberal First World; and the Church is ascendent in parts of the super-secular Second. Even in societies not torn by ethnic passions, a new cultural pride and exclusivism are visible. American Blacks and Hispanics are examples. Though often viewed as unique, the self-affirmation of parts of the Muslim world can also be seen as a part of this larger picture. The Muslims now find themselves at the center of the world stage precisely because for long they were treated as the etceteras and the and-so-forths of the world, whereas their ethnic self-affirmation is now backed by wealth and a new capacity to be a political nuisance.

This is not the world where one can talk glibly about the marginalization of faith. Yet the fact remains that the affirmation of religion in our times has gone hand in hand with the erosion of religions; exactly as the victory of the idea of the nation-state has coextended with a new cultural and psychological crisis in the modern nation-state system. The two crises however become one in the Third World, and each society in that part of the world is faced with a dilemma.

On the one hand, the existing hierarchy of nations and the cultural domination of the modern West have created a new concern for, and defensiveness about, nonmodern cultures. Modernity no longer looks like something in the distant future or a marginal strain in the Third World, as it looked to the first generation of public figures who led the newly independent countries in the 1950s and 1960s. Modernity is now hegemonic globally.

This sensitivity to the power of modernity has been sharpened by the Orwellian awareness that one by one the main modern theories of manmade suffering and this-worldly liberation have themselves been coopted by new forces of oppression; these theories themselves now legitimize new forms of greed, violence and obscurantism. In such a world, the older objectivist interpretations of religious intolerance are bound to look incapable of handling the need of many cultural groups for survival with justice and dignity.

On the other hand, the pathologies of religion have become more obvious, due to the greater visibility of many forms of religion and due to the attempts to empower some of them. Even in the few Third World polities where democratic participation has expanded, religion has ridden piggy-back on the newly politicized to enter visible politics and move center stage. Democratization and politicization have not eliminated religion from politics; they have given xenophobic and anti-democratic forms of religion new power and salience. On the one hand is Coca Cola, on the other Ayatollah Khomeini. The choice, even in this terribly crude formulation, is painful.

II

The modern concept of secularism in India, I have already said, is borrowed from Western history and it has a clear normative component: religion and ethnicity should be banished from the public sphere and an area should be marked out in politics where rationality, contractual social relationships, and *realpolitik* would reign. This sanitized sphere of politics may throw up rulers who are believers, but if it does do so, these leaders should be weak, secret or apologetic believers. It also follows from the same normative frame that in open societies some citizens may choose their leaders on religious grounds or the leaders may exploit this weakness of the citizens, but both sides – the leaders and the led – should be embarrassed about this state of affairs and know the limits of their game.

Thus, a section of the Indian citizenry too feels more at home with a temple-going Prime Minister such as the late Indira Gandhi, the same way a section of the American public applauds a church-going President and sees him as potentially more honest or straightforward. Yet, most vocal Hindu Indians will be shocked if Nepal is declared a natural ally of India because it is the world's only Hindu Kingdom, exactly as most vocal Americans, irrespective of party affiliations, would express genuine surprise if the United States takes a position in international relations solely on the grounds of Christian ethics. A majority of the vocal citizens in both countries will be happier to be led by leaders who are good Christians or Hindus but who know how to set limits on their religiosity.

There is a tacit theory behind this ambivalence to religion. And it cuts across nearly all state-centered ideologies in the Indian polity. It posits two secular trends in history: (1) the gradual erosion of faith and culture because of the growth of science, rationality and modern education; (2) the consequent expansion of a homogenous, universal, contractual, impersonal, public sphere where only values like self-interest, *realpolitik* and national security rule. The theory is an indirect plea to educate, guide and 'break in' the citizenry into this secular sphere, the sphere of *rajdharma*, with the help of a modern vanguard acting as a pace-setter in matters of social change. The vanguard sets the pace by exercising its political choices in a rational and, hence, moral fashion from the point of view of the state. It may not be the Christian, the Hindu or the Islamic concept of morality, the theory goes, but it is morality all right; it is the morality of modern statecraft. In other words, the vanguard sets the pace by being a collection of exemplary persons who live with their fellow humans without illusions, yet ethically, and by building their ethics not on myths or compassion but on scientific rationality, history and reasons of the state.

The influence of such theories on the public life in other parts of the world explains the sigh of relief when the *faith* in communism gave way to communist interests in the Russian nation-state in the 1940s and 1950s, and the even greater sigh of relief when post-Maoist China returned from the 'Little Red Book' of Chairman Mao to the principles of the four modernizations in the 1970s. Though the changes are often cited as a proof of the falsity of Marxism and the hypocrisy of the Marxists, they are almost universally interpreted in the modern world as a return to sanity, normality and adulthood.

It should be admitted straightaway that, howsoever limited its concept of human nature, howsoever contemptuous its attitude toward ethnic peripheries, such secularism has served the Indian citizenry reasonably well for long periods of time. Especially so in the early years after Independence under the easy, benign modernist, Jawaharlal Nehru. At the time, political mobilization, despite the existence of a powerful nationalist movement since the 1920s, was still at a manageably low level. The Indian power elite was choosy about whom it admitted to the highest levels of the government, and the memory of what could be done in the name of religion in public life was fresh in the minds of the citizens. There was a wide consensus that an area of sanity had to be maintained in the polity, community-based nepotism had to be contained, confidence had to be created in the new political institutions and in the impartiality of the peace-keeping forces. Above all, there was a consensus which acknowledged – against the beliefs of the various forms of liberal, Fabian and Marxist ideologies which informed the ruling ideology of the Indian state – that Hindu and Islamic exclusivism and zealotry were the strongest among the urban middle classes, not among the so-called peripheries of the country, and therefore the main battle against religious and ethnic conflicts had to be fought among the middle classes which dominated the Indian political consciousness. The secularization of Indian politics, so far as it involved mainly the middle classes, did hold such conflicts in check.

That consensus and that strategy have gone as far as they could have gone. They have now not only begun to break down but to work against many forms of ethnic tolerance. First, political participation has grown enormously, thanks to the eight general and innumerable local elections since Independence and thanks to the way politics has entered virtually every sphere of Indian life. No longer is it possible to screen those entering politics for their commitment to modern secular ethics. This is another way of saying that democratization itself has set limits on the secularization of Indian politics. Indeed, the new political institutions in India have acquired popular support and cultural content from exactly the new entrants from what was, till recently, a part of the ethnic 'backwaters' of India. They, the new incumbents, have given Indian democracy its power and resilience.

Second, partly negating the first process, the new entrants carrying their religion or ethnicity into their politics have self-consciously begun to shed their ethnic consciousness while retaining their ethnic links. These links they use in a secular fashion for electoral, especially factional ends. That is, they end up by joining the second category of political participants (exemplified by persons like Jinnah and Savarkar) rather than the third or the fourth (exemplified by Indira Gandhi and Nehru respectively – see Figure 1 on page 246). Instead of religious use of politics, they make political use of religion. I need hardly add that such use of religion only apparently gives them more power. In reality, it makes religion not a principle of moderation or restraint in politics nor a source of values; it makes religion an instrument of political mobilization within a psephocratic model – a model in which elections and elected 'kings' dominate the system. Thus religion as a depository or expression of cultural values no longer remains available for checking the pure politics of public life, often seen by the newly politicized as an area where only the laws of the jungle apply. But religion as an idiom manages to extend the domination of pure politics and the ubiquitous hand of the state to the sphere of religion. All this is another way of saying that there is now a peculiar double-bind in Indian politics: the ills of religion have found political expression but the strengths of it have not been available for checking corruption and violence in public life.

Third, self-doubts have arisen in many modern Indians because the older concept of secularism has been losing its shine since the late 1960s in exactly those countries which were said to be way ahead of India on the road to secularization and nation-building. The positivist, science-centered ideologies of nationality and the conservative and radical theories of progress have come under attack in these countries as the new opiates of the masses which allow the new ruling classes to hand over the state to the technocrats and to the controllers of mass media. After rejecting and very nearly defeating religion as a false consciousness in society after society in the First and Second worlds, the social critics and activists there have found that the secular state has begun to claim – along with its new priestly classes like the scientists, the bureaucrats and the development experts – exactly the same blind faith from its followers as the church once did. After undermining the concept of an omniscient, omnipotent and omnipresent God, and after popularizing the concepts of science, history and progress as gods, the secular state, to the chagrin of some statists, has begun to equip itself with the technological means to be omniscient, omnipotent and omnipresent itself. In the North that process is called scientific advancement, in the South development.

All these experiences have been unkind to the modern secularists in India. Recently, they have been subjected to further stress because, as part of secularization itself, the private lives of politicians have become a public property. This has revealed that the best of the secular politicians in twentieth-century India have not been as aseptically secular in private as they have been made out to be. Jawaharlal Nehru, it now turns out, was a votary of astrology and a sneaking Hindu in personal life; Subhas Chandra Bose was a *Gita*-devouring crypto-*sanyasi*; and by now it is well-known that Indira Gandhi, that open worshipper of the secular Indian nation-state, did not like to miss a *havan* or pilgrimage, given half a chance. The clear line drawn earlier between the secular and the nonsecular, and the believer and the nonbeliever, is now blurred. And even some of the ultra-secular Indians have begun to suspect that secularization and ethnic tolerance are partly independent of each other.

Even the implicit, third model of secularism used by the *bête noire* of Indian secularists, Mohammed Ali Jinnah, is in a crisis today. Most well-known Indian secularists of the recent decades would have by their personal faith put to shame Jinnah, who was in private life a nonbeliever. But Jinnah made a rather profitable mix of private agnosticism and public religiosity, which of course was the exact reverse of the dominant mode of linking religion to politics in Indian nationalism: a private faith and public non-belief. Jinnah's goal was to create a political culture in Pakistan which ultimately would not be much different from the liberal secular culture he himself had at one time wanted for the whole of India. He hoped gradually to delink Islam from the Pakistani state and to confine it to private life, and then to move towards a secular modern state where a highly Westernized, lapsed Muslim like him would not be a misfit. At least, that is the meaning I impute to his first speech after taking over as the Governor General of Pakistan.

Jinnah's main fear, the fear which made him leave the Congress camp, was that the Gandhian movement would create a culture of politics in which, under the guise of Gandhian 'secularism', a Hindu culture would discomfit both the Indian secularist and the Indian Muslim. Being a Westernized ethnic, Jinnah could not differentiate between a Hindu zealot and a spokesman of the peripheral Hindus. He had no clue as to why a zealot like D. V. Savarkar should be more hostile to Gandhi than to a modernist like Nehru. However, if Jinnah had been alive, he would have been happy to see that his political style, even though in crisis because it has been taken over by the zealots in his 'homeland', survives in other parts of the subcontinent. In India, often fully secular, even anti-religious, Muslim politicians get access to power in the name of their Muslim origins which they themselves see in purely instrumental terms. In Pakistan and Bangladesh, the Zulfikar Ali Bhuttos and the Zia-ur-Rahmans, who are nonbelievers or weak believers themselves, have constantly tried to profit politically from the appeal of Islam.

The experience of Islam in this respect has been the experience of every religion of the subcontinent. It is the experience of being often reduced to the status of a handmaiden of politics, subservient to the needs of a nation-state and of the class interests of the zealot and the Westernized secularist, both of whom hold in contempt the vast majority of the people of their own religion – one for their lack of zealotry, the other for their incomplete Westernization.

In sum, formal, Western-style secularization has shown an incapacity to keep pace with politicization in this part of the world, and it shows no sign of being able to do so in the future. As with countries long held up as models of development for India (at different times Britain, the United States, the Soviet Union, Maoist China and even the Shah's Iran), in this subcontinent too ethnicity is refusing to fade. Yet, as I have already said, the survival of ethnicity has not strengthened ethnic or religious traditions; it has only allowed the pathologies of the latter to find political expression.

You will notice that I have tried to make this point in quasi-empirical terms. To avoid polemics, I am ignoring for the moment the worm's-eye-view argument that a modern secular state can never be that secular, for it is built on another form of religion, namely the ideology of modernity, and that this religious status of modernity is recognized by the population in every Third World society which resists it as the faith of the rulers and as the faith of a part of the intelligentsia shadow-boxing with the power-holders.

We thus come to the 'method' of a small minority of those working for religious or ethnic tolerance in India, though the method paradoxically is based on the faith and the culture of the majority of Indians. The method is implied in the unofficial Indian use of the word 'secularism'; it is explicit in the Gandhian and proto-Gandhian theories of interreligious harmony.

Those loyal to the modern idea of nation-state accept the idiom of secularism and try to hitch ethnicity to politics in a more or less pragmatic way. They try to create a social basis for secularism by linking it to the reward system of the state, thus creating a vested interest in at least the secular political style. Those sympathetic to the Gandhian vision – to the utter embarrassment of the modern Indian state with its new-found global power ambitions and its fear of the growing political self-affirmation of the nonmodern Indians – try to shift the emphasis from actors to texts, and from outer to inner incentives, so as to reaffirm 'true' religion and 'true' culture which they see as definitionally tolerant of the other religions and cultures.

Such a vision has many features. The most crucial of them is the recognition that the clash between modernity and religious traditions in the Third World elicits from each culture four political responses to ethnicity. The responses can be called half idealtypes, half mythic structures.

The first of the four, which does not really fit in with the other three, is the ethnic construction of the *Western man* whose personality is viewed as the cause of the West's success and the non-West's failure. This Western man is a shadow category or a dummy variable. Not merely because he is often physically absent in the Third World but also because the way the non-West construes him is not how he sees himself. Nor even the way he has 'really' existed in history. However, the category is not unreal either; millions of human beings have lived by that image and millions have suffered because of the existence of that image.

Sometimes the Western man is construed by a non-Western culture as an 'other' – to criticize or correct the allegedly faulty personality types available in the culture. The shadowy Western man then becomes a critique of the indigenous personality as well as a projection of the ego-ideal of some sections of the indigenous population. If these sections are powerful, they may even manage to set up this ego-ideal as the ideal of the entire society. It then begins to represent a new eupsychia (to use Abraham Maslow's concept of an utopian concept of personality) in opposition to the traditional eupsychias surviving in the society.

Along with this image of the Western-man-as-the-ideal-political-man goes a managerial attitude to ethnic and religious groupings, often expressed in the belief that successful nation-building involves hard decisions relating to ethnic minorities, decisions not based on the chauvinism of the majority, but on inspired, hard-headed statecraft. What is in store for the minorities in the model is not very different from what is generally in store for them in a theocratic state. Only, instead of facing the prospect of being Islamized under, say, an Islamic theocracy, the minorities face the prospect of being Westernized in a Western nation-state. However, in the second case, the situation is morally 'redeemed' by the fact that what is in store for the ethnic minorities in the long run is no different from what is in store for the ethnic majority in the long run. Both become objects of social engineering and both face cultural extinction.

The second category of response is that of the *Westernized native*, the ethnic who has internalized and approximated the Western man (though his syncretism may include sometimes a touch of defiance, too). From a Rammohun Roy (1772–1833) who took a Brahmin cook with him to England after life-long defiance of Hindu caste codes, to a Jawaharlal Nehru (1889–1964) who in his weaker moments gave in to astrologers and *tantriks* of all hues, a long and colorful list of individuals provides clues to the inner contradictions of the Westernized native. But it also happens to be a list of men who have fought for the Western secular ideals in their part of the world and turned against their own cultural self, to partly identify with their Western tormentors.

Corresponding to the personality type is a reconstructed history which locates in the past persons who reportedly represented the same ideals. Thus modern India has rediscovered Ashoka from the third century BC and Akbar from the sixteenth century as proper 'secular' rulers and it has reinterpreted traditional texts (such as the ones dealing with the different *dharmas* of the king and the brahman, or the ones dealing with the morality of statecraft) to legitimize the Western ideals of secular statecraft.

The Westernized native may differ politically from the Western man, he may even be the Western man's political antagonist but his ultimate aim is to Westernize – he prefers to say 'modernize' or 'universalize' – his own culture. He takes the ideal of one world seriously and he believes in a theory of progress in which progress stands for uniformity according to the model of the European nineteenth-century visions of a desirable society. He believes that the Western nations – or, if the Westernized native happens to be orthodox socialist or positivist Marxist, the socialist West – is more advanced culturally; that the peripheries of the world will have slowly and painfully to traverse the same path of progress. The two main obstacles to this he sees as the backward, religious masses, unexposed to modern scientific rationality, and their false leadership, ever willing to take advantage of irrational, superstitious faiths. To fight the two obstacles, he invokes the image of the Western man and constantly compares it with the realities of the non-Western cultures.

Thirdly, there is the *zealot* – the aggressive Hindu, Muslim or Sikh who, reacting to and yet internalizing the humiliation inflicted on all faiths by a triumphant antifaith called Western modernity, has accepted the modern attitude to all faiths including his own. He is the one the Westernized native fears the most as the fanatic who might mobilize the otherwise-unmobilizable masses suffering from an acute case of false consciousness (even though such zealots mostly operate from urban bases and appeal to the semimodern). If such a zealot is a Muslim or a Sikh we call him a fundamentalist; if he is a Hindu we call him a revivalist or a Hindu nationalist.

Strangely enough, the zealot only *uses* the traditional religious or ethnic boundaries as units of mobilization, means of coalition building and settling scores. To him the faith of the ordinary Hindu, Muslim or Sikh is an embarrassment. The latter does not seem to show the right kind of respect to the purity of his own faith; he has no sense of unity; his commitment to *realpolitik* is partial; and he lacks the martial spirit shown by the zealot himself. For instance, the Hindu zealot constantly bemoans the betrayal of Hinduism by the Hindus; the Muslim zealot laments the inadequacy of the Muslims. Both lack basic confidence in their own communities and in the day-to-day culture of their co-believers. For both, a religious community exists only for the purpose of fulfilling the drive for potency and parity of its zealots.

In this respect, the Hindu revivalist or Muslim fundamentalist is often only a variation on the secular political man of post-Enlightenment Europe and his ethnicity is skin-deep and reactive.

He, too, has identified with the aggressors; he, too, has turned against his cultural self. Ultimately, the zealot's is more a political than a civilizational self-affirmation. To the zealot the idea of his own religion or culture is appealing, not the actuality of it. (That is the reason for his strong commitment to the classical version of his religion and culture.) He is one who has internalized the 'defeat' of his religion or culture in the hands of the modern world and he is the one who believes that that defeat can be avenged only when the peripheral faiths or ethnicities have internalized the technology of victory of the Western man and decided to fight under the flag of their own faiths. The zealot hates the Westernized ethnic as one who has sold himself to the Western man but his hatred for the peripheral ethnic is deeper. For he shares with the Westernized ethnic the reference point called the Western man.

Finally, there are the numerically preponderant, *peripheral believers* (who are peripheral only because the zealots and the secularists have declared them so). These believers have learned to fight with, as also to survive, the zealots of the other faiths as well as their own. The modern secularist and the crypto-modern zealot know of the battles for survival against the zealots of other faiths, not of the other battle against the zealots of their own. Neither the secularist nor the zealot has the sensitivity to stand witness to this other battle for survival. Neither has the time to remember the experience of neighborliness and co-survival which characterize the relationships among the peripheral believers of different faiths.

The nonmodern, peripheral ethnic has a longer and deeper memory. And it is to him and his ideology that Gandhi turned to give a political basis to his concept of religious and ethnic tolerance. A number of scholars, most recently T. K. Mahadevan and Agehananda Bharati, have written about Gandhi's poor knowledge of textual Hinduism. An impartial scholar of classical Hinduism cannot but agree with them. Surely Gandhi had little patience with the greater Sanskritic culture. He sometimes paid lip service to it but there could be little doubt that his primary allegiance was to the folk theologies of Hinduism and Islam. His family belonged to the Pranami sect, a sect deeply influenced by Islam and he belonged to a region where Muslim communities were in turn deeply influenced by Hindu folk theology. He had reasons to be confident that religions not merely divided but also united human aggregates.

Once you have classified the ethnic personality in politics thus (see the table below), it becomes obvious that in societies like India, there are two affinities and three enmities in any situation involving two religious communities.

Political Responses to Ethnicity

Response Category	Ethnic Examples	
The modern secular-rationalist	Westernized Hindu	Westernized Muslim
The semi-modern zealot	Hindu revivalist	Muslim fundamentalist
The modern ethnic	Peripheral or everyday Hindu	Peripheral or everyday Muslim

The overt affinity is between the Westernized believers of the two communities. The Westernized Hindu and the Westernized Muslim, for instance, can spend days discussing their commonness, especially how the two of them are different from the common run of Hindus and Muslims who are willing to kill each other for the sake of their faiths, and how in the distant future, they, the barbarians, might be persuaded to shed their faith, modernize and then live happily ever after. The covert affinity is between the peripheral Hindus and peripheral Muslims, much less accessible to the modern Indian and to modern scholarship.

The overt hostility is that between the Hindu and the Muslim zealots who hate each other but understand each other's motivations perfectly. The less overt one is the hostility of the Westernized ethnic towards the peripherals of his own as well as other faiths whom the Westernized ethnic sees as passive or prospective zealots. The covert hostility is that of the zealot whose hatred for the everyday practitioner of his own faith is total.

III

I have more or less completed my analysis. All that remains to be done is to mention briefly some features of the peripheral majority, their folk religions and folk theologies, and the politics of tolerance implicit in them. This tolerance bypasses the three enmities mentioned above and has the capacity to survive and even enrich the process of democratic participation. Unlike the tolerance of the modernized sectors which proves fragile in a situation of expanding participation.

First, the peripheral believers in a traditional society face a worldview which seeks to pre-empt and frequently deny the existence of their traditional ideology of tolerance. Thus, modern India talks of Ashoka and Akbar without admitting that they did not build a tolerant state in a sense in which a Lenin or a Jawaharlal Nehru would have wanted them to; they built their tolerance on the tenets of Buddhism and Islam. Likewise the chieftains of the Hindu zealots like to refer to the profound truth that India is tolerant because it is Hindu. But their claim has a dishonest ring about it, for they violently disagree when someone parodies them and says that Akbar was tolerant because he was Muslim or Ashoka was great because he was Buddhist first and a king second.

All Gandhi did as a *sanatani* or traditional Hindu was to take seriously both these positions – the one which says that India is secular because it is Hindu and the one which says Akbar was tolerant because he was a Muslim – and to openly admit the religious basis of ethnic tolerance in India. He did the same thing with Christianity and tried to do so haphazardly with Sikhism and Judaism, too. Instead of committing himself to the hopeless task of banishing religion from politics while expanding democratic participation, he dared to seek a politics which would be infused with the right kind of religion and be tolerant. That is why a Hindu zealot found him a serious opposition and killed him. As I have already said, Hindu zealotry has never found the modernist a serious enemy; it has found in him only an effete, self-hating Hindu.

Secondly, Gandhi recognized that India's most effective preachers of inter-communal harmony in the past have mostly been either pre-modern, nonmodern or anti-modern. Men like Nehru, he felt, were only a partial or apparent exception to this rule. Sensing the critique of modernity implied in this recognition, the embarrassed modernists have tried to integrate Gandhi in their framework by conceptualizing Hinduism and Islam as two cultures which could be freed from their religious moorings and fitted into a composite whole called the Indian culture to which all right-thinking Indians should be allegiant. Unfortunately, religions are not machine-parts and politicians and scholars make bad cultural machinists. The best of Hinduism and the best of Islam may go

An Anti-Secularist Manifesto

together as the titles of two paperback books of readings in the same series, but it hardly invokes two living religious traditions trying to cope with each other or with real-life issues.

Those outside the modern sector in India sense this. They are conscious of the existence of two religions called Hinduism and Islam as well as one of the Hindu construction of Islam and the Muslim construction of Hinduism. It is on the basis of such constructions – and by this I certainly mean something more than stereotypes – that they operate in everyday life. At this plane the 'languages' of Hinduism and Islam – and for that matter all major religions and ethnic traditions in India – have now interlocking and/or common grammars. These grammars survive, in spite of the efforts of learned scholars to read them as folk theologies – as inferior, peripheral versions of Hinduism and Islam. They survive as a mode of mutuality and a major source of Indian creativity. Creativity, after all, presumes a certain marginality and, in the matter of culture, a certain dialectic between the classical and the folk. It has to transcend the classicist – and elite – formulation that classicism is the center of the culture, to protect the classicism itself from becoming a two-dimensional frozen instance of a culture museumized and commoditified.

Let us consider for a moment what many consider to be the finest expression of Indian creativity: north Indian classical music. Is it Hindu? Is it Muslim? Is it secular? One need not do a very imaginative empirical work on Indian creative musicians – though some such works are available – to pierce through their derived sloganeering about secularism and to find out that the Muslim musicians think north Indian classical music to be mainly Muslim, the Hindu musicians think it to be mainly Hindu. This could be read as a source of possible conflict; it could be read as the possible source of the cultural power of such music. Abdul Karim Khan and Bade Ghulam Ali Khan when they composed their majestic *bhajans* implicity recognized this; so do Mallikarjun Mansur and Gangubai Hangal when they sing their odes to Hazrat Turkman or celebrate Muhammadshah Rangeele. Some musicians like Ali Akbar Khan pay their homage to this awareness by being devotees of the goddesses Saraswati or Durga; others have done so by undertaking polluting domestic chores – such as cleaning cooking utensils or even *pan* spitoons at their Muslim gurus' homes – even though Brahmins themselves. Some others are even more direct. One of the major symbols of the north Indian classical tradition in this century, Allauddin Khan, when he wanted to honor his wife Madina Begum by composing a new *raga* in her name, could not apparently find anything less Vaishnava than *madanmanjari*. Modern secularism fails to see the religious sources of such creativity and tolerance of other faiths. It sees the refusal of Bade Ghulam Ali to sing paeans to Pakistan or to its founder during his brief stay in that country as an expression of his secularism. Traditional theories of ethnic tolerance see it as an expression of *his* Islam or of a truer Islam. They recognize that song texts in north Indian classical music have a tradition behind them and they bear a direct relationship with an artist's or a *gharana's* mode of creativity. That tradition has a direct religious meaning – simultaneously Hindu and Islamic. It cannot be artificially given a religious meaning exclusively identified with one faith. Nor can it be ever fully secularized.

Similarly with architecture, P. N. Oak has worked for years on a 'Hindu' history of the Taj Mahal. Now carbon dating seems to be lending partial support to this theory. Trying pathetically to be a proper modern historian, Oak never owns up the psychological insight he is tacitly articulating: the Taj Mahal does seem sanctified to a religious Hindu, and deeply Islamic to the believing Muslim. There lies the Indian meaning of its grandeur as well as appeal. Disconnect Taj from either of the two traditions, and it becomes a monument purely for the non-Indian tourists and orientalists. Oak's history, thus, is not only irrelevant to the majority of Hindus; it is anti-Hindu. It is meant only to cope with the sense of inferiority of the Hindu zealot *vis-à-vis* other faiths. It is directed against the ideology of the living Hindu in the name of a dead Hindu, derived from texts and from the post-seventeeth-century, Western concept of scientific history. The everyday Hindu ceases to be a Hindu, *lokachar* affirms, if he begins to define his places of worship by their histories. The Taj to him is a place of worship as a mosque. For him its Hindu history, even if true, neither adds to nor subtracts from its meaning.

What is true of the zealot's approach to culture is also true of the Westernized native's attitude to culture. The modern secularist and the modern Hindu try to preserve the Taj as a monument for tourists and build an oil refinery next to it. Their modernity is linked to the Taj through the market and through sulphuric acid. The traditional concept of ethnic tolerance, cornered, powerless and at bay, can only pray at the mosque hoping that the modern world will pass it by.

Both examples provide clues to an alternative awareness of the culture of India. This awareness admits that on one plane Hinduism has become a part of Indian Islam and Islam a part of Hinduism. The ordinary Indian Muslim knows – even if being part of a minority he finds it more difficult to admit – that Indian Islam, one of the most creative in the world, owes its creativity to its encounter with the other faiths of India, exactly the way the everyday Hindu knows that the creativity of Hinduism has been sharpened over the centuries by its encounters with other faiths, mainly Islam, Buddhism, Christianity and Sikhism. True that the uprooted or marginalized Muslim, urbanized and frequently lumpenized, often looks to the Middle East for salvation. And so does sometimes the Mullah trying desperately to protect his place among followers whose peripheral Islam does not often grant him the centrality he seeks. But can one not make a strong case that such defensiveness follows not so much from his faith as from his frustration and insecurity in his immediate political environs? The Gandhian response to this question is clear. If the rules governing the treatment of *mlechchas* and *vidharmis* in Manu, Yajnavalkya and Kautilya do not handicap the Hindu in a democratic order, because he has other *shastras* and traditions to fall back upon, the concept of *dar'ul Islam* also should not make the Muslim a congenital misfit in a plural society. There are alternative traditions in Islam, too.

Even within the folds of Islamic orthodoxy there has always been a substantial proportion of those who have represented the will to live and die, as their forefathers have lived and died, in a culture they know and have internalized. The subcontinental Muslims live not only with the myth of one thousand years of Muslim rule, as is often mentioned, but also with two hundred years of more recent memories of the recession of the political power of Indian Islam and with – this is never mentioned – one thousand years of conflicted but meaningful neighborliness. (Has anyone measured the psychological impact of one thousand years of distant past against the impact of the more immediate past of two hundred years? Or against the experience of one riot in which one's family has been a victim? Has any psychologist assessed the influence of immediate neighborhood as opposed to that of distant political authorities in an apolitical society? The existing empirical understanding of interreligious and ethnic conflicts in India is not on as firm ground as it pretends.)

I find in the *Indian Express* of January 29 1983, a brief biographical note written by a journalist which, in an abbreviated form and with minor editing, I want to reproduce for the scholarly secularist as my last word on the inner capacities of faiths in the matter of ethnic tolerance.

On January 9, the house of a young Telegu poet in the old city of Hyderabad was raided by a band of communalists. They stabbed him, his wife and his child ... Communal frenzy does not know what it claims. They ... did not know that they were destroying a promising Telegu poet, who was writing the 17th version of ... Ramayana.

His ambition was to become a *vidwaan* of Sanskrit. But Kashi Vidyapeeth rejected him ... Then he met a scholar, Pandit Gunday Rao Harkarey, who taught him the secret of learning a language by the self-taught method ... Thus, studying privately, he obtained Master's degrees in three ... languages – Sanskrit, Telegu and Hindi.

He had started composing small poems in Telegu when he was just 12 years old. After his marriage, he produced four volumes of *kaavyas* and three volumes of *khanda kaavyas* ... The young poet now began studying all the versions of Ramayana – Valmiki, Ranganatha, Bhaskara, Kambha, Molla, Viswanatha, Kalpa Vruksha and Tulsi. 'I have discovered rational and logical flaws in Valmiki in his description of places and situation,' he said, 'I want to write my version of Ramayana ... I want to name it "Yaseen Ramayana." It will be my gift to posterity.' That is what Ghulaam Yaseen, the teacher and the poet, was busy doing when fanaticism struck its deathly blow ... And the Ramayana which Ghulaam Yaseen wanted to leave behind him ... remains unfinished.

Who was Ghulaam Yaseen? A secular Muslim who did not know his real vocation? A good man with a Muslim name who could be *used* by dedicated social reformers or by the Indian state to establish bridges between faiths? A crypto-Hindu killed by the Hindus by mistake? Or a true Muslim who could express his religious sensitivities through other people's faiths? Or an Indian whose assassination has simultaneously impoverished Hinduism, Islam and Indianness?

Gandhi's response to these questions, I am sure, would have been unambiguous. What about ours?

Glossary

Ahimsa	Nonviolence
Atma	Soul
Bapu	Gujarati term for father; a title of respect applied to Gandhi
Bhagavad Gita	A Hindu sacred poem of 700 stanzas which describe the teachings of Lord Krishna
Bodhissatvas	Buddhist saint in the last stage before attaining complete knowledge
Brahmacharya	Self-disciplined conduct, including celibacy
Charkha	Spinning wheel; wheel of life
Dharma	Religion, moral practice, duty
Gandhiji	A title of respect bestowed on Gandhi
Gita	See *Bhagavad Gita*
Harijans	Gandhi's term for the Untouchables of the Indian caste system
Himsa	Violence
Karma	The force created by personal actions which accompanies the transmigrating soul
Khaddar	Homespun cloth (also called *Khadi*)
Locachar	Ostentation, pretense, conforming to the world
Mahatma	Great soul
Marga	The right path or approach
Moksha	Liberation from the cycle of death and rebirth
Samvrittisatya	Common truth
Sattvik	Spirited; inner feelings or sentiments
Satyagraha	Holding fast to Truth; used by Gandhi to describe actions of nonviolent or passive resistance
Satyagrahi	A follower of *satyagraha*
Sevagram	Gandhi's last ashram
Swadeshi	National self-reliance; used by Gandhi to label his movement for the boycott of foreign goods
Swaraj	Indian independence, self-rule
Tapas	Religious vow
Vaishnava	A Hindu sect that worships Vishnu as the one supreme God
Varna	Caste

Index

Absolute Truth 95, 97-8, 101, 102, 124, 168, 169, 174, 238
affection and desire, obscuring vision of reality 91
agape 242
agraha 38
ahimsa 3, 23, 32-3, 105, 123, 124, 125, 129, 163, 171, 176, 228, 229, 237–9, 242
  see also nonviolence
alternative traditions 263
Ambedkar, Untouchable leader 41–2
Amritsar massacre 27
anarchism, Indian 210
anasakt yoga 16
anasakti 124
Andrews, C.F. 157–8
Ansbro, John J.
  Martin Luther King, Jr.: The Making of a Mind 239–41
anti-Indian policy 77,78
apartheid 3
appropriate technology 12, 23
arms race, ending of 185
Arnold, Sir Edwin
  The Light of Asia 153, 167
  The Song Celestial 139, 167
artha 130
artificial needs, creation of 199
asceticism 157
  and nonviolence 240–1
ashrama 123
ashrams 16, 75
  discipline of 100
  observances to deepen faith 171
'Asiatic question' in South Africa, distortion of history 65–6
atheism 105–6
Aurobindo 'school', interpretations of the four varnas 145–6
Aurobindo, Sri 138, 141–2, 148

Bannerjee, Kali Charan 158–9

Bannerjee, W.C. 159
Bardoli campaign 24, 25
Bardoli Conference 33
benign forebearance 115–16
Bennett, Lerone (Jr), *What Manner of Man* 236
Bhagavad Gita 90, 130, 131, 167
  Gandhi's interpretation of 86, 137–50
Bhana, Dr Surendra 72
Bhave, Vinoba (constructive worker)
  see Vinoba
Bhoodan (voluntary gift of land to the landless) 206–7, 222
Bihar 219
  sulabh gramdan 211, 212–13
Bihar movement 214–16
'Black Act' (Black Ordinance), Transvaal 26, 76–7
Boer War 62
brahmacharya 22, 56, 171
  see also celibacy
bread labor 186–7, 199, 227–8
British, the, and India, Gandhi's views 27–8
British Indian Association 71
Buddhism 131–2, 149, 152, 176, 260
  nonviolence 10
'Buddhist Economics' 12–13

capitalism 193
caste 145
  and varna 147–8
  see also varna
caste hatred 3
caste system 247
casteism 193
celibacy 22, 51–7, 62, 171
  contraceptive approach to 51, 54
  cultural approach to 51–2
  experiments in 55–7
  taking the vow 54–5

Chatterjee, Dr Margaret, *Gandhi's Religious Thought* 74–5
Chauri Chaura 25–6, 33
Christian missionaries 176
Christianity 132, 149, 260
  cultural packaging of 156–7
  evangelical 154
  and Gandhi 87, 152–64
  in Gandhi's religious formation 74–5
civil disobedience 24, 25, 62, 63, 76–7
civil rights movement in USA 187
civilization
  Gandhian view 125
  modern, decried by Gandhi 125–7
class interests, divergent 69
coercion 216
  detentive 47
  a form of violence 43–4
  and moral attachment 114–15, 116
  nonviolent 46
  permissible 46–8
  to achieve moral ends 117
collectivist theories, rejected by Gandhi 128
colour discrimination, Gandhi's opposition to 85
colour prejudice, South Africa 92
communalism 193
communitarian societies 198
conflict
  can be moral 39
  concept of 38
  resolution of 38, 101
confrontation, state power and people's movement 216
confrontations, nonviolent 102
Congress Party 216
conscience 94, 99, 135, 170
consensus democracy 193
constructive program 187, 205
constructive work 205
  and combative struggle 220
constructive workers 213
  role of 209–10
consumerism, curtailment of 199
conversion 156–7, 160, 175
  a non-issue for Hindus 154–5
  not recommended by Gandhi generally 88

cottage industries 199
courage 239
cow slaughter, ban on 221–2
creativity, Indian 261–2, 263
cultures
  marginalization of 248
  politics of 248
dan concepts 207
  new 211
Dandi Beach, march to 96–7, 191
Daridranarayana (the God of the poor) 93–4
Deity, concept of 133–4, 168
del Vasto, Lanza 8
democracy, participatory 219
democratization, and secularization of Indian politics 251-2
Desai, Mahadev (scholar) 138
  interpretations of the four varnas 142–5
Desai, Morarji 218
detachment 134
development, as violence 186, 192–4
  based on colonial exploitation 192–3
devotion 132
dharma 33, 130, 134, 144, 154, 156, 172
disciplines in the pursuit of Truth 100
discrimination 62
diversity, religious 101–2
dogmas 134
dogmatism 103, 131, 168
  of Gandhi 42
Doke, Rev. Joseph 63, 65
dual power 215
Dumezil, Georges 147
Dumont, Louis 147–8
Duphelia, Miss Uma 72
Durban demonstration 69
Durban–Westville, University of 72–3
duty 134–228
  Gandhian view 231
economic development, *see* development

Index

economic system, Gandhian 227–8
economics
  historical function of 197
  holistic approach to 195
  new: does not restrict production 197; profile of 198–9; visions of 195–6
  traditional 197–8
  and violence 195–9
economy, traditional 199
enemy within 194
epic fast, the 39–41
  was this satyagraha? 41–3
equability 139–40
equal rights 14
equality 227–8
  Gandhian view 231
ethics, central to religion 176
ethnic tolerance 251, 255
ethnicity 248
  political responses to 255–9
  refuses to fade 254
evangelism 154, 155
exploitation 186, 221
  origins in violence 192

facts, and Truth 100
faith 170–1
  marginalization of 248
  and politics 15
fasting 42, 43
feminism
  Gandhian 228–33
  modern 226, 227; seen as anti-feminist 227
feminist activities, Gandhian view 232
fetishism 103, 104
fighting (Gandhian), two levels of 45
Fischer, Louis 54
foreign cloth, boycott of 32
fundamentalists *see* zealots

Gandhi, Mohandas K.
  attitude to religion 102–6
  and Aurobindo 145–7
  biographical research 61–3
  blindness to Ambedkar's position 41–2, 43
  campaign for Independence for India 239
  career as lawyer 76–7; legal work 72–3
  and Christianity 152–64
  and Christians from overseas 157–8
  and Christians in India 158–64
  development as a moral thinker 109–10
  and exploitation 186
  Hind Swaraj 126–7, 195
  inner journey 31–3
  lifestyle, changes in 93–4
  limited writings on 190
  misunderstood by Indians and British 30–1
  a moral activist 111–12
  moral and political insights 123
  moral practice 114–20
  a moral reformer 118
  philosophy of life 67, 203
  public and private life linked 52–3
  pursuit of the spiritual path 118
  relationships with Blacks and Colored community in South Africa 78
  responded to initiatives of others 78–9
  reticence in spiritual matters 167
  Satyagraha in South Africa 62, 92, 118
  seen as saint 36
  social and political revolutionary 204
  The Story of My Experiments with Truth 62, 63, 90, 94
  as a thinker 122
  writing old-fashioned 141
Gandhi, Mrs Indira 216–17, 218, 223
Gandhi, Prabhudas 76
Gandhian feminism 228–33
  defined 232–3
Gandhian society 227–8
Gandhian vision, of 'true' religion and 'true' culture 255
George, S.K. 161–2
  Gandhi's Challenge to Christianity 161

Ginwala, Dr Frene, Gandhi's role and relation to economic classes 68–70
goals and programs, Gandhi and Martin Luther King Jr. 241
God 17, 94, 170
   man's oneness with, doctrine of 133–4
   real and imagined 168–9, 170
God is Truth 124, 169
governmental action in South Africa, focus on 65–6
gram sabhas 210, 221
gramdan (gift of the village) 207, 220, 222
   campaign for 210–11
   implied power changes in the villages 212

Harijans 137, 161, 163
   see also Untouchables
health 228
Hindu–Muslim unity 57, 205
Hinduism 131–2, 148, 149, 153, 154, 167, 173, 245, 258, 261
   creativity of 263
   and diversity of religious needs 155
   zealots 260
history, secular trends 250
human experience, religion and religious concepts 131–2
human rights, and social justice 13–14
humanity, to reach Truth 178
Huttenback, Robert, *Gandhi in South Africa* 64–5

imperialism 193
indentured labor 73
independence, Gandhi's advice 220–1
India
   Gandhi's vision of 204
   liberation of 204
   rural life 186–7
   secular politicians in 253
   secularization: of politics 251; of the state 245
   to be a society of village republics 204
Indian Community in South Africa 64–73

Indian culture, alternative awareness of 263
Indian National Congress 205
Indian people, swaraj and nonviolence 25
Indian political community in Natal and Transvaal 70–1
Indian 'question' in the Transvaal 62, 64
Indian rights in Natal 62
Indian South African scholars, emergence of 67
industrial capitalism 226
industrial development 192
industrial labor rights 13, 14
industrial society
   Gandhi's antipathy towards 186–7
   hampered in understanding Gandhi 187
inner experience, self-validating 172
insight 171
   Ghandi 99
institutional Gandhism 206, 221
intellectual and spiritual growth 168
inter-communal harmony, preachers of 260–1
interfaith understanding 178
international peace 185
interreligious dialogue 178
interreligious harmony/understanding 174–6, 255
inward Truth, concept of 99–100
irreligion 174
Islam 132, 149, 152, 245, 258, 260, 261
   creativity of 263
Iyer, Professor Raghavan 96
   on vows 173

Jainism 131, 152, 176
Janata experiment 223
Janata government 215, 218, 219–20
Janata (People's Party), and Gandhian socialism 217–18, 219
jatidharmah 145
Jesus, Gandhian view 158
Jinnah, Mohammed Ali 253–4
Jinnah, Qaid-e-Azam 57
Jones, E. Stanley 157, 158
Joshi, Pranshankar (activist) 67

'JP' (Jayaprakash Narayan) 208, 212, 213, 215, 217
 aimed to unite opposition parties 216
 failure of strategy 223
 first jeevandan 207
 and nonviolent struggle 222–3
 and Sarvodaya movement 207–8, 216
 and sulabh gramdan in Bihar 212–13
JP movement 214–16
Judaism 176, 260
justice, achievement of 113

karma 95, 127, 131
karma yogin 16
Kasturbai 55
khadi 13, 32, 205, 207
King, Martin Luther (Jr) 14
 and asceticism 240–1
 differing from Gandhi 239–41
 Gandhi's influence on 236–42
 nonviolence movement 242
 Strength to Love 237
 stressed nonviolence as active resistance 239
 Stride Toward Freedom 240
Kingsley, Ben (actor) 191
Kumarappa, Bharatan 161
Kumarappa, Dr J.C. 161, 195

labor, Gandhian view on division of 230
land revolution, peaceful 206–7
life, fundamental unity of 130
Lok Sevak Sangh (Association for the Service of the People) 205, 206, 213
love 164, 238–9
 victory of 239
Love Force 242

mankind, moral solidarity of 133–4
man's oneness with God, doctrine of 133–4
Manu (granddaughter of Kasturbai) 55–6
Marxism 105, 251
materialism 226
maya (illusion) 85, 86, 100, 125
 social 93

means and ends 113, 208
Meer, Dr Fatima (scholar), Gandhi's neglect of working-class Indians 67–8
minorities, representation of 40–1
modern civilization 193–4
modernity
 ideology of 254–5
 power of 249
moha (delusion) 125
moksha 5, 53, 90, 111, 124, 130
Montgomery boycott 241
moral action 112
moral activism 4
 and moral attachment 118
moral attachment 114–15, 116–17, 119
moral codes 195
moral conflict 41
moral courage, and Truth 96
moral discipline 109
moral economy 197, 199
moral fighting 39
moral growth, individual 128–9
moral integrity 21
moral intuitions 110
moral involvement 114–18
Moral Law 127, 129
moral non-attachment 115–16, 116–17
moral philosophy 109–20
moral power 22
moral principles 110
moral progress 185
moral purity, dangers in assumption of 114
moral strength, of women 229
moral suasion, dangers of 109
moral theories 110
moral thought, evolution of 110–11
morality, of modern statecraft 250
morals 198
motherhood, Gandhian view on power of 230
Mukherjee, Dr Radhakamal, rebuked by Gandhi 191–2

Narain, Iqbal, *The Politics of Racialism* 65

Index

Narayan, Jayaprakash *see* 'JP'
Natal Indian Association 69
Natal Indian Congress 69, 72–3
nation-states, modern 246–9
national regeneration 221
nationalism, challenged 248
nationalist movement 159–60, 161–2
nationalists *see* zealots
nature, reverence for 12
Nayer, Payarelal 65
Nehru, Jawaharlal 41, 159, 251
neo-romanticism 145, 148, 149, 150
non-cooperation movement 24, 29, 129
   ended 29, 31
non-exploitation 227–8
'Non-Party Alternative' 221
non-possession 139–40, 140, 171, 227–8
   culture of 196
   ideal of 186
non-registration vow 71
nonstealing 171
nonviolence 5–6, 13–14, 16, 21, 25, 125, 132, 138, 162-3, 168, 171, 176, 194, 203, 208, 209, 216, 227–8, 237, 238, 242
   of Christ 163
   combative/resistive 205
   and Indian National Congress 205
   and moral non-attachment 117–18
   truth of 7–8, 23
   under Gandhi 222
nonviolent communes, growth of 12
nonviolent movements
   at world level 11
   spread of 8–11
nonviolent resistance 186
nonviolent revolution 203–4, 214, 218, 220, 221
nonviolent society, creation of 200
nostalgia for the future 148–9

Oak, P.N. (architect), and Taj Mahal 262

Pachai, Dr Bridglal (academic historian) 68

pacifism, Martin Luther King 237
Pahad, Essop 68
parliamentary action 216
partition 56–7
'passing over' 102, 105
passive resistance 71
   English examples 75
Peace research 11
peasant society 204
peasant welfare 12
'people's candidates' 213
People's Committees 219
People's Front 216
People's Government (Janata Sarkar) *see* Janata Government
people's movement 216
   silenced 217
people's power 219
people's socialism 208
perception
   individual's own 98
   personal, partiality of 102
peripheral believers 258–9
   in a traditional society 260
perseverance 176
Phoenix Farm 54, 62, 74, 75, 78
Pillay, Puballan, *British Indians in the Transvaal* 64
Polak, Henry S. 63
Polak, Millie 76
   Mr Gandhi - The Man 63
political economy 197
political Gandhism 206
political morality 128
political participation 251
'politics' 130
politics
   Gandhian view of 127–30
   and religion 57
potentiality, positive 101
poverty 192
   just distribution of 197
   voluntary 129
prayer 132, 156
professions and parliamentary institutions, attacked by Gandhi 193
profit 226
progress, theory of 257

property as theft 196
purification, of religion and individual 174

racial discrimination 13
racial segregation, in South Africa 78
racism 193, 248
reality, enriched understanding of 101
reason 170
reason and experience, Gandhi distinguishes between 169–70
reflexive causation 53
relative truth 95, 97–8, 168, 169, 174, 209
religion 52, 53, 101–2, 174, 198
  ambivalence to 249–50
  divisive and oppressive 103
  and Gandhi 130–5; attitude to 102–6
  international ties 149
  and politics 91, 247, 248, 249, 251–2
religions
  equality of 15, 174
  as human mediations of the Truth 104
  marginalization of 248
religious education, Gandhian concept of 175
religious and ethnic tolerance, non-secular concept of 246–9
religious pluralism 88, 152
religious tolerance 15, 244, 245, 255
religious universalism 166–79
religious values 130–1
renunciation 240
resistance, nonviolent 138
resources
  communization of 196
  conservation of 12
respect 244
revivalists *see* zealots
revolutionary Gandhism 206
Rolland, Romain, *Mahatma Gandhi: The Man Who Became One With The Universal Being* 63
Romero, Archbishop (El Salvador), assassination of 10
Roy, Anilbaran (translator) 138, 145

rural development projects 13
rural land reform 13
rural society, preservation of 12

saintliness 48
Salt March 16, 237
Salt Tax campaign 96
Sarva Seva Sangh (The Association of Service of All) 138, 206, 214, 219–20, 221, 223
sarvodaya 187, 203, 227–8
Sarvodaya movement 12–13, 187, 205–6, 207, 218, 223
  divisions within 216, 221–2
  rethink of strategy 213–14
  to move into cities 213
sarvodaya society 196
satya 39, 85, 86, 123, 124, 125, 129, 171, 176
  see also Truth
satyagraha 3, 16, 24–34, 68, 85, 87, 92, 96, 97, 109, 113, 114, 118–19, 203, 221, 237–8
  an epistemological concept 46
  clarify what coercion is permissible 46–8
  concept of 38–9
  derivation of 26
  as form of moral order 47
  fundamentally opposed to coercion 46
  and Gandhi's rural communities 75–6
  and introduction of religious values into politics 128
  and moral non-attachment 117
  negative 209, 213
  non-coercive 208–9
  political techniques of 102
  positive 209
  profound insights of 110–11
  religious component in 130
  some suggestions for improvement of 36–48
  struggle created by Gandhi 73–4
  and Truth-search 44–6
  view of S.K. George 161
  women natural leaders 229

Satyagraha in South Africa, Mohandas K. Gandhi 62, 92, 118
Schumacher, E.F. 195
Schweitzer, Albert 158
secular state, acting as church 252–3
secularism 105, 188
  meanings of 244–5
  modern: concept of in India 249–59; fails to see religious sources of creativity 262
  official 247–8
Seedat, Hassim (amateur historian) 72
self-analysis 241
self-control 16, 124–5
self-direction, moral judgment on one's own behavior 128–9
self-discipline 113
self-employment 199
self-examination 170, 174
self-fulfillment, for women 226
self-help programs 240
self-knowledge 172
self-purification 42, 176, 240, 241
self-realization 31, 53, 91, 124, 125, 228
  see also swaraj
self-reliance 171, 227–8
self-rule *see* swaraj
self-sacrifice 124
self-suffering 124, 130
self-sufficiency 12, 187, 199
self-transcendence 177
selfless action 105
selfless service 124
selflessness 90, 228
service 228
Shanti Sena (volunteer Peace army) 207
  new 222
Sikhism 176, 245, 260
simplicity
  Gandhian view 230–1
  of Gandhi's religious universalism 177
social action 96–7
social aspect of Truth 100
social attitudes, in South Africa 93
social consciousness, critical 248
social institutions, and moral values 126
social justice 109, 237

and human rights 13–14
social norms, India and South Africa 193
social reform 14
social relationships 47–8
social structures 198
societal exploitation 192
society
  comprising the poor 198
  Gandhi's concept of 195
society of nonviolence 196
soul-force 164, 239, 242
South Africa 38, 110, 167
  Gandhi in 61–79
  Indian policy related to Native policy 78
South African communities, social milieu of 66
South African society, modern, and the 'Indian question' 77–9
spinning wheels 12, 28, 32
spiritual force 31
spiritual insight 171
spiritual purity and moral power 118
spiritual research 72
spiritual strength 30, 31
spiritual superiority 175
state, concept of in India 245–6
state of emergency (imposed by Mrs Gandhi) 216–17
state power 219
  challenge to 215
  growth of in India 245
state tolerance 245
Story of My Experiments with Truth, The, Mohandas K. Gandhi 62, 63, 90, 94
strength, nonviolent mobilization of 46
struggle 45, 194, 204
  concept of 38
  of nonviolence 194
  a war between Truth and untruth 46
student agitation 214
subsistence standard of living 199
suffering
  unearned, value of 239, 241
  without retaliation 113
suffering love 162

Index

suffragettes 75
sulabh gramdan 211
　concept of clarified 211–12
surplus, the source of exploitation and poverty 197
svadharma 142, 144, 154
Swan, Dr Maureen, research on Gandhi 70ff
swadeshi 32, 163, 171, 227–8
swaraj 4, 24, 25, 27, 31, 33, 195, 199, 227
　Gandhi's scheme for 28–9
Swaraj Sangam 221

Tagore, Rabindranath 259, 160
tapas 124, 134, 170, 176, 130
technological progress 185
technology
　and concentration of economic power 199
　nonviolent 196
　repressive 193
theology and ethics, Martin Luther King 237
Third World development problems, Ghandian solutions for 12–13
Thomas, M.M. 162–3
　The Acknowledged Christ of the Indian Renaissance 162
tolerance 134, 171, 179
　politics of 259–65
Tolstoy Farm 62, 74, 75
transformation, inner, of Gandhi 26–34
trust 116
　role of 115–16
trusteeship, concept of 140–1
Truth 6, 17, 21, 39, 86, 87, 105, 123, 124, 125, 131, 168, 170, 172, 176, 198, 203, 208, 238
　and ahimsa 238
　an ultimate moral reality 44
　differences in perception of 98, 101
　experiments with 100–1
　Gandhi's concept of 90–106
　Gandhi's philosophy of 16–17
　has a social dimension 93
　possibility of realization 95
　power of 95-6

　pursuit of 132
　spiritual 123
　ultimate 240
Truth is God 85, 87–8, 124, 169, 172, 173
Truth and love, politics of 209
Truth-search 44–6
truth-seeking, social and political forms of 96–7
truthforce 7–11, 242
truthful fighting, concept of 39
truth 171
　relativity of 94–102; in religion 102–3
　truth claims 156
truths 169
'two truths' doctrine 172

unemployment, eradication of 200
unity of diversity 179
untouchability 3, 33, 93, 176
　abolition of 28, 205
Untouchables 3, 13, 22, 39, 40
　and the epic fast 40
　fighting for a truthful principle 41–2
untruth 39
uplift of the whole 177
USA
　expansion of nonviolent politics 8–9
　social rights movement 14

Vaishnava tradition 162
van Onselen, Charles, *Studies in the Social and Economic History of the Witwatersrand* 77–8
vanaprastha 55
varna 229
varna-system 142–6, 147
varnas, universalization of 146
vegetarianism 12
village culture 186–7
village industries 205, 207
village welfare 13
Vinoba 12, 206–10, 218, 219, 223
　flawed approach to social change 212
　self-imposed silence 216–17
　would countenance resistive satyagraha 222

violence 185, 209
　and economics 195–9
　elimination of 194
　equated with exploitation 192
　prohibited by Gandhi 47
visions, marginalization of 248
voluntary service 186
vows 173
　observance of 171–2

wealth, a handicap to society 192
Western man 255–6
Western philosophy 142
　influence on Gandhi and
　　Aurobindo 148–50

Westernized native 256–7
　attitude to culture 262
wheel of life 135
women
　attributes of 229
　traditional role 228; Gandhian
　　view 229–33
　and war, Gandhian view 231–2
women's liberation 187
women's rights 13
world resources 126

zealots 257–8, 260
　approach to culture 262
Zoroastrianism 176